D0840014

RUNAWAY SLAVE SETTLEMENTS IN CUBA

Envisioning Cuba / LOUIS A. PÉREZ JR., EDITOR

Gabino La Rosa Corzo

Translated by Mary Todd

RUNAWAY SLAVE SETTLEMENTS IN CUBA

Resistance and Repression

The University of North Carolina Press

Chapel Hill and London

Originally published as *Los palenques del oriente de Cuba: Resistencia y acoso* by Editorial Academia, Havana.
© 1988 by Gabino La Rosa Corzo

English translation © 2003 The University of North Carolina Press
All rights reserved

Designed by Heidi Perov
Set in ITC Charter
by Keystone Typesetting, Inc.

Manufactured in the United States of America

This English-language edition was made possible thanks to a translation grant provided by the American Council of Learned Societies / Social Science Research Council Working Group on Cuba, with funds from the John D. and Catherine T. MacArthur Foundation and the Christopher Reynolds Foundation.

The paper in this book meets the guidelines for permanence and durability of the Committee on Production Guidelines for Book Longevity of the Council on Library Resources.

Library of Congress Cataloging-in-Publication Data
La Rosa Corzo, Gabino.
[Palenques del oriente de Cuba. English]
Runaway slave settlements in Cuba: resistance and repression / Gabino La Rosa Corzo; translated by Mary Todd.
p. cm.—(Envisioning Cuba)
Includes bibliographical references and index.
ISBN 0-8078-2803-3 (cloth: alk. paper)
ISBN 0-8078-5479-4 (pbk.: alk. paper)
1. Holguín (Cuba: Province)—History. 2. Slavery—Cuba—Holguín (Province)—History. 3. Fugitive slaves—Cuba—Holguín (Province)—History.
4. Government, Resistance to—Cuba—Holguín (Province)—History. I. Title.
II. Series.
F1845 .L3713 2003
973.91'64—dc21
2003005071

cloth 07 06 05 04 03 5 4 3 2 1
paper 07 06 05 04 03 5 4 3 2 1

THIS BOOK WAS DIGITALLY PRINTED.

Contents

Figures and Tables

Figures

Tables

RUNAWAY SLAVE SETTLEMENTS IN CUBA

Introduction

The eastern region of Cuba is very important for the study of runaway slave settlements, since it is the part of the island's territory that, it is supposed, contained the largest number of those settlements. Therefore, I took that region as a starting point in studying this form of slave resistance in greater detail, testing the truth of those suppositions and creating the basis for showing the common features of such settlements. The social phenomenon of runaway slave settlements took the form of small, almost inaccessible rural hamlets that abounded in Cuba during most of the period when the island's economy was based on slave plantations.

An earlier work (La Rosa Corzo 1986, 86–123) set forth the need for fieldwork and even for use of the resources offered by archaeology and ethnography in putting together a reliable historical reconstruction of the system of clandestine settlements, which were continually attacked by the colonial authorities and by the slave owners. The studies on this topic that have been made public in Cuba so far are based entirely on the information provided by a part of the abundant colonial documentation, but the critical approach required in historical work has been utterly lacking; moreover, some of those who were interested in this subject wrote their works as literary fiction. In order to write the history of this social phenomenon of runaway slave settlements, known in Cuba as *palenques*, I had to clear away enormous obstacles that had been created by fantasy and the lack of historical precision.

Therefore, while taking the first steps in fieldwork—which is important, though complementary—I based my interpretation of the subject on as many documents as possible; my goal was to propose conceptual definitions that would make it possible to break through the wall raised by the positivist approach that has prevailed in this sphere of historical research up until now. This last aspect is of cardinal importance. The line of work that has been adopted lacks a language of its own, an adequate formulation of the research done. The authors who have written on this topic in Cuba have not used a common terminology—which, I believe, has led to a lack of clarity in the results attained. The use of the same term in identifying different concepts or several terms for defining the same concept is the most common defect in the studies made on this topic.

A large number of documentary sources have not been used previously—such as the diaries or notebooks in which the slavehunters and authorities recorded military operations they had engaged in against vagabond runaway slaves and those living in *palenques* in Cuba. When such sources were taken into consideration (see appendix 1), knowledge of the repressive system that had been created to oppose runaways was increased, and the number of known runaway slave settlements and the amount of information about them were considerably increased, as well. Thus, thanks to the information contained in the notebooks of the captains of the bands and commandants of the militias that went after runaways and attacked the *palenques*,[1] it has been possible to discover the most important characteristics of the lives of the slaves who, after escaping, joined together and established settlements in isolated areas in order to remain free.

As had been supposed and as this study corroborates, the eastern region of the island was where this form of slave resistance was the strongest and most widespread—which made it necessary to create a repressive system that differed considerably from the one used on the rest of the island against this same form of slave resistance. This book seeks neither to present a history of the eastern region of Cuba nor to explore all the ways in which the slaves expressed their lack of conformity with their lot. The former would require a much longer, more encompassing work in which the economic, political, and social aspects would have to be taken up from a viewpoint that could explore the complex mechanisms of colonial society through which various socioeconomic formations were manifested. The latter would imply examining the varied forms of slave resistance and rebelliousness, such as suicide, running away and becoming vagabonds, and uprisings by all the slaves on a single plantation—manifestations or forms that are not included in this book. The present work focuses instead on the runaway slaves' establishment of settlements in isolated areas, where, in many cases, they managed to live and defend themselves against the continual attacks to which they were subjected.

Here the reader will find descriptions of previously ignored real-life happenings that I have culled from meticulous colonial documents in order to reveal the general and particular aspects of this subject. I have also tried to get to the bottom of the problem—showing that the social phenomenon of the *palenque* was really expressed as a process—by seeking its genesis, explaining its development and decline, bringing out the social relations of colonial society, and assessing this particular form of slave resistance as a system consisting of many factors and incidents that may at first appear to be unrelated. The form of slave resistance described in this book is simply one of the many ways in which slaves struggled, and, even though not inclusive, it contributes to a clearer understanding of the history of slavery in Cuba.

As a specific form of slave resistance, runaway slave settlements were, for several centuries, one of the thorniest problems with which the colonial power structures were beset. This study on the *palenques* in Cuba should lead to other studies that will bring out the regional characteristics of the problem, since this book focuses only on the easternmost part of the island. Therefore, comparisons on how the phenomenon was expressed in different regions are, for the moment, of a limited nature. In order to compare specific and general aspects of this subject throughout the island, one would first need monographic studies to facilitate a historical synthesis of the facts and characteristics prevailing in each region.

Several aspects are crucial for a true understanding of the *palenques*: the geographic location of the clandestine hamlets created by the runaway slaves, the elements that upheld their precarious economy, their demographic density, their greater concentration in certain areas, the most common tactics used in their defense, the places from which the people living in them came, and the ways in which those settlements were adapted to meet the changes that were made in the repressive system created to crush them. It is also important to note that this specific form of slave resistance, although expressed throughout the island, did not attain the same level or the same notoriety in all regions.

This last point can be inferred from the regional variations in the repressive system, a point that escaped previous studies on this topic, in which the hunting down of runaway slaves was described as similar in all geographic-economic regions, especially after the creation of the Royal Consulate, or Board of Development, in 1794. Working from its seat in Havana through its consular representatives in the main centers in the rest of the country, that institution directed and administered the network that hunted down, captured, and returned runaway slaves to their owners. In the western and central parts of the island, bands of men who were paid a fixed wage to make daily tours of the areas assigned to them were in charge of bringing back runaway slaves and destroying their settlements. This policy, which led to the creation of a large number of bands of slavehunters, shows that the repressive system in the western and central parts of the island reflected the fact that those areas contained large numbers of vagabond runaway slaves.

In the eastern part of the island, however, those operations were not carried out on a permanent basis, and the bands of slavehunters were far from small. There, large slavehunting militias of civilians and military personnel were formed to comb the areas containing runaway slave settlements for two or three months at a time. It is clear that those operations were aimed mainly against the groups of runaways who established fortified settlements in isolated areas—not vagabond runaways, who stayed near the plantations.

Therefore, I believe that, in Cuba, the historical reconstruction of the system of runaway slave settlements should begin in the eastern region of the island, the only part of its territory in which the repressive system took a different form. The transcription and comparison of diaries concerning operations in the western, central, and eastern regions made it possible to confirm what had been guessed: the existence of a different strategy and tactics in the Eastern Jurisdiction. Those notebooks, in which everything that happened to the bands or slavehunting militias was recorded, show which geographic areas had the most incidents and when the problem was most acute.

A detailed study of twenty-eight slavehunters' diaries referring to different parts of the island and a large number of the colonial documents related to this subject confirmed that the main form of active slave resistance in the Vuelta Abajo region, in the westernmost part of the island, was the formation of bands of vagabond runaway slaves.

Likewise, despite economic and geographic differences, something similar occurred on the plains of Puerto Príncipe (now Camagüey). However, in the Matanzas area, which had many sugarcane plantations and a higher concentration of slaves, even though there were many vagabond runaway slaves and runaway slave settlements at one time in history, slave uprisings were the main form of protest. But, as I have already said, the monographic method should precede the comparative, which is why I concentrated on studying runaway slave settlements in the eastern region as a starting point for future comparisons.

In line with what is set forth above, I must describe the system of concepts used in this book. The confusion that exists concerning the most common terms employed to date in theoretical discussions and studies makes it absolutely necessary to relate, describe precisely, and assign hierarchy to the terms used in this presentation. Therefore, I propose the following definitions of the forms of slave resistance,[2] which were made on the basis of the essential distinction of the variants and a detailed analysis of analogies and differences and also on the basis of their connections with external elements or other factors. This model was used for the study and tabulation of the data contained in the works that were consulted.

Slaves reacted in different ways to the cruel exploitation to which they were subjected, depending on the conditions of their environment, personal and ethnic characteristics, level of development, and social awareness. Thus, they adopted different attitudes or channeled their actions toward different goals.

I propose the concept of *passive resistance* to describe the series of acts through which slaves expressed their unhappiness with and held back their incorporation in the system in a very elementary or primary way. This kind of resistance includes failure to do the work assigned, the breaking of equipment and tools, a conscious brake on productivity, resistance to work, and even suicide—the most desperate form of resistance slaves employed, not only to find escape but also, in some cases, to harm their owners' interests. Overseers, managers, and owners—the people most closely linked to the slaves—used physical and moral chastisement to repress all expressions of this kind, both to punish those who committed infractions and to keep the captured runaways and other slaves from committing crimes in the future. Therefore, punishments were almost always administered publicly, in front of all the slaves on the plantation. Suicide was punished with the help of Christian morality, but preventive actions were also carried out on occasion. Father J. B. Labat described one of these methods used in the Antilles: "It was that of cutting off the head and hands of those of his blacks who had hanged themselves and placing them in an iron cage suspended from a tree in his yard, because the blacks believed that, when they were buried, spirits would come and take their bodies back to their own country" ([1772] 1979, 52).

Thus, the rest of the slaves were pressured not to commit suicide because they believed that the caged heads and hands would keep them from going back to Africa. This and many other methods were used against this form of passive resistance. The incidents caused by this kind of resistance always had a very local character in Cuba.

The concept of *active resistance* includes the three main ways in which slaves put up tenacious resistance against the system that oppressed them. Each of the forms in this category expressed a different level of the collective nature of the protests and gave rise to a different response by the colonial government in its efforts to eliminate it.

The first level in this kind of resistance was that of *vagabond runaway slaves* and consisted of flight by one or a very few slaves from the plantation or estate on which they were exploited. In 1796, when the first regulations specifically punishing this form of slave resistance were promulgated, the difference between the concept of vagabond runaway slaves and that of runaways living in a settlement was clearly established. In Cuba, this makes it inadmissible to use the former term for both phenomena or to use other terms for the same purpose. According to those regulations, a vagabond runaway slave was "a slave or slaves who are found three leagues [roughly eight miles] from the plantation on which they live and work or one and a half leagues [about four miles] from the fields where they labor, without a document issued by their owner, overseer, or administrator" (Real Consulado/Junta de Fomento 1796, 6), whereas runaway slaves living in settlements were those who joined together in groups of more than seven—a concept that was amplified later on with the constant practice of hunting them down. Thus, a document dating from the mid-nineteenth century states that the term "vagabond runaway slave" "is applied, by antonomasia, to a fugitive black slave who wanders through the countryside" (Erenchun 1856, 986); runaway slaves living in settlements were the fugitive slaves or slaves who had rebelled and who joined together "for strength, choosing mountain locations that are difficult of access and working the land" (Pichardo 1976, 458).

At that time it was also made very clear that, whereas a runaway slave settlement, or *palenque*, was a place where a subsistence agricultural economy was being developed, a temporary settlement of runaways slaves, or *ranchería*—a term that appears with great frequency in the slavehunters' diaries and that many confuse with the runaway slave settlements—was simply a group of rude huts providing temporary shelter for fugitive slaves.

Whereas vagabond runaway slaves might be hunted down and captured by "anyone, no matter what his class," the runaways living in settlements could be "attacked only by the territorial authorities or other persons authorized to do so by the Higher Civil Government" (Real Consulado/Junta de Fomento 1846, 4, 9). Even though some runaway slaves traveled great distances and the repressive system created island-wide networks, most of those runaway communities were a regional phenomenon, operating in a very local way in certain regions, where each territorial division or jurisdiction had different problems and its own resources for repressing them.

There was another category in addition to the vagabond runaway slaves and runaway slaves living in settlements, however. This third group—midway between the other two, if you will—appeared with great frequency in the documents of the period but has not been included in earlier studies made in Cuba. This specific form of active resistance was that of armed bands of runaway slaves.

Each armed band of runaway slaves kept on the move through isolated areas, occasionally spending the night in a cave or temporary settlement of runaway slaves. These runaways did not engage in agriculture but lived by hunting, fishing, bartering, and—especially—stealing. Such groups were very numerous in the western part of the island; several famous ones in Vuelta Abajo roamed between the Cuzco Hills and the Cajío and Batabanó Swamps. The band headed by José Dolores, which scourged some plantations near Matanzas in the 1840s, was notorious.[3]

There were several groups of this kind in the eastern region, as well. According to the statements of a woman runaway whom Santiago Guerra captured at the El Cedro runaway slave settlement in the Sierra Maestra in 1842, the blacks there had formed two bands of fourteen men each that kept on the march separately in order to elude the bands and militias of slavehunters (Archivo Nacional de Cuba [hereafter cited as ANC], Asuntos Políticos [hereafter cited as AP], leg. 41, no. 38). That same year, Leandro Melgarez, who headed the slavehunting militia that had gone out from Manzanillo to operate in the Sierra Maestra, reported the existence of two other bands of runaways: one of thirty members, under Lorenzo, and the other of twenty-two members, commanded by a man called Elías (ANC, Miscelánea de libros [hereafter cited as ML], no. 7,531).

The armed bands of runaway slaves nearly always stayed in a single territory, which they knew like the back of their hand, and so managed to elude the continual persecution to which they were subjected. I believe that groups of runaways whose settlements had been attacked or who lived in areas that did not offer much safety for forming permanent settlements adopted this form of active resistance, which was of a basically tactical and temporary nature.

A *palenque*, or runaway slave settlement, was the socioeconomic unit in which a group of runaway slaves tried to live together. The action of seeking refuge in those isolated settlements that were subjected to attacks has been known since the eighteenth century as *apalencamiento*.

The concept of the runaway slave settlement implies the existence of rudimentary crops at that place. When there were not any such crops, the place was referred to as a *ranchería*, or temporary settlement of runaway slaves. On occasion, the *rancherías* offered shelter to armed bands of runaway slaves, and many of them were also used occasionally by groups of runaways who lived in settlements when they went out in search of certain foods, such as the honey from wild bee hives. It is necessary to distinguish between these two concepts, not only to understand the contents of the slavehunters' diaries of operations and to establish quantitative and qualitative differences between the various forms of slave resistance but also to explain the level of development of the runaway slaves' settlements and the regional differences of that phenomenon.

Some of the many slave rebellions that took place in Cuba have been studied, as have some of the runaway slave settlements. Franco (1973) even put together a historical synthesis of several forms of slave resistance. However, the necessary differences between them have not always been established, and consequently there is a great deal of confusion, not only in understanding what happened but also regarding the validity of the opinions expressed. And, far from contributing to a correct historical assessment, this type of work has raised doubts about the subject matter described. Therefore, it is even more necessary than ever to undertake separate monographic studies of each of the forms of slave resistance.

In addition, the regional expressions of these forms need to be differentiated. Even though it is not advisable to establish categorical differences in the way of life and conditions of the slaves on the island based on the regions in which they were exploited—which might tend to hinder understanding of the common features of the problem throughout the island's territory—it is necessary to point out that some elements defined differences in the system of exploitation, which in turn were reflected in the slaves' living conditions and therefore in their reactions, generalized regionally.

In the western part of the island, where large plantation economies based on slavery predominated, the proportion of the slave to free population was always at very shocking levels, and there were very few large, unexploited regions that were isolated geographically.

In the central and eastern parts of the island, however, a cattle-raising economy predominated. In addition, small areas were planted to tobacco and still smaller ones to sugarcane and coffee. This resulted in some differences in how the slaves were exploited and in the relations between those in power and those subordinated to them, but it never meant that the slaves did not rebel; rather, some forms of rebellion were more common than others. The economic situation also affected the character of rebellion. If other factors—such as the population density, terrain, immigration, and racial mixing, which were different in each territory—are also taken into account, it is only to be expected that these expressions should have been slightly different in different regions. The diaries of operations against runaway slaves in each region contain data and anecdotes that express the more general characteristics of the problem, but they also include descriptions of the specific characteristics imposed by the terrain, the economy, production, the level of development of the slave plantation, and even the personalities of the members of the pursuing band.

The expressions of slave resistance usually conformed to a general pattern, but specific forms were adopted to meet the combination of interregional factors. In Puerto Príncipe, for example, there were few runaway slave settlements but many vagabond runaway slaves and armed bands of runaways, many of whom were captured by men on horseback. This characteristic was not repeated anywhere else. However, no great distinctions can be made between the level and development of Puerto Príncipe's economy and that of the eastern part of the island, a territory in which slave resistance mainly took the form of runaway slave settlements. Geographic conditions had much to do with these differences. In Puerto Príncipe, large plains used for cattle raising abounded; in the eastern part of the island, unpopulated mountain areas predominated. Therefore, even though all the existing documentation is valid for a general study of the matter, it also recorded the distinguishing regional characteristics of the problem in each territory, since the factors that led to the different forms of resistance were combined in a different way in each of them. Thus, differences between the specific and the general can be established for the phenomenon studied—a key aspect. However, this aspect has not been handled consistently, which has made it impossible to raise the theoretical levels of the studies on this topic in Cuba, since it was precisely these two categories that expressed the diverse connections that existed within the phenomenon and between it and the other components of colonial society.

The runaway slave settlements, as historical events linked to an infinity of changing realities and factors, reflected different levels of connection: first of all, among themselves; second, with the other forms of slave resistance; and, finally, with the other factors in the society that gave rise to them. It is absolutely necessary to understand the oneness of the unique, the specific, and the universal in the phenomenon and also the relative nature of each, depending on the level of the connection, in order to avoid making absurd generalizations—which have been made on occasion and which seem to characterize a social problem that has not changed in the course of years or expressed moments of development and of decline promoted by the internal mechanisms of the phenomenon.

Like any other historical fact, the runaway slave settlements had their distinguishing characteristics and specific qualities that depended on the combination of all their relations with their surroundings; therefore, runaway slave settlements were developed, went through stages, and consequently suffered a decline. They did not exist in the same way throughout all the centuries in which slavery lasted in the colony. Their internal conditions varied over the years, depending on the temporal and spatial connections they had with the phenomena surrounding them.

External factors exerted an influence on the *palenques*: when the repressive system that was created to oppose them was adapted to suit the regional conditions, the runaway slave settlements were adapted and changed, as well. And the opposite was also true: changes in the system of runaways' settlements led to adjustments in the repressive system. The cause-and-effect relationship was not only lineal; it involved the universal linking of all phenomena. External factors such as the Haitian revolution also influenced the runaway slave settlements, but that revolution was never their main cause, at least in the case of Cuba.

With runaway slave settlements viewed as a system produced by certain spatial and temporal objective conditions, each such settlement (whether permanent or temporary) expressed a different moment or reality of the system as a whole. Only studies that go beyond the limits of mere description can get to the bottom of the many multifaceted connections that each of them had with the system. However, once uncovered, the causal connections of the establishment of runaway slave settlements allow us to infer the possible extension and extinction of the phenomenon.

The establishment of *palenques* as a system evolved in accord with its own internal elements, but, as an open system, it was also affected by external factors. When the war of national liberation—which had a very direct effect on the central and eastern parts of the island—broke out in 1868, those settlements were already on the decline. The regime that had given rise to their establishment was in crisis, and the struggle for independence that was aimed against colonial despotism and against the system of slavery itself declared the inhabitants of runaway slave settlements to be free. After ten years of war, both slavery and the colonial regime continued to exist, though clearly weakened. Documents dating from the era contain almost no reports of runaway slave settlements. I return to this polemical point in the final chapters.

When economic development led to the advance of capitalism and capitalism supported the interests of the ruling sectors in Cuba, the regimen of forced labor that had engendered resistance and rebelliousness by the slaves on the island became obsolete. Therefore, the decline of the runaway slave settlements began with the crisis of slavery, and, even though a few of those settlements still existed when the war of 1868 broke out, *palenques* no longer constituted as serious a problem for the colonial authorities as they had prior to the outbreak of the war.

Earlier Historical Studies

Traditional historiography did not include special studies of runaway slave settlements as a social phenomenon linked to the history of Cuba. Very limited references were made to slave rebellions and to runaway slaves. Prior to 1960, when the triumph of the revolution wrought changes in education, the teaching manuals that circulated in Cuba stated in reference to such matters, "There were some sugarcane growers who mistreated the blacks, just as they did the Indians, so many of the blacks fled from the area of one plantation to that of another or hid out in the woods to rob and murder passersby, for which they were hunted down" (Aguilar Flores n.d., 174).

This quotation may lead readers to believe that the only reason slaves ran away was because of the harsh punishment meted out to them, and even though a distinction was made between the runaways who wandered from one place to another and those who stayed in the woods, the latter were considered thieves and murderers who hid in the woods for those purposes. It may also be supposed that they were hunted down because of the excesses they committed. I have mentioned this opinion not because it was accurate but because it sums up the feeling of the era and the assessment the people of that time made of the subject treated by this book.

Not all the interpretations were along that line. Renowned researchers who spent years studying various historical matters approached the subject more objectively, though nearly all their studies were rough outlines. Their opinions include Sánchez Guerra's statement that he considered the El Frijol runaway slave settlement to have been the most important one because it constituted an economic unit (Sánchez Guerra, Guilarte Abreu, and Dranquet Rodríguez 1986, 22). This aspect is analyzed in its corresponding chapter, but for the moment it should be emphasized that, whatever their nature, all the opinions about the forms of slave resistance were limited by the absence of monographic studies that would provide all-encompassing replies to the great questions that existed—and continue to exist, in large measure—concerning this topic. An additional limitation is the position taken by each author—who, in line with his ideology, culture, and prejudices, shows himself to be more or less inclined to identify with the hunted or the hunters.

In particular, before Franco (1973) dusted off a large number of records in the National Archives of Cuba and made the first, most serious attempt to write a history of the subject, there were only two brief works to serve that researcher as a base. Those works were two essays, one by Pérez Landa and Jústiz del Valle (1947) and the other by F. Pérez de la Riva (1952).[4]

The goal of Pérez Landa and Jústiz del Valle, both members of the Academy of History of Cuba, was to study the historical contribution made by fugitive slaves who lived in runaway slave settlements, not those who, suffering from an overseer's cruelty, thought the solution of their problems lay in the nearest woods but did not join in a common struggle. These authors concentrated their attention on the runaways who joined together in groups and put up resistance. Their starting point—differentiating between the vagabond runaway slaves and the ones living in runaway slave settlements—was correct, but that good beginning did not wind up as an essay interpreting runaway slave settlements, as they had proposed. The absence of documentary studies led the authors to base their hypotheses and arguments on aspects contributed by the oral tradition and, perhaps, the extrapolation of anecdotes and events from other countries in the Americas. As a result, they offered inexact data and expressed incorrect opinions about the system of settlements, defense tactics, and internal social organization of the runaway slave settlements.

Some of the authors' criteria are analyzed in later chapters, when they are developed—my analysis being the result of my having studied and compared a considerable amount of the information that is now available. For the present, I will simply comment on some of the main ideas, especially those that, inexplicably, have been repeated uncritically, mechanically, in later works.

For those authors, each runaway slave settlement consisted of a "circular area containing the group of huts," and "all of the huts faced inward, toward the middle of the circular clearing" (Pérez Landa and Jústiz del Valle 1947, 20). I do not know if this criterion was drawn from an anecdote or from the supposition that the runaway slave settlements repeated the design of a specific kind of African hamlet, but all the documents I have consulted show that, of the dozens of runaway slave settlements whose designs or forms have been described in sufficient detail, this kind of circular construction seems to have been used in only one: the El Cedro *palenque* in the Sierra Maestra.

The first logistical requirement for a settlement in an isolated place was that it offer sufficient safety for the group of fugitive slaves who decided to build a camp or group of huts. The area occupied and the type of housing were determined by the materials and characteristics prevailing in the area. The size, height, shape, and number of buildings; the living, storage, and planting areas; and the means of access to the settlement were determined by the size, elevation, and slope of the terrain; the existence of a nearby source of water; the kinds of vegetation; and the experience and tools the runaways had. The most important factor, however—the one that prevailed over and complemented all the others—was the degree of safety provided by the area that had been selected. To the extent that the characteristics of those locations were different, so were the characteristics of the settlements. Generalizing one type or form of settlement is one of the most typical errors, reflecting a lack of knowledge of the general and specific features of the various runaway slave settlements. In this regard, the norm was that they differed; what was true of each and every one of the settlements was a diversity of forms, styles, and resources.

Some runaway slave settlements were built under thick thatches of wild reeds, on piles standing on bare rock. In deciding where to establish their settlements, the runaway slaves considered the characteristics of the terrain. There were three prerequisites for guaranteeing that their settlement would last and that its inhabitants would retain their freedom: it had to be far from populated areas, inaccessible, and hidden. The former slaves wanted to settle down and live as well as they could—but always ensuring that they did not run the risk of being discovered easily.

In addition, no matter what kind of temporary or permanent settlement the former slaves built, even though the huts were all in one area, they were widely separated within it. This guaranteed two essential aspects: it was impossible for all the settlement's members to be caught off guard at the same time, and rapid flight was made possible because they were scattered.

In this regard, Pérez Landa and Jústiz del Valle stated, "In the middle of the clearing and at the widest part of the settlement, wooden props supported a roof of fan palms over the place where the second- and third-rank chiefs, who were in charge of the government, administration, and security of the settlement, met with the young men who worked in agriculture, fishing, or hunting. Another group selected and cut down trees from which to build canoes, piles, mallets, stakes, and palisades. The women usually worked the plots of land and raised sheep. Each settlement sought to meet its own needs, and barter was the only form of exchange in that attempt to form a nation" (1947, 20).

So far, no documents have been discovered in Cuba proving that the internal organization of runaway slave settlements was, in fact, like this; nor do I know of any witness who described it in this way. I think that, in their work, the authors let themselves be carried away by isolated anecdotes or perhaps by descriptions of large settlements of runaway slaves that existed in other parts of the Caribbean or the Americas. In Cuba, the examples studied to date—a broad sample of which is included in this book—do not contain enough elements to confirm that kind of description. The detail of sheep raising at the *palenques* on the island is noteworthy. There are no reports at all concerning this, which leads me to think that this information was based on reports from other countries.

This lack of sufficient data and these suppositions, with which the main ideas of the work are plagued, show how risky it is to accept some of the propositions presented in the essay by Pérez Landa and Jústiz del Valle. Lack of documentary proof even meant that they failed to substantiate their main hypothesis. According to those authors, there was a "mythical route" in Cuba that all runaway slaves followed; it consisted of a migratory movement eastward, which led all the fugitives to seek refuge in runaway slave settlements in the eastern part of the island. This hypothesis was based on an African legend that was passed on to the authors, according to which, in order to find the land of their ancestors, all lost Africans traveled toward the rising sun. This is how Pérez Landa and Jústiz del Valle explained the existence of a large number of runaway slave settlements in the easternmost part of the island. However, nowhere in their work do they provide any information proving the existence of this supposed "mythical" motivation. Yet, despite the absence of any corroborating proof, that element is always found—either explicitly or implicitly—in the views that were spread later on about the runaway slave settlements in Cuba.

In this regard, it is sufficient to emphasize that the accounts of the origins of the slaves who had lived in the *palenques* in eastern Cuba and had been captured—accounts that are included in this book—do not include any data proving that runaways from the western part of the island were in the majority or even constituted large numbers of those inhabitants. This aspect is the subject of another study that will be made public in future works, but it may be said that the research done so far shows, for example, that hundreds of the slaves captured in Matanzas, in the west-central part of the island, came from the central and eastern regions. There were many varied internal migratory movements on the island.

A book kept in the quarters where captured runaways were held in the city of Matanzas recorded the number of runaway slaves in 1851; according to this source, a total of eighty fugitive slaves from Havana were captured that year, twenty-one of whom were caught very close to the city of Matanzas. In all these cases, there was a migratory movement toward the east. But why did the runaways stay near the city of Matanzas if they wanted to go to the eastern *palenques*? Why did not they go through the central or southern part of that region instead of toward the city on the northern coast?

Moreover, toward which *palenque* was the slave María—a twenty-two-year-old Congolese woman who had run away from a plantation in Bayamo, in the eastern part of the island, and was captured in Ceiba Mocha, Matanzas, in 1851 (ANC, ML, no. 8,553)—headed?

Nor can it be stated that all the runaways who headed toward the eastern part of the island did so in order to join the eastern runaway slave settlements. An anecdote recorded in the diary of operations of the slave-hunter Rafael Parrado on February 17, 1831, in Puerto Príncipe shows a custom that prevailed at that time: "At Guanamaquilla, my men were examining a black who was making a pilgrimage to the El Cobre Sanctuary. After they had inspected his permit, he went off, and my men thought nothing of it, but, after he was on his way, they called him back, ... and he fled, so desperate that he even abandoned his horse, permit, and food" (Parrado 1830, 26).

The fugitive in question had been authorized to make a pilgrimage to the El Cobre Sanctuary, but his accidental meeting with the slavehunters filled him with so much panic that he fled, abandoning all his belongings. He was going toward the eastern part of the island, but it cannot be thought that he was doing so to find the land of his ancestors. Rather, he was making a kind of religious pilgrimage, in accordance with the degree to which he had assimilated the new pantheon of gods created by the merging of African cults with popular beliefs linked to Catholicism. In short, the "mythical route" is nothing more than speculation lacking any scientific foundation.

The other work that, together with the essay by Pérez Landa and Jústiz del Valle, served as the basis for Professor Franco's studies was that by Pérez de la Riva (1952). It contains some approximations about the run-away slave settlements as part of a possible study of rural housing, and thus it constitutes an important milestone in the historical studies specifically concerned with this matter, approaching it from a new angle and viewing it as part of a system—rural housing. Unfortunately, other authors have not taken up this aspect with regard to runaway slave settlements. Despite the work's importance, the opinions expressed in it should be evaluated carefully, for historical judgment did not always prevail over imagination in the analysis.

In line with the knowledge available concerning rural communities at the time, the author studied *bateyes*, or sugar mill communities, as a kind of settlement typologically counterbalancing the plots of land and run-away slave settlements, which he described as dispersion settlements.[5] Later, he went into an analysis of the kinds of housing, which ranged from thatched-roof huts and houses to *barracones*, or large slave quarters.[6] Regarding thatched-roof huts as the housing used by small groups of people, he focused attention on the close links between those huts and the small plots of land attached to housing, which were cultivated in a very rudimentary way and which originated with the people who had lived in Cuba prior to the Spanish conquest. He also noted the persistence of both forms in the colonial period, viewing them during that period both as part of settlements of poor farmers and as the ideal way in which runaway slaves met their needs. He took it for granted that the concept of *palenques* implied the existence of not only thatched-roof huts but also plots of land, in line with the way in which, in the colonial era, temporary settlements of runaway slaves were distinguished from permanent ones. Even though this was one of the most important conceptual contributions made by Pérez de la Riva's work, no later works have been consistent with this statement; nor has his criterion on the runaway slave settlements as forms of settlement been taken up again.

This author has been cited extensively, and many of his ideas have been repeated in publications, papers, and short works, but, paradoxically, it is the anecdotal aspects and those in which fantasy has prevailed that have been repeated, rather than his main thesis. One of the most important opinions that this author expressed was that there were fewer runaway slave settlements in the western part of the country and that they did not last as long as the ones in the east. Since the author did not make any mention of what sources he had used, it is impossible to know what he based that statement on; however, it coincides with the results obtained in this book. Despite this, Pérez de la Riva made a historical mistake that destroyed any possible scientific foundation for that statement: he explained that the difference was due to the fact that the slaves in the western part of the island were subjected to closer vigilance and were "less numerous" (1952, 314) whereas it was easier to hide in the eastern region because the slaves were not so closely watched. It is well known, however, that there were many more slaves in the western part of the island than in the central and eastern regions, and the authorities in those territories were far from indulgent with the vagabond runaways and slaves in *palenques* whom they caught—a matter to which I return later.

As for the internal workings of the runaway slave settlements, Pérez de la Riva made unverified statements that contradict what is set forth in the colonial documents. According to the author, when a runaway slave settlement was founded, the chief chose a group of men to form his band, "with the system of killing those who did not defend themselves against their pursuers" (1952, 315). Now, studies made of the diaries of operations against those living in *palenques* and of the dozens of other documents concerning this matter show not even one reference to this strange form of defense. Nor is it mentioned in the oral tradition or press of the period.

In only three of the runaway slave settlements studied here did the inhabitants put up stubborn resistance against occupation of the settlement by the slavehunters. Sometimes, when an attack was made, a small group of inhabitants—nearly always headed by the captain—fought the slavehunters while the rest dispersed along the various paths prepared for that purpose. Usually, the defense tactics of the runaway slaves living in settlements in the eastern part of the island consisted of falling back when attacked and abandoning the settlement as soon as the presence of slavehunters was detected nearby. Later, after the attackers had left, the runaways returned to their settlement. The view that those members of the settlement who did not defend themselves were killed by the others has no historical basis in fact, and its formulation shows how little the tactics and psychology of those who lived in the *palenques* were understood.

The author also wrote that newborn babies were killed in the runaway slave settlements so as not to give the others away, though, once again, he did not say what his source was for this statement. It may have been based on a letter that the captain of the Cayajabos Division, west of Havana, sent to the captain general in 1820 (ANC, Real Consulado/Junta de Fomento [hereafter cited as RC/JF], leg. 141, no. 3,935), the only document in which such information has been found. In this regard, it should be remembered that this was a local authority who was denouncing the threat posed by the runaway slave settlements and who portrayed the runaways as pitiless and bloodthirsty. In no other source of the period has any proof of this practice been found; to the contrary, there are many references and reports of newborn babies and young children captured during attacks on the runaway slave settlements. This occurred, for example, at El Portillo in 1747, at Todos Tenemos in 1848, and at many other such settlements.

Another of that author's opinions that has been repeated frequently was that the purpose of the attacks on plantations was to sow terror in the district, to make the owners leave the plantations so the runaways could trade freely (Pérez de la Riva 1952). As in the earlier cases, this view is not based on any documents, and its analysis should begin from the following point: the main goal of the slaves who fled and settled in isolated areas was to survive and avoid discovery. To make attacks and sow terror for the sole purpose of trading freely would be equivalent to announcing their existence and endangering their fragile peace and threatened freedom.

The runaway slaves living in settlements who, in those historical conditions, wanted to and could (because they had surpluses) engage in barter with free blacks and farmers did not need to sow terror or destroy plantations. The facts that are narrated in subsequent chapters show that every aggressive action by the inhabitants of *palenques* was inevitably followed by a raid by slavehunters—a lesson that the runaway slaves learned quickly.

Moreover, every attack on a plantation was prompted either by revenge for some offense to the attackers when they had been slaves or by the need to get women or the resources necessary for survival in the settlement. Plantations were attacked, burned, and robbed, but such actions were not frequent, and it cannot be said that all those actions were carried out by runaways who lived in settlements. The documents report attacks made by bands of runaways whose nonsedentary way of life gave rise to those practices. Only in one of the attacks that are studied here was it possible to show that runaways who lived in settlements in the mountains near the plantation took part in the attack: the one made on the San Andrés plantation in 1815. In that action, the runaways chopped down all the coffee plants in three coffee-growing areas belonging to the San Andrés plantation in the Sierra Maestra Division (Archivo Histórico de Santiago de Cuba [hereafter cited as AHSC], Gobierno Provincial [hereafter cited as GP], leg. 554, no. 1), but it sealed their fate, for a troop of forty slavehunters headed by Felipe Quintero was launched against them. According to another account taken from an official report sent from Baracoa on October 6, 1819, a group of runaways who lived in a settlement and had attacked several plantations had dared "to mistreat the owners with cruel whippings" (ANC, RC/JF, leg. 141, no. 6,935).

All the above makes it a rather speculative matter to sustain that the attacks were made for the purpose of sowing terror in the district in order to trade freely later on. The runaways living in settlements were not traders; they were marginalized and hunted down. Their lives revolved around a problem that did not have any easy solution—that of remaining free—which meant that they had to survive despite the continual attacks to which they were subjected.

Nor can we ignore the supposition concerning the existence of present-day towns whose origins date from runaway slave settlements. Starting in the mid-nineteenth century, Pezuela (1863) and Pichardo ([1875] 1986) reported the existence of several places called Palenque whose name originated from former settlements of runaway slaves. For example, one of the heights in Matanzas has been known as Palenque ever since the eighteenth century, but that territory, like most of the others that bear that name in Cuba, is not now a population center, and its present inhabitants are not descended from the runaways who founded the settlement.

The eastern town called El Palenque is a special case, for all documentation dating from the nineteenth century describes it as a plantation; thus its origins, or the time when it served as a runaway slave settlement, must go back to the eighteenth century.[7] The El Palenque plantation served as the camp or rendezvous for many bands of slavehunters during the nineteenth century because it was located halfway between the town of Tiguabos and the El Frijol (now the Cuchillas del Toa) Mountains.

The authors cited above used that example to show the existence of population centers that had their origins in runaway slave settlements. If their view is accepted as correct, it may be said that those towns were first runaway slave settlements, then plantations owned by settlers, and then (at the end of the nineteenth century) rural towns that kept their original name, Palenque. However, Pérez de la Riva (1952) cites some examples regarding this point that never had anything to do with this process or levels of settlement. One of them is that of the eastern town of El Cobre.

The present town of El Cobre (just west of Santiago de Cuba) had its origins in the first European settlement on Cardenillo Hill, which was founded to exploit the copper deposits that were discovered there. In 1534, unskilled black slaves were brought in to work the mines. The mines were abandoned some years later, and the slaves, left to their own devices, took up farming. It is true—Franco studied this aspect—that descendants of those slaves took part in an uprising in the mountains around the mines some years later, when an attempt was made to return them to slavery, and created several runaway slave settlements, but the town of El Cobre was never one of them. Moreover, there are no communities inhabited by the descendants of those runaways in the nearby mountains now, as was shown in the fieldwork done for this book. Nor did the other examples that Pérez de la Riva cited—such as Alto Songo and Bemba—have their origins in runaway slave settlements (1952, 320).

Finally, one of the aspects that Pérez de la Riva commented on was life in the runaway slave settlements, which he described as rudimentary and "primitive, men and women living in the utmost promiscuity, ruled by chiefs whom they called captains and the witch doctor, or *santero*, who was also the medicine man" (1952, 318). This may have been the way of life in some runaway slave settlements, but the view should not be gener-

alized. This form was more characteristic of the bands of vagabond runaways who went from one place to another with no permanent home and
led a more precarious life, but it does not correspond to such cases as
the El Cedro *palenque*, which had houses with bedrooms and a plot of
land for each member of the community, and the Todos Tenemos settlement, which had blocks of houses with a church in the center.

Apart from the critical aspects noted above concerning Pérez de la
Riva's view of how the runaway slave settlements were established and
his description of life in them, and even though his work has been indiscriminately copied, it has never been surpassed.

Of all the Cuban authors who have studied this subject, Franco made
the greatest contribution to knowledge about runaway slave settlements.
On the basis of one of his works that appeared in 1961 and was later
reworked for inclusion in the collection that R. Price (Franco 1981, 43–54)
published on the subject twenty years later, the noted Cuban writer enlarged his original ideas and offered a title that has been the only monographic work on this subject in Cuba (Franco 1973).

From the first view of the subject until the appearance of that book,
Franco's study maintained a similar structure, though amplified at the
end. After a short introduction containing a large number of incidents—in
which vagabond runaway slaves, rebellion, and runaway slave settlements in Santo Domingo, Mexico, Peru, Venezuela, and other regions in
the Americas are mixed—he listed events related to the existence of many
runaway slave settlements in Cuba. Immediately after that, after noting
some isolated incidents that took place in the sixteenth, seventeenth, and
eighteenth centuries, he went on to a study of runaway slave settlements
in the nineteenth century and, in this instance, separated the items referring to vagabond runaways from those relating to settlements.

That description was made on the basis of territorial units that corresponded to the political-administrative division in effect at the time
the work was published, which did not coincide with the geographic-
economic regions or with the political-administrative division in effect
when the events described took place. This, along with the fact that the
author did not make a comparative analysis of the regional differences
among runaway slave settlements, resulted in a lineal presentation of

events, which included everything from west to east without differentiating between the various levels of the phenomenon as a process.

In that section, he presented a very brief synthesis of many incidents and evaluations concerning the phenomenon in the eastern part of the island—a summary that constitutes the broadest view of the subject in that region to date.

In that work, the outstanding professor summed up a view that has been cited frequently in similar works since then and that has served as the basis for some rather unfortunate generalizations: "In Cuba," he said, "for many years, the runaway slave settlements were the only signs of nonconformity with the colonial regime, a virile protest against the infamies of slavery" (1973, 54). The content of that statement is true, but its intention should not be exaggerated when taken out of context, since recognizing the existence and historical-political importance of the *palenques* at a time when there were not any manifestations against colonial and slave-owner interests does not necessarily mean that they were the means for solving the fundamental contradictions of colonial society— and much less that the slaves were bearers of an ideology and class awareness that led them to struggle against a political system. Although slaves in Cuba fought in many ways against the cruel exploitation to which they were subjected, they never proposed to overthrow the social regime. Their goal was to achieve the freedom that had been wrested from them, but their condition, with all its attendant elements, kept them from developing a collective awareness and social goals that were beyond their mission as a class.

By gathering various denunciations of the existence of *palenques*, reports of attacks, and correspondence by officials that revealed the colonial power structures' constant concern over the danger posed by the existence of clandestine hamlets where fugitive slaves lived, the author summed up the experience of a *palenque* captained by Ventura Sánchez, known as "Coba," and thus revealed an event that had been ignored in previous historical studies. The little space dedicated to the problem in the eastern region made it impossible to detect any specific regional characteristics, but even though the information gathered on this point was scanty for assessing the historical nature of the problem in that region, it was not enlarged as a general analysis later on, except for the specific example of the El Frijol runaway slave settlement, to which Franco made some references and which the researcher Danger (1977) developed.

Franco's work contains many anecdotes and several opinions, the latter including his noting that the runaways in the El Frijol settlement engaged in considerable trade with Haiti and Jamaica and that three hundred people lived in the settlement—aspects that were subsequently analyzed as part of this study. The examination of statements such as these required contrasting them with other data, which will be presented at the correct time.

After Franco's work, the next research effort that was crowned with a monograph—the only one published in Cuba to date that was entirely dedicated to a runaway slave settlement—was the publication of Danger's (1977) work in a book, a third of which was dedicated to the study of that runaway slave settlement; the rest consisted of an introduction to the social phenomena of vagabond runaway slaves and runaways living in settlements (but without establishing the necessary qualitative differences between the two forms of slave resistance) and an appendix of documents containing a considerable proportion of the official documents generated by the attack that was made on that settlement in 1816.

Believing that that a runaway slave settlement was important because it constituted an economic unit, Danger gathered all the elements presented in the earlier works I have analyzed. Pérez de la Riva's (1952) and Franco's (1973) views are included, and some documentary elements are added, but, as in the earlier cases, the information taken from the sources was not examined critically. The frequently contradictory data contributed by the documents were accepted at face value.

The statements of Sergeant Alfonso Martínez, who made the first attack on the El Frijol runaway slave settlement, in 1815 (ANC, Miscelánea de expedients [hereafter cited as ME], leg. 4,070-Ai), had contributed a wealth of data—testimony that cleared up many questionable aspects that appeared in a distorted form in later reports, such as the number of people who lived in the settlement and their defense tactics. Danger did not use these data, however, in writing her work.

Nor did the author consult the accounts that correct the initial figures concerning the objects seized in the second attack, which was made in 1816, even though they appeared in the same file from which the data contained in the book were taken.[8] Further, Danger made no reference to the later statements by the governor of Santiago de Cuba when the third and fourth attacks on that runaway slave settlement were planned (ANC, RC/JF, leg. 25, no. 98) or to the final report of the number of runaways from the settlement who were captured and those who turned themselves in after the attack of 1816. These omissions limit understanding of the real importance of the settlement and of that historical event.

The work retained the narrative style that has prevailed in studies on this topic, though it considerably enlarged the framework of the documentary information. Because it is the only monographic study about a runaway slave settlement and because, as the author herself pointed out, the topic has not been exhausted, it is one of the studies on forms of slave resistance that should be considered required reading.

The present volume is not the appropriate place for evaluating the large number of articles and papers presented in congresses that contain opinions about this specific form of slave resistance, since none of them have surpassed the information contained in the works already mentioned or the line of presentation that has prevailed in them. The works in this category include a pamphlet by Duharte (1986) that sums up three other published works but, because of the brevity with which he set forth his ideas and goals, did not add anything new to the treatment of the subject of runaway slave slave settlements. Nor, in writing this book, have I taken into consideration some short works that referred very directly to other parts of the island and that will be used as sources for future monographs.

In short, the studies on runaway slave settlements that have been published in Cuba to date have proved deficient in theoretical elaboration, failed to approach the phenomenon as a process, demonstrated ignorance of nuances and chronological levels, and placed more weight on racial than on class factors in judging group and class attitudes. Even so, they constitute a necessary step in the learning process and should not be ignored. We must study them again—but not repeat them, since, as José Martí said, "every man contains within him the duty to add, to master, to reveal. Lives spent in the easy repetition of already discovered truths are culpable" (1953, 1006).

Methodology

As the preceding paragraphs show, this study seeks to broaden the chronological view of the events that took place in a selected region, evaluate them as a process, view that process as part of a system of slave resistance, differentiate between the possible levels shown in the evolution of the process, analyze runaway slave settlements as a specific expression of prolonged active resistance, show that the runaways living in those settlements were representative of the mass of slaves, analyze the also prolonged system of hunting down and destroying runaways, and show the special characteristics that both systems had in the eastern part of the island. By so doing, I hope to lay the bases for a historical reconstruction of runaway slave settlements throughout the island so that, in the future, other monographic studies may analyze other forms of slave resistance.

To achieve these goals, I have consulted new, previously unused documentary sources and broadened the view on the basis of the oral tradition and fieldwork in some previously selected geographic areas. Within these aspects, the incorporation of new sources—such as diaries of slavehunters operating in the eastern part of the island—was an important step toward obtaining new knowledge. Because of the absence of any studies on this subject related to its historical evolution, I felt it necessary to record the development of the main events chronologically.

Very often, the diaries of prominent figures who have taken part in wars are used for the reconstruction of historical events and for evaluating the roles played by certain individuals, groups, or social classes. Christopher Columbus's log and especially the campaign diaries of notable figures in the war of national liberation have been used for forming important reconstructions of historical periods and events in Cuban history. However, this is the first time that anyone studying the various forms of slave resistance has referred to the campaign diaries or diaries of operations of the slavehunters or of members of the mixed militias (consisting of both civilians and military personnel) that were used against the *palenques*.

The Royal Consulate—which in 1796, in response to the interests of the slave owners and colonial authorities, organized and financed bands and militias for hunting down and exterminating runaway slaves and the hamlets they established in Cuba—insisted that those groups keep diaries of operations.[9] In line with this requirement, the captain of each band (which had six members) and commandant of each slavehunting militia (which had more than twenty-five men) had to turn in a summary of the operations carried out. Each of the bands that operated on an ongoing basis in a single territory had provide a monthly report of its activities: the incidents, runaway slave settlements attacked, and fugitive slaves captured or killed on each day. Payment for the operations that had been carried out was made at the end of each month, when the summary was submitted.

In the case of the mixed slavehunting militias—which so far have been recorded only in a generalized way as a regional tactic employed in the Eastern Jurisdiction—the diaries were kept as a final accounting of all their operations, which might have lasted for up to three months in very isolated areas. This second kind of diary recorded the route taken (which had been agreed on with the higher-ranking authorities of the jurisdiction) and included the plantations visited, the denunciations received, and the places where encounters had taken place (including the names of the runaway slave settlements, how many huts and beds they had, and the kind of crops they raised). Often, lists of the names of the members of the slavehunting militia, of the runaways captured, and of the expenses incurred during the operations were attached to the diaries of operations.

Therefore, the slavehunters' diaries of operations constitute a very important source for the historical reconstruction of *palenques* in Cuba. Since the only diary of this kind that has been published is the one that was kept by Francisco Estévez (Villaverde 1982), a slavehunter who operated in the Cayajabos area (west of Havana), many historical and fictional works have been based on that source, but serious inconsistencies arise when attempts are made to generalize from that experience throughout the island.

Here, again, critical monographic studies on this subject are lacking. Not all the bands of slavehunters were motivated by identical circumstances or operated in the same geographic conditions or even in the same periods. All the slavehunting militias and bands served a general repressive system, but in every instance the characteristics of that system were determined by specific conditions and regional interests. All the diaries recording operations in a single area reflected the key aspects of the general repressive system, but the specific geographic, economic, and political factors in each region also had an important effect.

I do not claim that my analysis of the diaries included in this book exhausts this aspect. Rather, it opens the discussion, seeking a new approach to the topic. Subjected to further examination, the documents selected may reveal new aspects that have escaped me. Moreover, far from constituting all the diaries of this type that are in existence, the ones studied here are simply a small sample; their selection was sometimes determined by chance, since some have been lost or destroyed and others are scattered in various files in Cuban archives. The sources consulted also make frequent reference to operations that were carried out in years for which I have not found any diaries.

One aspect of interest related to the sources used in this study has to do with knowledge of the repressive system in which these documents were produced. In order to interpret the data provided in each diary correctly, it is necessary to know how the various bands operated in their regions and the differences that may have existed among them.

Both the bands of slavehunters and the mixed slavehunting militias that operated in the eastern region moved around on foot. Only in very few cases and for very short distances did they use horses or other means of transportation. When an operation was directed against one runaway slave settlement in particular and resources contributed from various points were employed, boats might be used for moving one of the groups, as was the case in the 1747 attack on the El Portillo *palenque* and in the 1816 attack on the El Frijol settlement. But, apart from this type of complex joint operation, the attacks were usually carried out by men on foot, since the terrain they had to cover was very uneven and beset with difficulties.

Even though this is a topic that should be taken up again when studying how the various systems of repression functioned in each region, I know of only one band that carried out all its operations as a mounted force. It operated on the plains of Puerto Príncipe between 1830 and 1832, and it was no coincidence that it was headed by Rafael Parrado.

This point—that most operations were conducted on foot—may seem irrelevant, but it is necessary for a full understanding of the style and work of each of the bands or slavehunting militias. Failure to acknowledge its importance makes it very difficult to reproduce the routes followed in the operations. Keeping this aspect in mind, analyzing the contents of the diaries, and being aware of the geographic conditions of the areas in which the operations were carried out makes it possible to reconstruct the marches and calculate distances and the possible locations of runaway slave settlements. It is the basis for the on-the-spot work that enables us to deduce important facts related to the economy, communications, defense tactics, and many other aspects that enrich our knowledge about this form of slave resistance. In this context, the distances covered by the slavehunters or the calculations they made concerning the distances separating various geographic points or features should also be kept in mind.

Distances in the nineteenth century were measured in leagues (one league being equivalent to 2.63 miles). However, we should not take the calculations in leagues that appear in the slavehunters' diaries of operations literally. Apart from probable errors caused by the personal characteristics, knowledge, and interests of the people who made the calculations, other circumstances have been substantiated. Rafael Parrado (in Puerto Príncipe), for example, always used a set number of leagues for each day's journey. He traveled on horseback, almost always on the plains, and divided the day's march into halves so the band could rest and eat; in his diary, he almost invariably recorded very stable journeys of six or seven leagues for each section of the day. However, if one calculates the length of the journey on the basis of modern maps and notes the points to which he referred, one finds that the real distances are generally very different.

The same was true of the diaries of operations in the eastern part of the island, since they were kept by bands or slavehunting militias that usually operated in very mountainous areas. They, too, calculated how many leagues they had traveled each day, but they always moved very slowly, covering very short distances; therefore, the calculations the eastern slavehunters made concerning how many leagues they had traveled should be taken with a grain of salt. If one takes into account the heights that had to be climbed, the many river crossings that had to be made, and other problems posed by the uneven terrain, one sometimes comes up with the same figures they recorded, which can be verified on modern maps; however, if the distance is calculated as the crow flies, the journey was always much shorter.

Most distances, however, were measured by the number of days' journey required. One example of this is found in the note Santiago Guerra made concerning the operations he headed in 1842, when he said that he had "walked fourteen leagues, or two days' journey" (ANC, AP, leg. 41, no. 38).

In general, the distances the slavehunters reported they had covered were nearly always exaggerated in their diaries and should be subjected to careful analysis. This problem occurred frequently in all the diaries and can be solved by comparing the data with the real distances between the points they described. For example, the report on the attack on the El Frijol runaway slave settlement included the following description: "From the point of Guinea, where the garrison was established recently, the runaway slave settlement was eighteen leagues from Monte Serrano, without any trail or path open to even difficult passage. It was impossible to ride animals, so the men had to endure almost unbearable labor, carrying the provisions on their backs" (AHSC, GP, leg. 554, no. 4).

This quotation confirms what has already been said concerning conditions in the areas of operation, which made it nearly impossible to use beasts of burden, and it also makes it possible to compare the slavehunters' calculations of distances. An analysis of the diary showed that they were one and a half days' journey from the runaway slave settlement, but the lineal distance was much shorter than reported. It would have been impossible for them to cover more than forty-seven miles as the crow flies in a day and a half, making their way through mountainous terrain. In this case, the lineal distance was really much less, but in the report, three sections of march were calculated as eighteen leagues.

Thus, the impossibility of using beasts of burden for transportation, the calculation of distances covered each half day, the occasional absence of open trails, and the crossing of streams and rivers were all aspects that had to be taken into consideration when reconstructing routes from the diaries of operations. With those elements in mind, I proceeded to analyze the contents of the diaries, contrasting the information found in them with data contained in other documents and maps. In addition, I decided on a chronological framework of operations, selected the geographic areas of greatest importance in those operations, and tabulated all the measurable information in order to define magnitudes and trends. In this way, I drew up a list of the runaway slave settlements in the eastern part of the island—the most inclusive such list known to date—compared the levels of development of those settlements, and established some common features of the social phenomenon under study.

I did not take the easy path of recording the history of the slavehunters—easy because they were the ones who wrote the documents. I refer to or analyze them only when it is necessary to do so in order to help readers understand my subject, which is the runaway slave settlements and the variations that arose in that form of resistance as a result of the continual attacks to which they were subjected. In order to reconstruct the development of those settlements, I combined the results obtained from analyzing the contents of the diaries with other information related to this topic that was widely scattered in various archives. Using the place-names, names of properties, and geographic points mentioned, I mapped the routes taken by each of the slavehunting militias. Aided by Pichardo's ([1875] 1986) map, I traced the routes on 1:50,000 maps of the Republic of Cuba, which facilitated greater precision in my calculations, and then transferred the routes to 1:300,000 maps (Instituto Cubano de Geodesia y Cartografía [hereafter cited as ICGC] 1980).

Thus, every operation is marked on a map. I used broken lines for routes that were reconstructed with a considerable degree of accuracy and dotted lines for those sections of the routes that, either because the descriptions given were not precise or because the writer did not identify some of the points, cannot be considered more than possibilities. The plantations, territorial divisions, and runaway slave settlements are marked, using the same legend on all the maps in order to facilitate their reading (see figs. 2, 5, 8–10, 12–16, 18, 26, and 27).

When elements that are not included in the general legend are shown on a map, another legend is used. The main purpose of the maps showing the routes taken by the slavehunting militias was not illustrative, though that is one of their functions. Rather, they were used as a methodological means for defining the areas where the runaway slave settlements were located, the areas of operations, the geographic areas that contained most of them, and possible regional changes.

Symbols Used in the Figures

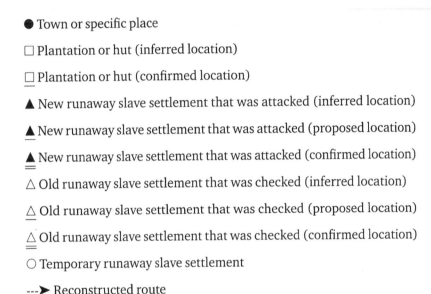

● Town or specific place

☐ Plantation or hut (inferred location)

☐ Plantation or hut (confirmed location)

▲ New runaway slave settlement that was attacked (inferred location)

▲ New runaway slave settlement that was attacked (proposed location)

▲ New runaway slave settlement that was attacked (confirmed location)

△ Old runaway slave settlement that was checked (inferred location)

△ Old runaway slave settlement that was checked (proposed location)

△ Old runaway slave settlement that was checked (confirmed location)

○ Temporary runaway slave settlement

---► Reconstructed route

Slave Resistance in Eastern Cuba
The First Few Centuries of Colonial Rule

The first part of Cuba that the Europeans who conquered the so-called West Indies saw was the rugged eastern region of the island. On Saturday, October 27, 1492, after leaving the eastern cays of the Great Bahama Bank, Admiral Christopher Columbus headed "to the south-southeast of the closest one of them . . . [and] sighted land before nightfall." On the next day, he continued the voyage and sailed up a very beautiful river. He recorded what he saw there in his log: "The island [is] full of extremely lovely mountains which are high but not very long, and all of the land is high . . . with many streams" (Colón 1961, 72).

Eighteen years later, Governor Diego Velázquez began the conquest of the island. He left Salvatierra de la Sabana, in the southwestern part of Hispaniola, on June 11, 1510. Early the next year, in the middle of a large Indian town called Baracoa, he founded the first European settlement on the northern coast of the easternmost part of Cuba, which he called

Nuestra Señora de la Asunción de Baracoa (Pichardo Viñals 1986, 11). Three years later, in November 1513, he founded a second town, which he called San Salvador de Bayamo. As in the other case, he added a Christian prefix to the Indian name of the town—and it is the Indian name that has survived.

After a long tour of the central and western parts of the island, during which they founded four other settlements, the conquerors went back east to where they had started and, in July 1515, founded the settlement of Santiago de Cuba. For many years, Baracoa, Bayamo, and Santiago de Cuba were the only European settlements in the eastern part of the island. Each was also the center of a jurisdiction whose borders had not been established precisely and that contained large areas that had not yet been settled.

Baracoa was considered the capital or focal point of the island, but Santiago de Cuba soon replaced it in importance. The rapid depletion of the sources of gold and the conquest of the so-called mainland turned Cuba into a kind of trampoline in that enormous enterprise, which halted the process of development throughout the island's territory—especially in the eastern region. Even though that part of the island had been inhabited by Indian groups with the highest level of development and greatest population density and had been the starting point of the conquest and colonization, it fell behind the populated areas in the western region.

Population growth is a good general index for calculating the development that took place during the first few centuries of Spanish colonization. The population in the eastern part of the island during that first century grew slowly because there was a rapid and considerable drop in the Indian population, many of the Europeans who had settled on the island left for the mainland, and few Africans were brought in.[1] During the first hundred years after the conquest, the population of Indians was considerably reduced, and from then on, their descendants—already mixed with whites, blacks, and other Indians who had been brought in as slaves from other islands and the continent—were concentrated in Guanabacoa (now Havana) and in El Caney, Jiguaní, and Tiguabos (in the eastern region). In a letter to the king dated September 22, 1608, Bishop Juan de Cabezas de Altamirano said, "Varacoa [sic] and Guanabacoa are towns that are far from the Spanish ones, but there are also

Table 1. Population of Santiago de Cuba in 1606

	WHITES		BLACKS		INDIANS		
PLACE	M	F	M	F	M	F	TOTAL
In the city	205	129	131	98	41	37	641
In the territorial divisions	12	0	7	0	1	0	20
Total	217	129	138	98	42	37	661

Source: AGI, Santo Domingo, leg. 116, 5.

Indians in Puerto del Príncipe [*sic*], Bayamo, and [Santiago de] Cuba, living on the outskirts of those towns" (Archivo General de Indias [hereafter cited as AGI], Santo Domingo, leg. 150).

In that same letter, concerning the black population, the bishop reported, "At a distance from some towns there are huts and *corrales* [small ranches] where there are always a number of blacks and some Spanish workers, depending on the plantation owner's possibilities" (AGI, Santo Domingo, leg. 150). This information agrees with other criteria of the era and was specifically stated in the census that was sent from Santiago de Cuba to the king in 1605, showing the composition of the population at that time (see Table 1).[2] Since Santiago de Cuba was the most important place in the eastern region, it may be inferred that the rest of the towns also had low demographic levels.

According to that census, nearly a century after the city of Santiago de Cuba was founded, it had 661 inhabitants, 12 percent of whom were Indians who had their own leaders and lived in a group of huts on the outskirts of the city per se. Black slaves constituted 36 percent of the inhabitants. This composition shows the changes that were taking place in the demographic process: whereas the Indians were disappearing, the population of African origin was experiencing a significant, though very slow, growth. If attention is paid to the way in which the black population was distributed in the census, some of the characteristics of slavery in those years can be inferred. Nearly always, there were fewer than five slaves for each family of Spaniards or whites who had been born on the island. With but few exceptions, the latter had more slaves than the former. These exceptions included the family of Andrés Estrada, who had twelve slaves, and that of Andrea Bernal, who had ten. The average was three slaves per house and seven per farm in the Guantánamo area in 1860. The proportion of male and female slaves did not yet show the important differences that arose some centuries later.

This fact is closely related to the stability and tranquillity of the groups of slaves, as was confirmed years later during the heyday of the slave plantations, when, in the interests of production, many more male than female slaves were brought in. In this regard, it is important to verify the relations that existed between the sexes and the different ethnic groups that, to a large extent, reflected where the slaves had come from in Africa (see Table 2).

Even though the sample presented in Table 2 is a very small one from which to draw inferences for generalizing about the situation on the island, it does reveal some characteristics of the problem of slavery in the colony at that time. It seems that this was the first census in which the slaves in Cuba were described by ethnic group—which is a reflection of the closed, domestic nature of the economy in those years. In this regard, legislation of the time advised owners to maintain a balance in the proportion of male and female slaves they brought in, since it was known that a disproportion in this regard was one of the causes of slaves' running away.

Another element that is brought out by an analysis of the census is that, of a total of 236 slaves in Santiago de Cuba, only 7 were listed as living on farms. These figures show that slaves were concentrated in the city or settlement, surely working as domestics and in manufacturing, transportation, grocery stores, and other small businesses, though many of them must have been hired out to work in agriculture, considering the importance that farming had in the era, according to the Cáceres Ordinances (Pichardo Viñals 1965, 108–29).

During the sixteenth and seventeenth centuries, the eastern region's economy was based on the exploitation of cattle- and hog-raising farms and other, smaller workplaces with diversified agricultural production that supplied their local areas and possibly engaged in smuggling. Hides, meat, and tobacco were some of the most important products, followed by sugar and cacao, the last two in very small amounts. This economy

Table 2. Ethnic Group and Gender of Slaves in Santiago de Cuba, 1605

ETHNIC GROUP	MALE	FEMALE	TOTAL
Unidentified	88	70	158
Biáfara	7	5	12
Angola	7	2	9
Criollo	4	5	9
Cape	3	3	6
Biocho	2	3	5
Bran	1	3	4
Arada	1	2	3
Mina	3	0	3
Congo	3	0	3
Barriga	2	0	2
Banon	2	0	2
Cumba	0	1	1
Batu	0	1	1
Batún	0	1	1
Moncauso	1	0	1
Chapala	1	0	1
Carabalí or Caravalí	2	0	2
Selandes	1	0	1
Banun	0	1	1
Viana or Biana	1	1	2
Ganga	1	0	1
Manguela	1	0	1
Bambra	1	0	1
Yalungá	1	0	1
Malangueta	1	0	1
Beruci	1	0	1
Enchico	1	0	1
Guayacan	1	0	1
Bela	1	0	1
Total	138	98	236

Source: AGI, Santo Domingo, leg. 116.

mainly favored Bayamo—and, to a lesser extent, Santiago de Cuba. The latter was also considerably helped by trade through its port. The other populated areas in the region had small groups of white inhabitants, most of whom had come from Spain; they raised cattle and grew tobacco, using the labor of descendants of Indians and African slaves.

This was the historical framework in which the first confrontations between slaves and slave owners took place. The first slave rebellion occurred in 1533, in the mines of Jobabo, in Oriente. During the rest of the first half of the sixteenth century, there were many uprisings and protests, both by Indians and by slaves of African origin, as may be inferred from a report that Hernando de Castro, a merchant, wrote in Santiago de Cuba in 1543: "In the twenty years that I have lived in Cuba, there has not been one in which a tax has not been levied for pacifying and conquering the runaway or rebellious Indians" (Pérez de la Riva 1952, 313).

All this is true, but we should keep the real importance of the facts in mind and not give them too much weight—as has happened on occasion. Only four slaves rebelled in the Jobabo mines in 1533, and no more than ten joined some Indians who had rebelled in Bayamo in that same decade. Such small numbers of participants were characteristic of that kind of protest in that era, and the protests were quickly drowned in blood. The isolated reports that came in from other places prove that the main method of resistance used by slaves was that of simply running away. There are no references to runaway slave settlements in Cuba during the sixteenth and seventeenth centuries—a response by the slaves that alarmed the owners when a plantation economy began to be developed at the end of the eighteenth century.

Documents dating from that period state that most of the first runaway slave settlements in Cuba were founded by Indians, though some were founded by Indians and blacks. However, no reference was made to runaways from the 1550s until the first half of the eighteenth century, when incidents related to the phenomenon of *palenques* were reported once again.

In 1731, some of the slaves in the Santiago del Prado (or El Cobre) mines, in the eastern part of the island, rebelled and founded runaway slave settlements in protest against attempts to return them to slavery after they—along with the mines—had been left to their own devices for several generations. Franco has studied that rebellion, so I will not do so here. It should be emphasized, however, that this incident was the first reference to the existence of runaway slave settlements in the history of Cuba.

Since 1607, the island had been divided into two departments—Eastern and Western—which corresponded to the jurisdictions of Santiago de Cuba and Havana, respectively. During the first few years of the seventeenth century, the Crown helped promote the sugar industry, but, as Wright (1916, 26–42) has shown, this assistance was more beneficial to the west than to the east. However, ten years after the industry began to be promoted by the granting of some small loans, the eastern region had thirty-nine sugar mills, owned by just a few people. Sánchez de Moya, administrator of the El Cobre mines, owned five of them in Santiago de Cuba, but eleven of the thirty-nine were in Bayamo. Total sugar production in 1617 was estimated at 28,000 arrobas, or 700,000 pounds (Jerez de Villarreal 1960, 68).

Reports dating from the end of that century show that some other lines of agriculture were being developed in the areas around Mayarí, El Caney, Guisa, and Yara (Jerez de Villarreal 1960, 71), all of which promoted small increases in the number of slaves brought to the island, many of whom were smuggled in. Many documents dating from that period attest to the importance that kind of smuggled goods acquired in the eastern region. As proof of this, all the runaways who lived in the El Portillo *palenque* and were captured in 1747 had been smuggled into Cuba from English ships along the coasts of Puerto Príncipe or Manzanillo.

Based on estimates made by A. de Humboldt, José Antonio Saco stated that around six thousand slaves were brought into Cuba between 1763 and 1789, a quarter of whom were smuggled in (1960, 173). As the slave population increased and the development of such production units as sugar mills concentrated them, reports of uprisings and other forms of active resistance by the slaves became more frequent. Vagabond runaway slaves were already commonplace in the city of Santiago de Cuba, as shown by announcements published in the press. In February 1742, the flight of two slaves who worked in a butcher's shop in the city was reported as follows: "They have run away again, and it is public knowledge that they are extremely depraved" (Bacardí Moreau 1925, 1:159).

A long process that began in the 1740s and lasted until the mid-nineteenth century showed the development of runaway slave settlements as a form of slave resistance—and the changes made in the repressive system that was created to oppose it. The first important development in this process was the founding of a runaway slave settlement that was much publicized in the mid-eighteenth century and was attacked for several years. A slavehunting militia composed of several columns of military men and civilians was sent against and attacked the settlement in 1747. It was the first important runaway slave settlement to exist on the island, not only because it was the first about which we have abundant information but also because it was the first against which an overwhelming force, of a size never before mobilized, was sent.

In the 1740s and 1750s, the eastern region experienced considerable—though still slow—demographic growth and economic development, which was reflected in the burgeoning of new towns, such as Holguín, which had begun to be a population center in 1731 (La Rosa Corzo 1987) and was officially founded in 1751. Likewise, places that had had few or no inhabitants up until then began to register a not insignificant increase in both respects. Jiguaní, where descendants of roving Indians had concentrated at the beginning of the eighteenth century, was declared to be a town in 1751. More than three hundred tobacco growers lived in the Mayarí area. The city of Santiago de Cuba began to surpass Bayamo in terms of economic importance. Slave plantations initiated a process of slow but steady growth in the region. The existence of an important runaway slave settlement in the mountain range between Santiago de Cuba and Bayamo was not unrelated to that phenomenon; nor was the fact that it was violently attacked and that the existence of two other *palenques* in the mountain ranges in the northern part of that region was denounced.

The 1747 attack on the El Portillo runaway slave settlement—which in colonial documents was initially called the Cabo Cruz settlement (because it was in the same general area as that cape) or the El Masío settlement (because it was near the Masío River)—had several important aspects. For one thing, the settlement had been in existence for twenty years; for another, even though the attack was the first to be organized against this kind of slave resistance, mixed forces were used—as had been done in Cartagena, Panama, and Jamaica. In Cuba, the absence of events as important as those that had taken place in those regions of the Americas in the sixteenth, seventeenth, and eighteenth centuries is proof of the links that existed between the social phenomenon of the runaway slave settlements and the levels of the slave population and the slaves' concentration in production units—mines, sugar mills, and coffee plantations—where they were exploited extensively.

In the southern part of the eastern region of Cuba, the authorities and plantation owners were terrified that incidents similar to those that had taken place in Jamaica—where the runaway slaves living in settlements had caused a veritable upheaval—would occur in Cuba because of Jamaica's geographic propinquity to the coasts of the region. Official documents even expressed fear, noting that the El Portillo runaway slave settlement was in an area that was "the closest to Jamaica" (AGI, Santo Domingo, leg. 367). This fear had considerable weight in the official decision to wage what in other colonies was known as a war on runaways—which had never been done in Cuba before.

El Portillo

Even though some sources that are frequently consulted, such as the work of Bacardí (1925), contain references to this runaway slave settlement and some students of this subject have also mentioned it, the El Portillo settlement has not been made the subject of an individual study, possibly because the basic documents concerning it are in Seville (AGI, Santo Domingo, leg. 367). From a chronological point of view, this *palenque*, which was attacked in 1747, was the first and most important expression of this specific form of slave resistance—that is, if no new documents, unexamined as yet, appear in the future to change this. Therefore, the detailed study of that settlement is a historiographic necessity. Moreover, even though limited to the colonial documents that have been located to date that were written as a result of the settlement's supposed extermination, such study yields results that broaden the chronological framework of the existence of runaway slave settlements in Cuba, since El Portillo was the most important expression of that phenomenon at a very early stage in the development of slave plantations.

Early in 1747, the *cabildo* (municipal council) of the city of Santiago de Cuba echoed rumors that had been circulating for some time, both in Bayamo and in Santiago de Cuba, to the effect that there was a runaway slave settlement at the place known as El Portillo in the Sierra Maestra.[3] According to the authorities in Santiago de Cuba, the runaway slave settlement had been in existence for more than twenty years, though with very few inhabitants, but the number of runaways living there at that time was increasing at a rate that the slave owners considered alarming. The runaways in the settlement farmed and also obtained sustenance from the woods, so "they lacked nothing" (AGI, Santo Domingo, leg. 367). The same documents issued by the *cabildo* of Santiago de Cuba also referred to the need to attack two other runaway slave settlements—one in the Mayarí area and the other near Moa (in the northern part of the region)—so it may be supposed that they were also attacked, but it has not been possible to confirm this as yet.

Those documents prove that, by the mid-eighteenth century, the authorities knew that there were three runaway slave settlements in the eastern part of Cuba—though there were no indications of similar settlements in the rest of the island's territory. It is important to emphasize that those three settlements were located in the three mountain regions in which the greatest number of combing operations and attacks on *palenques* were recorded during the first half of the nineteenth century. In this regard, it should be noted that a plan that the governor of Santiago de Cuba drew up in 1816 for capturing the runaways who lived in those settlements stated that around three hundred runaways had been living in the mountain ranges in the northern part of the region since the mid-eighteenth century. This aspect is discussed later on, since few of the figures and calculations contained in the colonial documents on the runaway slave settlements—documents that had a marked tendency to exaggerate and always cited the figure of three hundred, which was repeated indiscriminately when referring to different areas and times—have been corrected.

The scene of the operations undertaken against the runaway slaves who lived in the El Portillo settlement was a very high wooded area: the range of the Sierra Maestra, which is a clearly defined part of the landscape in eastern Cuba. That range, which includes the highest peaks on the island, extends eastward from Cruz Cape to the Guantánamo Basin, broken only by the basin and bay of Santiago de Cuba. It is estimated to be a little more than 150 miles long. At that time, this extensive mountain area could be reached only from the towns of Manzanillo, Bayamo, and Santiago de Cuba. Most of the area consisted of virgin forests, with paths too steep and narrow for beasts of burden.

The part of that great mountain range lying between Cruz Cape and Santiago de Cuba is known as the Turquino Range and is between six and eighteen miles wide. This was the area where the first runaway slave settlement was located, but it would also be an important zone of operations more than fifty years later. The easternmost part of the range before reaching Santiago de Cuba was called the El Cobre Range. The entire area was threaded with rivers whose courses were sometimes very steep, plunging down to the sea. Some of them—such as the Turquino, Bayamito, Guamá del Sur, and Sevilla—were very closely related to the runaway slave settlements.

The vegetation in this area is now very lush and thick. In the eighteenth century, the area was practically uninhabited, and its forests contained many mahogany and cedar trees. Only on the northern spurs of the mountain range were there a few farms and widely scattered work sites, with very few people. On the southern coast, there were three or four plantations, whose only buildings consisted of one or two fan-palm huts.

The Attack on El Portillo

Throughout August 1747, the *cabildo* of the city of Santiago de Cuba worked on the preparations for a general attack on the runaways living at El Portillo. On August 30, the authorities of the city of Bayamo received two letters signed by the governor of Santiago de Cuba, dated August 21 and 24, ordering them "to contribute fifty men with their main and subordinate chiefs, in two slavehunting militias." That is, Bayamo was to contribute two slavehunting militias of twenty-five men each, captained by military men; together with a similar number of slavehunting militias formed at El Caney and El Cobre, they were to "explore the mountains where runaway blacks [were] reported to be living in settlements" (AGI, Santo Domingo, leg. 367). The second letter stated that each of the men in the slavehunting militias would be paid three pesos in advance and would be given three silver reals when the troops set out.

The authorities in Bayamo quickly carried out those orders. Recruiting began on the same day the letters were received. Miguel Muñoz, head of the Bayamo branch of the Holy Brotherhood, led the troops from Bayamo and was in charge of directing the operations.[4] Muñoz named Bernardino Polanco as his subordinate, and the two headed one of the slavehunting militias. Francisco Joseph Noranco headed the other, with Andrés de Guevara as his subordinate.

That same day, they recruited thirty-one men, to each of whom they paid the advance of three pesos. On leaving Bayamo, they headed toward Lora, recruiting more men along the way: one at Peralejo and seven at Lora. On September 2, two men joined them at Jibacoa, and then five at Guá. On September 4, ten more men joined the troop, at the place known as Vicana.

Thus, Bayamo contributed a total of fifty-six men. However, their initial enthusiasm caused by the advance of three pesos soon turned to discouragement as a result of some misfortunes. Several men got sick, and five others deserted. By the time the men reached El Portillo, on the coast, where it had been agreed they would make camp and wait for the rest of the troops, seven men were sick, and an epidemic of measles broke out.

It had taken them seven days to travel from Bayamo to El Portillo, during which time three other recruits joined them. Three days after they had made camp, waiting became difficult because their food began to run out. They therefore sent six men to Betancourt's *corral* to get cassava bread, since twelve pesos' worth of it "was not enough to feed fifty-four men for ten days" (AGI, Santo Domingo, leg. 367). On September 15—that is, six days later—twelve pesos' worth of cassava bread, one hundred pounds of salt, and a jug of sugarcane aguardiente were sent to them from Bayamo, but they did not receive those items until September 20; therefore, when the troops that were coming from Santiago de Cuba arrived on the afternoon of September 16, the situation they found was not very encouraging. The head of the Santiago de Cuba branch of the Holy Brotherhood led the group of thirty-six men from Santiago de Cuba, but they were in "very bad shape and hungry." Their provisions had run out, several of them were sick, and some others had gone back. Thus, we can calculate that a troop composed of two bands of twenty-five men each, making a total of fifty, had set out initially from Santiago de Cuba.

El Caney had sent a troop of twenty-one men, only six of whom arrived at El Portillo. They were led by the head of the El Caney branch of the Holy Brotherhood. During their trek along the coast, the members of that slavehunting militia had captured two runaway slaves who lived in the settlement. The authorities of the mining town of El Cobre had outfitted another force—also composed of twenty-one men—but its arrival was not recorded. However, since that was the closest point to El Portillo and the troops from El Cobre were famed for their resistance, they must have had few, if any, losses. Because of this lack of precision concerning the final figure of participants in the operations, we can only estimate that the force that attacked the runaway slave settlement must have totaled slightly more than one hundred men—a force that would not be equaled in the eastern region until many years later, in the nineteenth century.[5]

A report dated September 20 that was sent from the camp at El Portillo to the representative of the *cabildo* stated, "We all continue to lack what is needed for setting out," and asked that four jugs of sugarcane aguardiente, salt, and cassava bread be sent. Another message was sent to Betancourt's *corral*, asking for more cassava bread. After some of the provisions that had been requested arrived and some cattle that had been purchased from nearby *corrales* were killed, the troops began the operations against the runaway slave settlement.

Moving in several small squads from the Masío River, the slavehunters combed the nearby mountains. A mountain man known as Manuel Peregrino, who lived in the area, served as their guide. Eleven runaway slaves who lived in the settlement—five of them women—were captured in those operations. The official list of the slaves who had been captured did not include two "small children," ages one and two, who, according to the statement of one of the captured slaves (discussed later in this chapter), had lived in the settlement. None of those prisoners were captured at the settlement; rather, they were seized while fleeing through the mountains, since the inhabitants of the settlement had scattered when they learned that the troops were nearby. It is interesting to observe that the tactic they used was the one that the runaways living in settlements employed most frequently up until a hundred years later.

From the first statements extracted from their prisoners, the attackers learned that the runaway slave settlement had a total of nineteen members. Thus the approximately one hundred men in the column—some of whom were sick, all of whom were tired from their march through thick underbrush, and who had little food left—contented themselves with having captured more than half the runaways and decided to withdraw, even though they had not found the runaways' settlement.

Therefore, it really cannot be said that the El Portillo runaway slave settlement was attacked. On that occasion, the attacking force did not reach the place that served as refuge for that small group of runaway slaves. Later references speak of its existence, but they offer no proof that it was destroyed. Its history was lost in the decades that followed, in which the colonial administration turned its attention to other runaway slave settlements. It may be that it was abandoned after that expedition and was covered by the undergrowth, or runaways may have lived in it again for many years, but this is a matter of speculation. What has been proved from the statements of those who were captured is that it had been in existence for more than twenty years.

The capture operations had been carried out in the hills between the Masío and Mota Rivers and ended on October 17, 1747. The area was really more than eighteen miles from Cruz Cape, so the runaway slave settlement should be identified as El Portillo—as it appeared in some later communications—rather than Cabo Cruz. The operations, including the capture of runaways who had lived in the settlement and were fleeing through the underbrush in an attempt to throw off their pursuers, took a total of twenty-five days. The first two runaways the slavehunting militia from El Cobre captured near the coast had been sent to Bayamo; one of the five women, called María Antonia, who had been born in Jamaica and was close to giving birth, was sent to Bayamo with her two young children. The captors formed the eight other runaways into a chain of prisoners and set out with them for the regional capital.

The Captured Runaways

In the case of Cuba, it is very difficult to create a full reconstruction of the way of life and motivations of a group of runaway slaves living in a settlement.[6] Most of the runaways who were captured in the nineteenth century were not tried in any legal proceedings—or, when such proceedings were held, they were not given much importance—so the document containing the statements made by the captured runaways from the El Portillo settlement is of great interest. It provides valuable data on the way of life in the settlement, the runaways' motivations, their experiences as slaves, why they fled, how they were brought to the island, how they had been branded, and how they had been treated by their owners.[7] In short, it is one of the few documents that record statements made by a group of runaways who had lived in a settlement. I have found nothing similar concerning the nineteenth century. Therefore, the inclusion of this section, which summarizes the statements made by the runaways who were interrogated, complements our knowledge of that social phenomenon and makes it possible to understand, in part, the runaways' point of view.

On October 24, 1747, Alonso de Arcos y Moreno, governor of Santiago de Cuba and its captain in time of war, received a letter from Pedro Sánchez de Lorenzana, mayor of the settlement of Bayamo, to which was attached a description of the events that had taken place, written by Bernardino Polanco, and a list of the runaways who had been caught "on the southern coast, below this [river] port," between the Masío and Mota Rivers. Descriptions of the captured runaways and the names of their owners were included.

The document stated that most of the runaways were of "bad entry"—had been smuggled onto the island—and had not been branded as proof that their owners had paid the tax required to legitimize their entry. The captured runaways were imprisoned in the castle of Santiago de Cuba and in the public jail. The governor ordered that they be tried. Few captured runaway slaves who had lived in settlements were tried in the following years, especially after a repressive system directed by the Royal Consulate was created in Havana in 1796 and adapted to the conditions in each region—in the eastern part of the country, with the creation of the Commission of Eastern Plantation Owners in 1814.

In the last few months of 1747, the captured runaways from the settlement were brought to the Hall of Justice of Santiago de Cuba, where they appeared before the minister of the Royal Treasury and Manuel González Prestelo, clerk of the royal court, who took careful notes. The same procedure was used in all cases to obtain statements from the runaways. After being asked if they had accepted the Christian doctrine, which was determined by whether they had been baptized, they were required to swear on the Bible, told they had to tell the truth, and asked the obligatory questions: Who is your master? Why did you run away? How long have you been a runaway? Where is the runaway slave settlement? How many runaways lived there?

Other questions were also asked, depending on the specifics of each case. Based on their answers, it is possible to reconstruct the experiences and views of each of the runaways who had lived in the El Portillo settlement and were captured in 1747.

The Congo Joaquín Eduardo. The first prisoner to appear in the court of Santiago de Cuba, on the morning of October 25, 1747, was Joaquín Eduardo, of the Congo ethnic group. He said that he was owned by Andrés de Guevara, who lived in Bayamo, and that he had been a runaway for a year and a half. He stated that he had been living in the settlement because his master had sent him as a spy to find out where the runaway slave settlement was; he said he had been offered his freedom in exchange for bringing back information on how many blacks lived there. He added that, after he had reached the runaway slave settlement, he realized that the deadline his master had set for "going and coming back with the information" (AGI, Santo Domingo, leg. 367) had passed, so he was afraid and stayed with the runaways.

In response to other questions, Joaquín Eduardo said that he had been brought in a ship and taken ashore along the southern coast of Puerto Príncipe around twenty years earlier and then sold in El Portillo, in the Sierra Maestra. His first master was called Gregorio Eduardo, but then he was passed on to another, named Gabriel Ignacio Palma, from whom he had run away. He went to and lived in the runaway slave settlement in the Sierra Maestra but was captured by Andrés de Guevara, who then purchased him from his former master in order to send him to the settlement as a spy. Asked if his master had presented him for branding as proof that his owner had paid the tax for legitimizing his entry and if he had been branded, he replied "no to both questions."[8] He added that he had heard what was going on when other slaves were being branded for that purpose in Bayamo but that his master did not bring him in from the tobacco plantation where he was working.

When asked where the runaway slave settlement was, where he had been captured, how many runaways were living in the settlement, and how many of them had managed to escape, he replied that the place where the settlement was situated was known as El Portillo but that he had been captured at a place known as Mota, around three leagues [eight miles] from the settlement. He said that nineteen runaways had been living in the settlement, eleven of whom were captured; eight escaped. He stated that seven of the nineteen runaways who had lived in the settlement were women. Joaquín Eduardo did not know how to sign his name, and an examination of his body showed that he had never been branded. He was thirty-two years old.

The Congo Antonio Felipe. The next prisoner to appear was the Congo called Antonio Felipe, who had been baptized some years earlier, so the obligatory procedure was followed with him. It was recorded that his master was Diego Felipe Silveira, who lived in Bayamo. Antonio Felipe said that he did not know how long he had lived in the runaway slave settlement but added that "it seemed to him that he had been there for five or six years, because he had not gone out of the woods at all after going there, and he had run away because he did not have any set place in which to work and raise food on a plot of land, because his master had him working in one place one day and another place the next; he said that his master had not given him any cause for running away" (AGI, Santo Domingo, leg. 367).

Antonio Felipe had been smuggled into Cuba on board an English ship along the Manzanillo coast twenty years earlier and had had only one master. When asked about the brandings as proof that masters had paid the tax required to legitimize the entry of slaves smuggled into Cuba, he said that "in the brandings that were carried out in Bayamo, the master took him to the house where the agent lived. It was in a tall house, and they burned him in two places on the chest and back" (AGI, Santo Domingo, leg. 367).

In response to other questions, the runaway gave answers similar to those given by the other defendant. With regard to where the runaway slave settlement was located, his information agreed with that of other witnesses, but he added one interesting bit of information, saying that the settlement was up in the mountains between the Masío and Mota Rivers, "near the seacoast" (AGI, Santo Domingo, leg. 367). Concerning the runaways who lived there, he said that, in addition to the nineteen adults, there were two children, making a total of twenty-one runaways living in the settlement. When the body of Antonio Felipe was examined, only one brand was found, on his left shoulder blade. He was forty years old and did not know how to sign his name.

The Congo Gregorio. Later, when the session was resumed, Gregorio, of the Congo ethnic group, who belonged to Juan de León Estrada, who lived in Bayamo, appeared in court. This slave had run away about two years earlier. As to why, he said "that he had done so because his master had taken away a pig he had raised to help his brother," who was going to Havana, and "also because his master had taken away a bale of tobacco that he had," giving nothing in exchange. He said that Juan de León Estrada had purchased him on board an English sloop along the Manzanillo coast. This proved that he had been smuggled in, but he had also been branded as proof that his owner had paid the tax for legitimizing his entry, since, as he reported, his master had taken him to the house of Captain Juan Guerra, "where they burned his chest, and then, later, he had been taken to a house with a balcony, where they burned his back" (AGI, Santo Domingo, leg. 367). The rest of his statements coincided with those given by the previous witnesses. Finally, his body was examined, showing the brands. He was thirty-five years old and did not know how to sign his name.

The Carabalí Miguel. That same day, Miguel, of the Carabalí ethnic group, appeared in court. Since he said that he had not been baptized and only Christians were required to swear to the truth of their statements, he was allowed to testify "in his own way, promising to tell the truth." His master was Captain Pedro Orellana, known as "Capacha." Miguel could not say how long he had been a runaway because, as he said, "when he ran away, he had just been brought from Africa and did not know any-thing about the woods. One day when he was working, another black called Francés asked him to go with him, and he took him to the runaway slave settlement where the other blacks were." When asked who had purchased him, Miguel said that "he had just been brought from Africa and did not know how to express his thoughts, and he did not remember who had purchased him" (AGI, Santo Domingo, leg. 367). He added that his present master had bought him in Bayamo from another, who had in turn purchased him on board an English ship along the Manzanillo coast and that he had then been taken up the Cauto River. He had never been branded, which was confirmed when his body was examined. He was fifty years old and did not know how to sign his name. Collateral investigations brought out the information that he had lived in the runaway slave settle-ment for sixteen years.

The Carabalí Mariana. The first of the women who had lived in the runaway slave settlement appeared in the court of Santiago de Cuba on October 27. A member of the Carabalí ethnic group, she was named Mariana. Since her arrival in Santiago de Cuba as a member of the chain of runaways from the settlement who had been captured, she had been kept in the city's public jail. She said that she was a Christian and took an oath. She belonged to Clara Núñez, of Bayamo, and had been a runaway for seventeen years. As to why she had run away, she said that "it was because her mistress was never pleased but punished her for trivial mis-takes, and that, when she ran away, she and another black woman named Juana María Riveros and five male blacks, including the witness's small son Bartolomé—who was captured after he had lived in the runaway slave settlement for some time—all left Bayamo together" (AGI, Santo Do-mingo, leg. 367). Concerning her entry in Cuba, she said that Francisco de Velazco had purchased her on the coast of Puerto Príncipe, to which she had been brought by an English sloop. Later, she was passed on to Basilia de Luna, who lived in Bayamo, who then passed her on to her sister. Still later, she was sold to a man called Pablo, who was also known as "El Isleño," and then to somebody called "Don Matheo." She was branded in Bayamo when Pedro Ignacio Ximenez was governor. When her body was examined, the marks were found on her right breast and on the left side of her back. She was thirty-five years old.

The Mina María de la Caridad. Another of the female runaways who had been captured—María de la Caridad, of the Mina ethnic group—was presented in court next. Since she was a Christian, she took an oath. Her owner was Juan Antonio Bosques, of Bayamo, and she had run away two years earlier. When asked why she had run away, she said that "she had done so because . . . Ana María Morales, her mistress, was very poor, so whatever money she, the witness, obtained was used to support her mistress. Because she had done this, when her mistress was dying, her mistress wanted to give her her freedom, but her son Juan Antonio did not agree to this. Later, he punished her a great deal even though the witness had not given him any reason for doing so, because she had done whatever he ordered her to do. So, she ran away" (AGI, Santo Domingo, leg. 367). Concerning her entry in Cuba, she said that a very big English ship had brought her to the coast of Puerto Príncipe. She had had several owners and had been taken to Bayamo so Colonel Carlos de Sucre, governor of Bayamo, would brand her as proof that her owner had paid the tax for legitimizing her entry. When her body was examined, the branding marks were found, though they were very indistinct. She was fifty years old.

The Congo Juana. Juana, of the Congo ethnic group, was the next to appear. She, too, was a Christian and took an oath. Her owner was named Juan Domínguez, and he, too, lived in Bayamo. She could not say exactly how long she had been a runaway but stated that she thought it was a long time. As for why she had run away, she said it was "because her mistress was not pleased by anything she did and punished her, so she felt plagued and ran away" (AGI, Santo Domingo, leg. 367). According to her statements, an English sloop had brought her to the Manzanillo coast, where Francis Verdecia bought her. After that, he died, and she was inherited by his widow, Felipa, whose last name she could not remember. After that, her mistress "hired her out to Pedro de Orellana, a free black," and, on his death, she was sold to her last owner, Juan Domínguez, from whom she immediately ran away. She had not been branded as proof that her owner had paid the tax required to legitimize her entry or for any other purpose. In this regard, she said that, when Governor Pedro Ignacio Ximenez was branding slaves as proof of payment of that tax in Bayamo, her mistress did not want her to be burned because she did not have enough money to pay for the branding. When her body was examined, no marks were found. She was thirty-five years old and, as was discovered from other statements, had lived in the runaway slave settlement for seven and a half years.

The Congo Rosa. Another of the runaway women who had been captured—Rosa, of the Congo ethnic group—was brought into court next. Considered a Christian because she had been baptized, she took the obligatory oath. She stated that her owner was Miguel Bosque, of Bayamo, and that she had run away three years earlier. On explaining why she had done so, she said "that the reason was that her mistress, her master's old mother-in-law, was a woman who was very hard to please and punished her every so often but that her master was a good man." She had been brought to the Manzanillo coast in an English ship with two masts, and, when she was taken to Bayamo, it was to Camaniguan. When asked if she had been presented for branding as proof that her owner had paid the tax for legitimizing her entry, she said that, when Governor Pedro Ximenez was conducting the branding in Bayamo, she was not presented "because she had been taken inside the house, and she did not know if any papers were required for branding as proof that owners had paid the tax required to legitimize the entry of their slaves" (AGI, Santo Domingo, leg. 367). When her body was examined, no brands were found. She was thirty years old.

On October 29 of that year, aware that Juan Antonio de Anaya, head of the Santiago de Cuba branch of the Holy Brotherhood, had just brought two of the captured runaways who had lived in the settlement from Bayamo, the governor of Santiago de Cuba ordered that they be held in the castle of San Francisco and that they make statements in the Court of Justice in the city.

The Mandinga Salvador. As a result, Salvador, of the Mandinga ethnic group, appeared before the judges on Thursday, October 30. Since he considered himself to be a Christian, he took an oath. He said that his master was Joseph Lopez, of Bayamo. He had been a runaway for five years and, when asked why he had run away, said it was because "he worked in his field of yucca on holy days but, when it came time to harvest it and make cassava bread, his master took the money and refused to give it to him so he could buy provisions" (AGI, Santo Domingo, leg. 367). As for when he was brought to Cuba, he said that he and many others had been sold from an English sloop that had put in along the Manzanillo coast forty years earlier. He had not had any other master, and he remembered that he had been presented for branding as proof that his owner had paid the tax required to legitimize his entry and had been branded. It was verified that he had the corresponding marks on his chest and back. At that time, he was sixty years old.

The Congo Antonio. The other runaway who had been captured was Antonio, of the Congo ethnic group. After the required formalities for beginning the trial, he said that he had lived in the runaway slave settlement for fifteen years. On referring to his motivation, he said "it was because his master sold his country house and the witness's plot of land, so his work had been for nothing, so he decided to run away" (AGI, Santo Domingo, leg. 367). His master, Diego Rodríguez, had purchased him, along with "many blacks," from a sloop that put in along the Manzanillo coast. He had never been presented for branding as proof that his owner had paid the tax legitimizing his entry or been marked in any way. When his body was examined, no brand was found. He was thirty-four years old.

After those statements, Joseph de las Cuevas, a lawyer from the royal courts of Santa Fe and Santo Domingo, was appointed prosecutor and was given the writs so that he could follow the normal procedures in handling the matter of the runaway slaves who had lived in a settlement and been captured in the hills between the Masío and Mota Rivers, in the leeward part of the island, all of whom belonged to residents of Bayamo.

But the trial was not over yet. The woman called María Antonia, who had been born in Jamaica, had lived in the runaway slave settlement, and had been captured along with her two small children when she was close to giving birth, still had to appear. Therefore, the Santiago de Cuba authorities asked their counterparts in Bayamo to turn her over to them. The continual requests from the authorities in Santiago de Cuba that María Antonia be handed over to them and the varied justifications that the Bayamo authorities gave for not doing so contained references to the trials that the runaway slave woman had gone through since her capture. Therefore, it is possible to form a detailed reconstruction of the facts and present a social and personal description seldom recorded in documents of this kind.

The Jamaican María Antonia. After having been captured near the Masío River, along with her two small children, María Antonia was sent in a chain of prisoners to Bayamo. In a certificate issued on December 23, 1747, a doctor stated that, after having gone through the "mistreatment and fatigue" of being sent in the chain of prisoners and having fallen in the river, she gave birth two days after being imprisoned in the Bayamo jail. Just before she gave birth, however, there was "a complication in the evolution of the matrix, from which she is suffering, with her legs and feet inflamed, and the baby has a serious catarrhal secretion. The mother . . . has a fever every day, which is why a close eye is being kept on them" (AGI, Santo Domingo, leg. 367).

A free fifty-year-old mulatto named Seberina Sánchez, one of the midwives in Bayamo, had assisted when María Antonia gave birth. In a written statement that was attached to the case, she gave testimony about the birth and the state of the mother and child. As for the former, she reported that she had had to apply "hot cloths and that the birth was achieved with much labor, leaving the mother with the same complication." The midwife stated that she was still working on her but had "not managed to halt the hemorrhage completely." María Antonia's feet were still swollen, and thus it was felt that her life would be endangered as a result of any exertion on her part. As for the newborn child, the midwife said, "There is no hope that the baby, her daughter, will live, because half of the side of her face is very swollen and she has a bad cough" (AGI, Santo Domingo, leg. 367).

Despite the midwife's statements, the authorities, who wanted to conclude the case quickly, requested the participation of Dr. Esteban de Fuente, who practiced medicine in the Bayamo garrison and who, after an examination made on December 30, 1747, expressed his opinion that the baby had "two apothems in both ears, that they [had] caused some sores that cover[ed] nearly all the ears' surfaces and another ulcer in the nostrils that interfere[d] with her breathing, and that the mother [had] a hemorrhage" (certificate signed by Dr. Esteban de la Fuente, December 30, 1747, AGI, Santo Domingo, leg. 367).

The baby died that same day, which led to an examination and report by Juan Rubio Polanco, who attested that the baby "was laid out on a mat, dressed like an angel, and had died of natural causes" (certificate issued by Juan Rubio Polanco, December 30, 1747, AGI, Santo Domingo, leg. 367).

Two and a half months later, María Antonia, completely recovered, was taken on horseback to Santiago de Cuba, along with her two small children, and imprisoned in the city jail. During her appearance in court, she corroborated many of the details that had been presented earlier in the trial. María Antonia had lived in the runaway slave settlement for seven years, during which time she had given birth to three children, one of whom had died in the settlement. The other two were captured along with her. Her owner was Juan Polanco, of Bayamo. When asked why she had run away, she said that "it was because of the bad conditions of captivity, bad food that her master gave her, and much punishment, because a good master makes for a good slave" (AGI, Santo Domingo, leg. 367). With regard to her entry into Cuba, she said that she had been taken from Jamaica to the Manzanillo coast in an English ship. She also said that she had never been branded, but when her body was examined, it was found that the initials S. M. had been burned on her left breast, which she identified as a mark her mistress had made. María Antonia was thirty years old.

This concluded the process of taking statements, and thus, after Joseph de las Cuevas had studied the writs, the court proceeded to the confiscation of the slaves whose illegal entry had been proved and who had not been submitted to branding as proof that their owners had paid the tax for legitimizing their entry. Some months earlier, the court had initiated a process of returning to their owners all those whose "legitimacy" had been proved. Hence, on November 6 of that year, Mariana the Carabalí had been returned to her owners after they had paid the expenses incurred for her upkeep and a jailer's fee.

Militia sergeant Andrés de Guevara presented a claim that the Congo Joaquín Eduardo be handed over to him because, as he explained, he had captured the runaway slave a year earlier, along with eight others who had lived in the El Portillo *palenque*. In view of the mission to destroy that refuge, the sergeant had promised to give Joaquín Eduardo his freedom—just as the latter had stated in the trial—if he told him where it was. This statement was corroborated by Joaquín Bosques, a participant in an earlier unsuccessful attack on the settlement in 1741 and witness to the events described. Guevara also claimed the Mandinga Salvador, since he had captured him in similar circumstances and used him for the same purpose. Guevara had purchased the two slaves from their respective owners after capturing them. With this as justification, the old owner was able to recover both slaves after making the established payment, a matter that was verified on October 1, 1747.

For his part, the owner of the Congo Antonio provided documents proving that Antonio, along with a group of his other slaves, had been presented for branding some years earlier but that, at the owner's request, they had not been branded, a point that was recorded in the handwritten certificate stating that their owner had paid the tax required to legitimize their entry. The document in question recorded the payment of the tax and a physical description of the slave. This permitted the owner to take him away after paying the costs of his capture, his keep, and a jailer's fee.[9]

On December 20, María de la Caridad was ordered turned over to her owner, who paid seventy-one pesos and six reals when he took her away.

The judge who heard the case, with the proof of illegal entries and testimony that some of the captured runaways from the settlement had not been branded, ordered that the owners of those slaves be subpoenaed to appear before the court within a given time. This was delayed because the owners did not respond to the repeated subpoenas that were issued. Therefore, the captured runaways who remained were auctioned off. On July 16, 1748, nearly a year after they had been captured, it was determined to sell the following slaves:

Miguel, a Carabalí. Slave of Pedro Orellana. Illegal entry and no brand showing that his owner had paid the tax for legitimizing his entry. He was fifty years old and suffered from pains in his spine and joints. As he was very thin, he was appraised at 125 pesos.

Antonio, a Congo. Slave of Diego Rodríguez. Illegal entry and no brand showing that his owner had paid the tax for legitimizing his entry. Because he had lived in the runaway slave settlement, which was considered a defect, he was appraised at 200 pesos.

Juana, a Congo. Slave of Juan Domínguez. Illegal entry and no brand

Table 3. Runaway Slaves Captured at the El Portillo *Palenque*, 1747

NAME	ETHNIC GROUP	AGE	YEARS AS A RUNAWAY
Miguel	Carabalí	50	16
Antonio	Congo	45	15
Antonio Felipa	Congo	40	6
Juaquín Eduardo	Congo	22	1.5
Gregorio	Congo	35	2.5
Salvador	Mandinga	66	5
Juana	Conga mondonga	35	7
Mariana	Carabalí	35	17
María de la Caridad	Mina	50	2
Rosa	Congo	30	3
María Antonia	Criollo (Jamaican)	30	7
No name recorded	Criollo (born in the settlement)	1	
No name recorded	Criollo (born in the settlement)	2	

Source: Based on information contained in the decrees of the trial (AGI, Santo Domingo, leg. 367).

showing that her owner had paid the tax for legitimizing her entry. She had no physical defects and was thirty years old. Since she had been a runaway for seven years, she was assessed at 150 pesos.

The day after the slaves were appraised, a slave who served as official town crier announced that the three slaves would be sold at the gates of Government Square in Santiago de Cuba. The announcement was repeated every day for the rest of July and the first few days of August, but no buyers appeared. At last, on August 14, an individual named Manuel de la Fuente, a watchman from the port of Santiago de Cuba, appeared and made an offer of 335 pesos for the three slaves—140 pesos less than the asking price. More announcements were made on August 15, 16, and 17, and a man named Miguel Cortina, who lived in the city, raised the offer to 400 pesos. A new announcement was made, and the first bidder,

OWNER	HOW BROUGHT INTO CUBA	FATE
Pedro de Orellana	Illegally, no tax paid	Sold
Diego Rodríguez	Illegally, no tax paid	Sold
Diego Felipe Silveiro	Illegally, no tax paid	Returned
Andrés de Guevara	Illegally, no tax paid	Returned
Juan León Estrada	Illegally, tax paid	Returned
Joseph López	Illegally, tax paid	Returned
Juan Domínguez	Illegally, no tax paid	Sold
Clara Núñez	Illegally, tax paid	Returned
Juan Antonio Vázquez	Illegally, tax paid	Returned
Miguel Bosques	Illegally, tax paid	Returned
Francisco Blanco	Illegally, no tax paid	Sold
		Sold
		Sold

Manuel de la Fuente, then offered 450 pesos if Juana was replaced with another of the captured slaves who was not included in the announcements. The announcements continued with this difference, and Cortina raised his offer to 600 pesos on August 19 for three men and a woman—"four head." This last announcement was repeated until September 7, on which date, since nobody could be found who would offer more, four of the runaways who had lived in the settlement were sold. Miguel, Antonio, Joaquín, and Juana were returned to slavery.

On September 9, an agent of Miguel Vázquez, owner of the Congo Rosa, paid sixty-six pesos and five reals to recover the runaway. The same thing happened in the case of the Carabalí Mariana, whose master recovered her at a cost of twenty pesos and five reals. The case of the Mandinga Salvador was closed in the same way.

Thus, the only case that remained open was that of María Antonia and her two children—who by then had turned two and three. Because of her youth and strength—and, certainly, even though this is not recorded in the documents, also because she had proved to be a good breeder—María Antonia was considered to have no defects and was sold as such, and each of her children brought a third of the price for an adult.[10] Once again, an announcement was heard at the gates of Government Square in Santiago de Cuba, and a few days later the three were handed over to their new owner.

This was the last mention in historical documents of eleven of the runaway slaves who had lived in the El Portillo *palenque*. After prolonged pursuit and a judicial proceeding that lasted for more than a year, they left a record for history of their rebellious attitudes and of their lives, which were filled with important events. Their names have remained unknown for many years, but they constitute the first important proof of active slave resistance in the history of Cuba. Table 3 lists the names of the runaway slaves who lived in the El Portillo settlement and the number of years they had spent there.

A Settling of Accounts

On January 12, 1748, just three months after the conclusion of the operations that were mounted against the runaways who lived in the *palenque* in the mountains in the El Portillo area, the *cabildo* of Santiago de Cuba discussed ways and means for defraying the costs of those operations. During that day's session, Juan Antonio de Anaya, head of the Santiago de Cuba branch of the Holy Brotherhood, presented the bill for what was owed to him and the troops that had hunted down the runaway slaves.

Total expenses for the four slavehunting militias came to 1,621 pesos and 6 reals, from which 680 pesos and 3 reals was subtracted because it was paid by the owners who had recovered their runaway slaves; thus the real debt was 941 pesos and 3 reals. In order to make up for that deficit, it was agreed to levy a tax on the residents of Santiago de Cuba and Bayamo under the provisions of Law 20, Book 7, Section 5, of the compiled Laws of the Indies. The amount to be paid in each case would be based on the number of slaves owned.

Juan Miguel Portuondo, the royal scribe, was therefore instructed to compile a list of the residents of the city, which he completed on August 22, 1749, noting the number of slaves owned by each and the amount each of them should contribute to pay off the debt incurred for the attack.

The most important aspect of all this from the historical point of view was the list of 327 slave owners who lived in Santiago de Cuba at the time and owned a total of 2,417 slaves. Even though no other data of a demographic nature are available for that same year, if we accept the figure that Bishop Pedro Agustín Morell de Santa Cruz reported during the visit he made in December 1756—that is, a little more than seven years later— when he stated that there were 3,678 slaves of both sexes and all ages living in Santiago de Cuba (García del Pino 1985), the figure of 2,417 slaves may be considered quite reliable, as may an increase of 1,261 slaves in seven years. That increase in the slave population in Santiago de Cuba reflected the development that was taking place in the eastern economy— and, within it, the growth of the sugar industry, since it was reported that there were fifty sugar mills in the eastern region as a whole in 1749 and seven years later Joseph de Rivera noted that there were fifty-two sugar-producing units in Santiago de Cuba alone (Portuondo Zúñiga 1986, 7).

In this regard, some of de Rivera's considerations when describing the eastern economy are noteworthy. According to him, few of those fifty-two sugar mills had more than two or three slaves, and only rarely did as many as twenty-five or thirty slaves work in a single sugar mill (Portuondo Zúñiga 1986, 190). This shows that most of those sugar mills were very rudimentary.

This same aspect was observed in the list of slave owners that was drawn up in Santiago de Cuba in order to recover the funds that had been spent on the attacks on the El Portillo settlement. As stated earlier, there were 2,417 slaves in all and 327 slave owners. This translates into an average of 7 slaves per owner, but the data included in that list, together with a scale grouping the owners by the number of slaves each owned, show that Joseph de Rivera was right about the concentration of slaves in production units (see Table 4).

Table 4. Concentration of Slaves Owned by Individuals in Santiago de Cuba, 1749

CATEGORY	NUMBER	PERCENTAGE
Owners of 1–4 slaves	171	52.29
Owners of 5–9 slaves	66	20.18
Owners of 10–19 slaves	51	15.59
Owners of 20–29 slaves	23	7.03
Owners of 30–39 slaves	8	2.45
Owners of 40 or more slaves	8	2.45
Total	327	

Source: Based on the list of slave owners in Santiago de Cuba (AGI, Santo Domingo, leg. 367).

As shown in Table 4, most of the slave owners had very few slaves, and a very few owners had a great many slaves. In addition, 30 percent of the 171 owners who owned four or fewer slaves owned only one, which shows what a small part slave plantations played in Santiago de Cuba's economy at that time.

All this is very symptomatic of the eastern economy. In this regard, de Rivera asserted that the low number of slaves in that part of the island was due to the difficulties involved in exporting their products (1986, 190). In those years, the eastern—self-supplying—economy was not basically market-oriented, and it imposed some very specific characteristics on slavery. In this regard, Portuondo Zúñiga has pointed out, "Because of economic demands, the slaves became free men. They worked in paternalistic conditions to guarantee consumption or became tenant farmers or day laborers. . . . The plantation owners needed the slaves to provide their own sustenance. Thus, they either made it possible for them to purchase their freedom or maintained slavery in an ambiguous patriarchal relationship" (18).

This correct view of the nature of slavery in the eastern region in that period was shown in the statements that all the captured runaways who had lived in the El Portillo settlement made during their trial. If attention is paid to the problems that led them to run away and seek refuge in that settlement and to the economic activities in which they were engaged, it is possible to confirm how far they still were from the merciless system of exploitation that was imposed many decades later by an economy at the service of the capitalist market.

But, to return to the number of slaves: six of the few owners who had forty or more slaves each owned between forty and fifty, and only two owned more than that—one had sixty-one slaves and the other sixty-six. It is also illustrative of the era that administrative authorities of the colonial government were among the owners of the most slaves. They included Mayor Mateo Hecheverría, Second Lieutenant Mario Juan Ferrer, Mayor Francisco Xavier Sisteneos, and the sergeant major of the fortress. A few women are listed as slave owners—for example, María Augusto, who had thirty-nine; Rosa Teresa Albaian, who owned sixty-six; and the widow of Martín Herrero, who had eight.

The debt of 941 pesos and 3 reals was divided equally among the residents of Santiago de Cuba included in Juan Miguel Portuondo's list, and they came up with 470 pesos and 5.5 reals of it. It is said that slave owners living in Bayamo paid the rest. Similar procedures had been used ever since 1600 for covering the costs of expeditions against vagabond runaways and runaways living in slave settlements, and this recourse would continue to be employed for many years to come.[11]

The royal order issued in Aranjuez on June 11, 1748—in which the Spanish monarch expressed his approval of the measures that had been taken against the runaways living in the El Portillo *palenque*—reiterated the duties of the heads of the local branches of the Holy Brotherhood, who were to keep an eye on everything related to runaways. Because this document placed the responsibility for such acts squarely on those authorities, the royal order recommended that those posts be assigned to "indefatigable, vigilant men, not lazy ones or men in delicate health," so that "most of that damage would be remedied" ("Real Orden fechada en Aranjuez el 11 de junio de 1748," AGI, Santo Domingo, leg. 116). The monarch also congratulated the eastern authorities on the actions they had undertaken and exhorted them to continue hunting down the rest of the runaways who lived in the settlement.

That was in addition to the support the king had already given to the events that took place in 1747, with the result that incursions into the mountainous region between the Masío and Mota Rivers continued in the 1750s. A letter from the governor of Santiago de Cuba that was written in 1752 (ANC, Correspondencia de los Capitanes Generales [hereafter cited as CCG], Caja 9, no. 403) mentioned a new attack on the runaways living in the El Portillo settlement, noting that three of them had been captured and that an unknown number had escaped. That operation was carried out by a band composed of four soldiers and an equal number of slave-hunters. In short, several attacks were made on that runaway slave settlement—in 1741; in 1747, by several slavehunting militias from El Caney, Santiago de Cuba, El Cobre, and Bayamo, making a total of slightly more than one hundred men; and later, in 1752, by a small band.

Later on, the El Portillo settlement—the first *palenque* in the history of Cuba that caught the attention not only of the authorities in the eastern region but also of the Spanish monarch, who praised the results of the 1747 attack even though he could not be assured that the attackers had located and destroyed the settlement—dropped out of historical records, leaving no further trace.

Decades of Economic Development

Starting in the mid-eighteenth century, seven towns attained considerable importance in the eastern region. The first three to have been founded continued to be large population centers, but they exhibited uneven development, as was characteristic of suppliers of the capitalist market. This meant that the functions and positions of each area or geographic region differed, depending on their possibilities for meeting demands. Baracoa, the first European settlement to have been founded, fell behind the others, and Joseph de Rivera described it in that period as a "poor town with few inhabitants." That Physiocrat, whose opinions are now one of our main sources for understanding eighteenth-century Cuba, summed up each of the eastern population centers in a short but apt phrase. Thus, he described Bayamo as a "large settlement"; Santiago de Cuba was a "small town of blacks and mulattoes, some free and some slave"; Jiguaní was a "very small town of Indians"; and San Luis de los Caneyes was a "small town of Indians" (Portuondo Zúñiga 1986).

Even though new population centers to which de Rivera paid little attention had already appeared, Bayamo and Santiago de Cuba continued to have the largest populations, closely followed by the new town of Holguín. The others had either declined in population or were growing very slowly. Santiago de Cuba had the largest sugar production in the region, and it also produced significant amounts of tobacco and processed foods. Bayamo had attained high levels in livestock raising and was also an important center in terms of growing tobacco and manufacturing such products as soap, candles, cloth, and cheese. For its part, Holguín exhibited advances in tobacco and cattle raising (Portuondo Zúñiga 1986, 145). The economies of the other population centers, though diversified, had not yet managed to make places for themselves in the available markets.

On referring to these aspects, the historian Portuondo Zúñiga asserted that even though "the historic, geographic, and demographic characteristics of that eastern region led to a situation whose key elements, up to the mid-18th century, were not different from those in the western part of the island, the development of social relations made the quantitative differences between the two territories very substantial" (1986, 5). However, it may be said that, because of the role that colonialism assigned to each of the regions and islands during the process of colonization in order to promote the conquest of new territories and because of the system of fleets, among other causes, each of the regions of Cuba developed differently—and therefore had different historical and demographic patterns, as well.

The demographic factor plays an important role in development, but, in turn, it is a result of the advances and progress in the economy (e.g., production and trade). Starting at the end of the sixteenth century, the population, amount of cultivated land, and trade in the eastern part of Cuba advanced more slowly than elsewhere, which had repercussions in the region's levels of development and history. It was the colonial system and the role it assigned to the eastern region that defined different levels. It is obvious that the consequences that stemmed from this situation became causative elements, as in the case of population.

The trade with other parts of the Caribbean that developed through the port of Santiago de Cuba during the eighteenth century defined the ever more important role played by the eastern economy, which began to shake off the lethargy imposed by a consumer economy (Portuondo Zúñiga 1986, 9). In the eastern region, the break with the consumer economy was initiated in the latter half of the eighteenth century, but the aristocrats and authorities kept complaining about the region's backwardness until well into the nineteenth century, which shows that differences not only continued to exist but became more marked with the development of the slave plantations. It was precisely with that kind of economy that the existing inequality in development—both between different regions of the island and within a single region—was accentuated. The western part of the island has always been considered more developed than the eastern part, but within the latter Santiago de Cuba was to the rest of the jurisdiction what the western part of the island was to the rest of Cuba. The same mechanisms that favored Havana over other regions favored Santiago de Cuba over Bayamo and the other eastern towns. In the latter half of the eighteenth century, Bayamo's development slowed to less than that of the capital of the region, whereas Holguín advanced impetuously, without pause.

In 1756 and 1757, Bishop Morell de Santa Cruz paid an ecclesiastical visit to the eastern towns; this enabled him to contribute data that, when compared with the 1778 census, show some of the significant changes that came about in the eastern economy and population. Over a period of twenty-one years, Santiago de Cuba's population grew from 11,793 to 12,644, and the number of slaves increased by 9 percent. According to the bishop's description, there were 3,678 slaves, who constituted 29 percent of the population. The 1778 census recorded 5,078 slaves, constituting 40 percent of the population. In nearly all the other towns in that jurisdiction, the number of slaves was insignificant. The sole exception was El Cobre, where slaves constituted 63 percent of the population, which is explained by the fact that the most important mining operations in the region were located there. Slaves constituted only 17 percent of the population in Bayamo, 8 percent in Holguín, and 7 percent in Baracoa. Those percentages did not register any significant growth in the period of time analyzed.

The growth in the slave population, which favored El Cobre and Santiago de Cuba, did not correspond to an increase in the number of sugar mills, however. The records show that there were fifty-two sugar mills in Santiago de Cuba in 1756 but only forty-eight in 1778. In Bayamo, the number of those production units dropped from sixty-three to fifty-three in the same period of time. In El Cobre, they went from six to just one, and the sugar mills that residents of Santiago de Cuba owned in El Caney dropped from eight to four. Therefore, the process that seems to have been at work in that kind of economic unit—which, along with the mines and, later, the coffee plantations, were the places where the largest slave workforces could be concentrated—served to enlarge production capacities rather than increase the number of units. It should be remembered that, when referring to the sugar mills in those regions, Bishop Morell de Santa Cruz said that they were more like "molasses mills" (García del Pino 1985, 112).

During that same period, according to the available data, the number of housing units in Santiago de Cuba increased by 18 percent and those in Bayamo by 8 percent, which testifies to not only demographic but also economic growth. In June 1756, referring to Holguín, the bishop emphasized that, even though it had very fertile land and abundant pastureland, it was "sparsely populated," lacking laborers to work the land. He concluded, "As a result, those people live in great poverty, being entirely dependent on their tobacco harvests" (García del Pino 1985, 88). Twenty years later, however, as noted earlier, slaves constituted 8 percent of Holguín's population.

The needs of an economy that was seeking foreign markets with products requiring the ever greater participation of a slave workforce spurred the ruling sectors on, and they demanded that more and more Africans be brought into the territory as slaves. The runaway slave settlements, vagabond runaway slaves, and slave rebellions did not make the enterprising plantation owners change their mind in the slightest. In 1745, the cabildo of Santiago de Cuba had sent a request to the Spanish Crown that one thousand more slaves be brought into Cuba to "benefit the rural plantations, which [were] in a state of total decline for lack of black slaves" (Bacardí Moreau 1925, 1:172).

It is clear that the "state of total decline" should be viewed skeptically. This was one of the most common expressions of the colonialist mentality of the wealthy sectors on the island, who exaggerated mishaps and calamities in order to get the Crown to grant their requests. In a report sent to King Carlos II in 1760, Joseph de Rivera insisted that the whites living in the eastern part of the island had to increase their imports of blacks from Africa, saying that there was "nothing more useful for progress" (Portuondo Zúñiga 1986, 190). The western part of Cuba always had more privileges than the eastern part regarding imports of slaves, but this does not mean that the demand was not met to some extent in the eastern region.

Many studies have been done on the number of slaves that were brought into Cuba during the sixteenth, seventeenth, and eighteenth centuries and in the early nineteenth century—the period when the slave trade on the island of Cuba was legal. The estimates made by Aimes (1907), Valle Hernández (1975), Ortiz (1975), Humboldt (1959), and Saco (1881) are often used, but, among the most recent studies made in Cuba, the ones by Pérez de la Riva (1979) are particularly outstanding. Pérez de la Riva agrees, in general, with the other authors concerning the upsurge in the number of slaves that were imported beginning in the latter half of the eighteenth century. An average of three hundred a year were brought in prior to 1761; an average of one thousand a year were brought in between 1761 and 1790; and the number grew spectacularly starting in 1790, reaching annual averages of more than twenty thousand in later decades. But, in general, all the studies that were done on this topic considered it in terms of Cuba as a whole. Only Saco made special note of some aspects related to the eastern region, calculating that around six thousand slaves were brought into that region between 1763 and 1789 (1960, 174).

It is clear that these calculations should be taken as approximations, since some slaves were brought into the region from the western part of the island, where slaves were purchased to be sold to eastern owners. Another consideration is the illegal entries, which seem to have been of considerable importance. As noted earlier, all eleven of the captured runaways who had lived at the El Portillo settlement had been smuggled into Cuba. It is important to note that English ships played an important role in that kind of smuggling—a subject that deserves a study of its own.

At first, the black slaves in the eastern region were concentrated in the urban centers and in the rural production areas that ringed the various towns. Many of them were in Santiago de Cuba and other cities, where there were many small businesses, such as grocery stores, butchers' shops, and laundries. Many others were concentrated in mining, whose most important area was El Cobre. In 1800, after long years of struggle, the descendants of the former slaves in the mines at El Cobre were acknowledged to be free, but slave labor did not disappear from those mines; nor was it even reduced there. According to the 1828 census, there were 279 slaves (ANC, Gobierno General [hereafter cited as GG], leg. 490, no. 25, 150), all of whom had been brought in after 1800.

In contrast, in the areas where cattle raising and tobacco growing prevailed—which required few hands and some degree of adaptation—fewer slaves were brought in, and the concentrations of slaves were always very small. The sugar mills and coffee plantations needed more workers; therefore, to the extent that production units in those branches were developed, areas with greater numbers of slaves appeared. Thus, in addition to Santiago de Cuba and El Cobre, new places with large concentrations of slaves soon appeared: Yateras, Alto Songo, San Luis, and Guantánamo. However, in Bayamo, Baracoa, and Holguín (after a slight increase caused by the development of the first sugarcane plantations), the number of blacks remained, generally speaking, at an insignificant level.

Even though these differences within the eastern region remained, the proportion of slaves increased during the latter half of the eighteenth century—a situation that was reflected in the growth of the forms of slave resistance.

In 1777, the *cabildo* of Santiago de Cuba echoed the lamentations of some plantation owners who had "many black vagabond runaway slaves wandering through the countryside without being able to capture them, due to the lack of experts working in this important sphere . . . required under the Laws of the Indies" (Bacardí Moreau 1925, 1:1225). Items of this sort, which are contained in documents dating from that era, attest to a slow increase in the problem but also show that the incidents caused by the slaves were still isolated and of minor importance, inasmuch as the local authorities had not created a full-time parallel system (such as bands and militias of slavehunters) for hunting down the runaways. In those years, the ruling sectors still solved contradictions of that kind by working through the heads of the local branches of the Holy Brotherhood, applying the regulations of the Laws of the Indies, since the Cáceres Ordinances—the legal instrument that governed most of the contradictions of that society—made few references to the hunting down of vagabond runaways and runaway slaves living in settlements (Pichardo Viñals 1986).

The agreements that the *cabildo* of Havana reached in 1600 for taking special measures against runaways in the western region had been adopted in order to create a fund that would cover the costs of pursuit. They also reflected the fact that, in the first few years of the seventeenth century, sugar mills had been built in areas close to Havana—which meant an increase both in the number of slaves and in associated social problems.

In fact, the absence of documents that specifically set forth norms and measures against this kind of problem, in both the western and eastern regions, is the most categorical historical proof of the low levels of slave resistance in Cuba during those years. Contrary to what has been supposed thus far, it may be stated that the Laws of the Indies were the legal underpinnings for the attacks that began to be made throughout the island against vagabond runaways and the runaway slaves who lived in settlements during the sixteenth, seventeenth, and eighteenth centuries.

The matter was discussed again eight years after the concern that some plantation owners felt over the existence of runaway slaves had first been recorded in the minutes of the *cabildo* of Santiago de Cuba. It seems that feeling was running high in this regard in April 1785, for the same source reported, "Greater numbers of runaways and rebels are found robbing and damaging the plantations, wounding and mistreating individuals, and putting up resistance to the ministers of justice, using weapons of all kinds. The insolence of these slaves even attracts others owned by residents in this city, so the number of slaves who have rebelled will grow, and it will be difficult to subdue them. Therefore, we should waste no time in applying the remedies contained in the laws concerning these things in Book 7, Section 5, . . . to the slaves who have rebelled and who have joined with other black slaves, free blacks, and other vagabonds and thieves. Together with the heads of the local branches of the Holy Brotherhood, members of bands, and volunteers, we should hunt them down" (Bacardí Moreau 1925, 1:254).

Such incidents that were recorded in colonial documents reflected the level of the problem at that time, and their analysis will contribute valuable data for studies on this topic—if those documents are approached critically. Alarmist reports of this kind have, on occasion, been accepted at face value, without establishing the necessary connections between them and the other factors affecting the situation. Such reports were surely made in order to inflate the importance of those expressions and are not supported by the findings of serious historical studies, which leave them out. An interest in reinstating forgotten truths should not lead us to ignore the real levels and nuances of the social phenomenon being studied.

When analyzed in context, reports such as the one just mentioned enable us to infer the real scope of the issue. The paragraph cited states clearly that the slaves who had rebelled went around "damaging," "wounding," "mistreating," and "putting up resistance." These terms show how serious the problem had become. The famous El Portillo *palenque*, which had sheltered a small number of runaway slaves for around twenty years, was attacked for nearly two decades, even though the runaways living there had never disturbed the peace of the plantations at all—which we know because there are no references to their having done anything of the kind. The mere fact that their action might serve as an example to others and the ridiculous fear that they might join forces with the runaways in Jamaica spurred the authorities to hunt them down.

The documents consulted contain no convincing proof that, in those years, runaway slaves went around attacking and killing people. The documents from that period would unquestionably have recorded such things if they had taken place. Rather, it seems that, in those decades, the groups of runaway slaves on the roads and in the woods were very small and preferred not to draw the attention of the plantation owners and authorities, even though a few incidents such as the ones mentioned in the quotation did take place.

The owners, frightened by the increase in the number of runaways and in incidents related to runaway slaves living in settlements (corresponding to the numerical growth of the slaves and to the ever harsher conditions of work on the plantations), called the authorities' attention to this problem. Because of their fear, they tended to exaggerate the threat posed by the runaways, and it is important to note that the quotation cited stated that the number of runaways would grow and that it would be difficult to subdue them. There were some cases of this kind of trouble, and the slave owners were worried by their conviction that the number of runaways would increase, but the runaway slaves were still far from making attacks in which they would kill owners and burn their property. The runaways posed a potential threat to the owners, which is why, at that time, the owners sought to apply a supposed remedy for that ill—to keep it from growing.

Earlier historical studies did not distinguish between stages and levels of the problem and, on occasion, exaggerated some of its expressions in a way that was not very convincing—which, far from helping to preserve the truth and to assess the important role played by the masses of slaves, created confusion and raised questions that have yet to be answered.

As seen earlier, the number of slaves in the eastern region had grown, but not many of them were concentrated on the plantations, and the plantation economy had not yet reached the levels it would attain in the nineteenth century. This leads to some considerations: in a letter dated June 12, 1764 (AGI, Cuba, leg. 1,071), four years before his death, Bishop Pedro Agustín Morell de Santa Cruz said that there were only four cities in the eastern region (Santiago de Cuba, Baracoa, Bayamo, and Holguín, this last founded in 1751) and three towns (Jiguaní, El Cobre, and El Caney); Tiguabos, Morón, Yateras, Las Piedras, and Las Tunas (which, at that time, was part of the Eastern Department) were rural hamlets. A very short time earlier, some descendants of Indians had founded a tiny town in Mayarí.

The eastern part of the island of Cuba was larger and more rugged than the western region. In addition, it had a smaller population and fewer demographic concentrations. A comparison of some figures reflecting the levels of development in the western and eastern parts of the island bears this out. In 1778, Havana and its divisions had 82,143 inhabitants, 25,896 (or 32 percent) of whom were slaves. Santiago de Cuba had both fewer inhabitants and fewer slaves, but in about the same proportions, since slaves constituted 32 percent of its population. With regard to the sugar industry, Santiago de Cuba had 48 sugar mills at that time, whereas Havana had 138, and the ones in Havana were better equipped and had higher production levels.

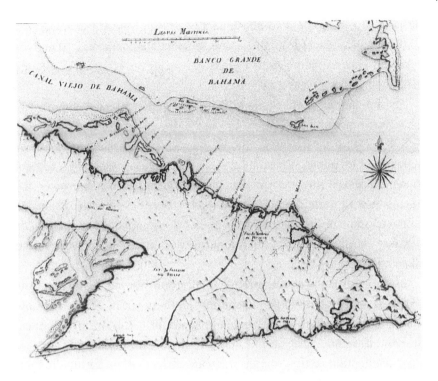

Figure 1. *Eastern part of the island of Cuba, as shown on an eighteenth-century map.*
(Pérez de la Riva 1979)

These figures show the differences that existed between the western
and eastern parts of Cuba in terms of the development of the sugarcane
plantations and the number of slaves—two aspects that had much to
do with the development of the forms of slave resistance. This leads to
a simple conclusion that is borne out by the statistics (La Rosa Corzo
1988a): more slaves ran away in the western part of the island than in the
eastern region, and there were more incidents such as rebellions and
refusals to work—and they were of a more serious nature—in the western
region, too.[12]

If we add the geographic factor—the fact that the eastern part of the
island contained large, sparsely populated areas that were hard to get to—
to the causes of slave resistance, it is easy to see why the establishment of
runaway slave settlements was the main form of slave resistance in the
eastern region but not in the western one. Moreover, there were enough
slaves and internal contradictions in the eastern region to generate a kind

of resistance such as the establishment of *palenques*, so it was not necessarily runaway slaves from the western region who founded or joined the runaway slave settlements in the eastern region (see fig. 1) (AGI, Santo Domingo, leg. 847, year 1789).

The remainder of this chapter begins to outline the development of slave resistance and the levels it reached in the eastern part of the island. In 1785, several slave owners who lived in Santiago de Cuba paid for the creation of an apparently small band of slavehunters who were to hunt down the slaves who had run away from their properties. However, the members of the band simply grabbed every black they came across, which annoyed some of the other slave owners, who complained to the *cabildo* because the slaves they had hired out to work in the fields were seized (Bacardí Moreau 1925, 1:225).

At the end of the 1780s, several small groups of vagabond runaway slaves roved through the woods on the southern coast. This is corroborated by the fact that, when Spain and Great Britain broke off relations in 1790, it became necessary to improve the fortifications and close the road leading to the city—that is, to create the conditions for holding out against a possible attack by enemy forces. Because manpower was required, the *cabildo* of Santiago de Cuba promised that, if they presented themselves, "the 100 blacks who rove along the coast" would be pardoned, would be paid one real a day for working exclusively on the fortifications, and would not be returned to their owners (Bacardí Moreau 1925, 1:276). The absence of later news concerning the results of this offer by the *cabild* of Santiago de Cuba seems to indicate that it met with little success.

During those years, there were continual reports of the existence of bands of vagabond runaways and runaway slaves living in settlements. Also in that period, the *cabildo* of Santiago de Cuba officially acknowledged the existence of a band of slavehunters headed by Francisco Labrada that worked full-time hunting down runaway slaves. This was the first mention of an officially recognized band of slavehunters in the eastern region—a means that would be used as a matter of course in the following century. Thus, the repressive apparatus was adapted to fit the levels of rebellion. It is possible that that band of slavehunters did not last for a long time, but it was an important milestone marking the end of the stage of economic development for the slave plantations. Starting in 1790, along with the development of slavery, important changes came about in the reactions of the slaves in the eastern region—a topic discussed in the next chapter.

Active Resistance in the Eastern Region, 1790–1820

As noted earlier, in response to the demands of economic mechanisms, the western and eastern regions of the island experienced unequal development internally. Santiago de Cuba, for example, had higher levels of development in some branches of the economy than many important towns in the western part of the island. Even though this element may seem unrelated to the levels and characteristics of the slaves' rebelliousness, this is not so, for it largely explains the internal contradictions of a region—contradictions that defined the size and specific features of the problem. Knowledge of the internal conditions of slavery in the eastern region serves to challenge the supposition that runaway slaves from the western region made a great contribution to the *palenques* in the eastern part of the island.

Along with such aspects as the concentration of the slave population, intensive forms of exploitation, and kinds of regional economies, an important consideration is the geographic factor and how it influenced the forms of resistance that prevailed in that region. Between 1778—which is used as a point of reference because of the census taken that year (which contained valuable data)—and the early 1790s, the eastern plantations registered considerable development. The 1792 census shows the composition of the population in the various jurisdictions into which the eastern region was divided (see Table 5).

According to that census, the four jurisdictions of the eastern part of the island had a population of 48,768, or 18 percent of the total population on the island. As may be seen, slaves constituted a large percentage of the total population in the Santiago de Cuba and Bayamo jurisdictions—a percentage that was very similar to that in several jurisdictions in the western region. For example, slaves constituted 31 percent of the population in Matanzas that same year.

This was the socioeconomic basis of the slaves' rebelliousness and resistance. Moreover, viewed from another angle, the data of the census bear out one of the criteria stated earlier: 43 percent of the 14,184 slaves in the region were concentrated in the jurisdiction of Santiago de Cuba, and 51 percent of them were concentrated in Bayamo. Meanwhile, only 6 percent of them were in Holguín and Baracoa combined. In Baracoa, which had no sugar- and coffee-production units, the slave population registered almost no increase; in Bayamo, however, where the sugar industry was growing, there was a corresponding increase in the slave population.

Whereas, because of the prevalence of old patriarchal characteristics in slavery and the very low number of Africans still being brought in, there were eight free blacks for every slave in Baracoa, there were more slaves than free blacks in Bayamo, illustrating the strength of an economy that was being projected toward the capitalist market.

That year—1792—the largest concentration of slaves in the eastern region was in Bayamo and Santiago de Cuba, but those jurisdictions had the highest number of free blacks, too—which, I believe, shows the combination of the old elements of patriarchal slavery and the natural economy of the large cattle-raising areas with the development of the sugar industry in those years.

All this was a reflection of the unequal development that was taking

Table 5. Population in the Eastern Part of the Island, 1792

	TOTAL		BLACKS			
JURISDICTION	POPULATION	WHITES	FREE	PERCENTAGE	SLAVE	PERCENTAGE
Santiago de Cuba	20,761	8,212	6,512	31.36	6,037	29.07
Bayamo	19,804	6,851	5,725	28.90	7,228	36.40
Holguín	5,837	4,028	1,056	18.09	753	12.90
Baracoa	2,366	886	1,314	55.53	166	7.01
Total	48,768	19,977	14,607		14,184	

Source: Based on data from the 1792 census, collected by Sagra (1831).

place in the eastern region and brings out the contradictions of that development. It also explains why class contradictions were more acute in some areas in the region than in others. All those aspects were related to the prevailing characteristics of the forms of slave resistance. In the Eastern Department, trade—which, on a national scale, favored the western region over the eastern one—benefited Santiago de Cuba more than the other jurisdictions. The importance of trade in the development of the plantation economy led to continual complaints by the eastern plantation owners and authorities. Royal letters patent that the Spanish monarch issued on December 18, 1793, had ordered a review and proposal of measures for promoting agriculture and industry in the eastern region and for increasing its population, since it still contained large areas that were sparsely populated or even unexplored.

Less than three years later, on August 31, 1796 (ANC, RC/JF, leg. 1, no. 15), acting on the orders of the administration, the Board of the Royal Consulate of Havana submitted for discussion a document on implementing the instructions of the royal order. An analysis of the document that was approved, which was sent to the monarch, shows some of the factors that were holding back the economy of the eastern region and promoting that of the western part of the island.

Summing up these matters with regard to promoting an increase in the population, it recommended that:

1. more slaves be brought in;
2. immigration from the Canary Islands be promoted and those immigrants be exempted from paying taxes for three years if they settled in the sparsely populated areas; and
3. poor farm laborers be exempted from having to present papers in order to get married.

As for promoting the agricultural economy, it suggested that:

1. small farms be promoted for raising coffee, cotton, and indigo;
2. the extraction of precious wood, which was abundant in the eastern forests, be facilitated; and
3. cattle raising and beekeeping be promoted.

With regard to trade, it emphasized that:

1. products (mainly tobacco) should be shipped directly from the port of Santiago de Cuba;
2. good roads should be built;
3. wood from the nearby forests should be shipped through the port of Santiago de Cuba; and
4. military control should be established along the southern coast.

Among these measures that were suggested to the monarch for promoting the development of the eastern region, the ones regarding trade were closely related to the growth of agriculture. It was not just a matter of increasing production and of exploiting agriculture by bringing in slaves and white immigrants; it also involved increasing production for trade and enlarging trade so as to promote agricultural production.

This criterion was included in the three categories within which the recommendations were grouped to facilitate their analysis—all of which were very closely linked. Concerning the measures that referred to promoting an increase in the population, even though the document requested that immigration from the Canary Islands be facilitated, it was more important to increase the number of black slaves brought into the region.

As the interests of the wealthy sectors were being directed toward this objective, the Haitian revolution—an earthshaking event in the history of the Caribbean and the Americas—took place. It greatly favored those interests and had enormous repercussions in Cuba, including its eastern part. A desire to take over Haiti's former sugar and coffee markets quickly transformed a large part of the Cuban countryside. The functions of many plantations changed, and land that had always been covered with underbrush and woods was cleared and typical slave-plantation economic units created there. This made it possible to increase new fortunes—which in turn were invested in developing new sugarcane and coffee plantations. All this had special repercussions in the development of coffee and cotton in the eastern region.

The Haitian revolution began on the night of August 14, 1791, as a rebellion by black slaves. Soon, more than 80 percent of the slaves were involved against a minority of white owners, free mulattoes, and even some slaves who followed their owners. Just a few months after the initial outbreak, the flames of the revolution engulfed the French part of the island of Hispaniola, which exported seventy-five thousand tons of sugar and twenty-seven thousand tons of coffee—28 and 40 percent, respectively, of the world consumption of those products—each year (Pérez de la Riva 1957, 367).

The repercussions that the Haitian revolution had in the development of slave plantations in Cuba have been studied many times, so I will not go into this subject apart from emphasizing two things. First, the influence that the Franco-Haitian immigration had in terms of the number of émigrés and their role in slave resistance in the eastern part of the country has been exaggerated. With regard to the figures, traditional historical studies used the figures given by the colonial authorities themselves. However, J. Pérez de la Riva showed some years ago that they were inflated (1957, 370). Second, the role that some authors have given to that immigration in the development of the slaves' resistance and rebelliousness is rather paradoxical, since the French and the slaves and free blacks who came with them were fleeing from a revolutionary process that put an end to slavery on that neighboring island. Far from being receptive to emancipating attitudes and ideas, all those émigrés spread lies about the emancipation process and whipped up fear of it.

Most of the Franco-Haitian émigrés who arrived on the coasts of Cuba in various waves during the years following the outbreak of the revolution settled in the eastern part of the island, for purposes that were expressed in documents dating from the colonial period. The eastern part of the island had a lower population density and a greater abundance of uncultivated land, and thus it was thought that it could absorb this kind of émigré with the least damage to the colonial authorities' and slave owners' interests, since the newcomers supported the plantation owners' interests in the region.

In February 1796, with the support of the king's legislation, the colonial authorities decided that families coming from Hispaniola should not be allowed to settle in Havana, reasoning that it was a "populous city, that its own inhabitants [did] not fit in it, and that its land [was] worth a thousand pesos a *caballería* [a little more than thirty pesos per acre]." Instead, they directed the flow toward the eastern part of the island, using the argument that "it [needed] a large number of inhabitants, and the land there [was] worth a hundred pesos a *caballería* [slightly more than three pesos per acre], the eastern region needing more inhabitants" (Bacardí Moreau 1925, 1297).

Thus, the waves of émigrés were directed toward the eastern end of the island, even though some settled in the western and central regions—in the Rosario Mountains, where they made an important contribution to the development of coffee plantations; in Alquízar, Guamutas, Santo Domingo, and Cienfuegos; and on the northern coast of Puerto Príncipe. The greatest concentration of immigrants, however, was in the eastern region, which was also the part of Cuba that was closest to Hispaniola.

In eastern Cuba, the immigrants formed groups that plied various skills in the cities, and projects for colonizing new land were drawn up, creating a wide agricultural belt around Santiago de Cuba and occupying some of the uncultivated areas in the Sierra Maestra, west of Santiago de Cuba and east of the Gran Piedra mountain range. Moreover, some of the mountain areas of what would later become Guantánamo Province were opened to this kind of colonization, in which priority was given to coffee growing.

One of the first important conspiracies in Cuba took place during this period of history. Known as Morales's Conspiracy, it centered in Bayamo in 1795 and then extended to Santiago de Cuba, Holguín, Manzanillo, and Jiguaní. Since the authorities assumed that it was aimed at promoting the equality of whites and free mulattoes, they crushed it with much bloodshed. Throughout the island, slave resistance became so great during the last decade of the eighteenth century that it led to the creation of the first regulations that specifically defined the legal, operational, and economic terms governing the catching of runaway slaves and the destruction of their settlements (Franco 1974).

Starting in 1796, all slave owners were supposed to make monthly reports to the members of the Royal Consulate, stating how many of their slaves had run away. In practice, however, they did not do this so frequently. Daily reality and the plantations' demands did not facilitate this kind of communication. Moreover, the law stated that slave owners had to report whatever temporary or permanent runaway slave settlements they heard of. This information tended to flow more expeditiously. The factors responsible for this included the plantation owners' own fears, since every runaway slave settlement not only posed a latent threat to the owners but also—and more important—was an incentive for all the slaves on their plantations to run away. Therefore, the documents in Cuban archives that date from the colonial period contain many denunciations of the existence of runaway slave settlements and reports about them.[1]

Even though the provincial courts were empowered to order attacks on the runaway slave settlements that were reported in their territories, the bands of slavehunters paid by the Royal Consulate assumed those functions after the regulations were published. This was so in general, but, as I show later on, the system for repressing the *palenques* in the eastern region had some distinguishing characteristics. Starting in the last few years of the eighteenth century, the practice of having bands of slavehunters or local authorities visit the sites of former temporary and permanent runaway slave settlements periodically, to keep them from being used again as refuges for runaway slaves, spread throughout the island.

In accord with the owners' economic interests, the repressive system encouraged capturing the runaways alive. Eighteen pesos were paid for each runaway who was captured alive if the group that had been living in the settlement numbered twenty or more (counting all those captured, whether alive or dead). This meant that if a total of twenty runaway slaves who had lived in the settlement were taken alive, 360 pesos were collected for their capture. The right ear of each runaway who had been killed was cut off and taken as proof, with the prisoners, of the total number.[2] Nothing was paid for captured runaways who "were in such bad condition that their owners did not want them" (Real Consulado/Junta de Fomento 1796, 9).

If the total number of captured runaways (both alive and dead) was between twelve and nineteen, only sixteen pesos were paid for each one captured alive; if the total number was between six and eleven, that amount was reduced to ten pesos for each one taken alive. This system not only promoted attacks on the runaway slave settlements and the hunting down of those who lived there, so as to capture as many of the runaways as possible, but also stimulated an interest in capturing them alive—disproving the supposition expressed in earlier works to the effect that, under the repressive system, the economic interests of the owners were subordinated to the license of the bands of slavehunters (Real Consulado/Junta de Fomento 1796). The diaries of operations that the slavehunters kept show that they killed only those runaways who forcibly resisted capture and that the ones who put up stubborn resistance constituted a minority of the runaways living in those settlements.

Right from the beginning, the law stated that the booty seized in the runaway slave settlements should be divided equally among the members of the attacking band, except that the captain of the band was entitled to a sixth of the total—a practice that remained in effect for more than fifty years.

At the end of the eighteenth century, the most important reports on vagabond runaway slaves and those living in settlements referred to the rural areas of Havana. There were very few reports—and those few, unimportant—referring to the eastern region. The most interesting data on this topic in the eastern region included the creation of a band of slavehunters to attack runaway slave settlements. This is known because the governor of Santiago de Cuba asked the Royal Consulate for fifty pesos for the purpose. The amount of money requested seems to indicate that it was a small-scale operation; moreover, no other references to it have been found (ANC, RC/JF, Libro 127).

On March 28, 1799, a new governor, Colonel Sebastián Kindelán—who became famous because the Franco-Haitian immigrations took place when he was in power—took charge in Santiago de Cuba and all the eastern territory. In 1803, a large number of émigrés fleeing from the Haitian revolution arrived on the Cuban coast at Baracoa and Santiago de Cuba. Using data from colonial documents, Rousset (1918, III, 104) gave the number of immigrants as twenty-seven thousand, but that seems exaggerated (Pérez de la Riva 1957). In any case, no matter how many or few they were, they did influence the eastern region's economy and society.

Boosted by the Franco-Haitian immigration, the development of units of production based on slave labor changed a part of the eastern landscape and added to the social and political problems in the region. The number of coffee—and, to a lesser extent, cotton—plantations grew in the eastern part of the island, especially in the Sierra Maestra and the Gran Piedra Mountains and in the mountain range north of the Bay of Guantánamo, a mountain system closely linked to the El Frijol Mountains, which was where many runaway slaves built their settlements.

Referring to the history of Santiago de Cuba during the first few years of the nineteenth century, Rousset stated, "Nothing of note happened" (1918, III, 104). Traditional histories do not support that view with regard to the economy and other matters commonly recorded in them, but they have agreed with it regarding the history of slave resistance and especially the runaway slave settlements. There is still a lack of knowledge— and therefore analysis—of what happened.

Even so, incidents of interest did take place during those first few years of the nineteenth century that brought out the class contradictions that existed in that important period of history. They included a series of events that took place in many isolated places in the island's territory and riveted the interest of the authorities—the uprisings and founding of settlements by rebellious Indians.

As mentioned earlier (based on documents referring to the early stages in the history of Cuba), the "Indians" were really descendants of Indians mixed with Africans, Spaniards, and Indians from the mainland who had been brought to Cuba as slaves. Even though these "Indians" had very little of the racial and ethnic characteristics of the original inhabitants of the island, fear of the bravery with which some of them had confronted the conquistadores and colonizers in the past was latent in the oral tradition and had permeated rural traditions and psychology. This, more than the fact that there were some rebellious "Indians" at the beginning of the nineteenth century, caused panic in some rural areas and towns.

In colonial society, there were always some individuals or small groups who lived from theft and banditry, and whether they were the descendants of Indians, blacks, or Europeans had nothing to do with it. The case of the rebellious Indians, however—who were described indiscriminately as "*mecas*," "*feroces*," and "*bravos*" and were occasionally joined by vagabond runaway blacks and runaway slaves who lived in settlements—was notorious at the beginning of the nineteenth century.

Documents written in 1800 reported a rebellious Indian who was terrorizing the inhabitants of the Puerto Príncipe jurisdiction (which consisted of vast plains lying to the west of the region studied here). He was described as a murderer and cannibal who attacked plantations, sometimes shooting his victims with a bow and arrow. The case attained so much notoriety that the town hall offered a reward of five hundred pesos for his capture, and the hullabaloo ended with the death of the "rebellious Indian" on June 11, 1803, killed by three men, one of whom was a "black slave." The importance of that event can be judged from the fact that, when his body was brought to the settlement of Puerto Príncipe, all the church bells were rung in celebration (Torres Lasqueti 1888, 112).

Similar events were recorded in many other places during the early years of the nineteenth century. On August 14, 1802, six "Mexican" Indians who worked as slaves in the munitions depot in Plaza, Havana, ran away. A month later, it was said that they had founded a runaway slave settlement in the San José de las Lajas woods. A band of slavehunters headed by José López Gavilán, a local authority, was formed to catch them. The six runaway Indians had sown terror in the district, for they had stolen some animals, which they cut up and ate, and had killed a black slave during a clash on a plantation they were robbing. After twenty-four days, the slavehunters managed to kill two of the runaways and capture three, who were badly wounded.

In October of that same year, the same slavehunter, López Gavilán, was sent to hunt down two other rebellious Indians who were attacking plantations in the Filipinas area, west of Havana. A reward of four hundred pesos was offered for each of their heads. López Gavilán managed to kill the taller of them, which give rise to the legend of the big Indian and the little Indian. The pursuit continued, but by September 1804 the little Indian had been joined by two "Mexican" Indians and eight blacks. A band of slavehunters was then formed, which pursued them for two months. Manuel Ortega, one of the slavehunters, lost his life in the course of the chase. In December 1804, the reward for the little Indian's head was increased to 2,250 pesos (ANC, RC/JF, leg. 141, no. 6,913). Investigations conducted to find out what finally happened to the group have been fruitless, and this case, like others mentioned here, requires a special study.

On February 7, 1803, the *cabildo* of the city of Santiago de Cuba passed a resolution offering a reward of two hundred pesos to anyone who managed to kill the bandit known as "the Indian," who had sown terror among workers in the eastern region with his continual attacks. There are isolated, inflated references to this case—gross distortions of the facts—but it is true that he was seen on some occasions accompanied by other runaways, and no few robberies were attributed to him. Both the Holy Brotherhood and the band of slavehunters headed by Miguel Ferrer went out after him (Bacardí Moreau 1925, II, 45).

These events—which, as has been seen, shook both the western and eastern parts of the island—reflected the contradictions of that historical period, in which large numbers of "Mexican" Indians were brought in as slaves. Their importance may have been exaggerated in the oral tradition and in documents dating from the era, but those accounts were based on fact, and the pursuit operations mounted against the "rebellious Indians"—especially the costs of those operations—show that such events really did take place. The Royal Consulate drew up a balance sheet of its expenses between July 21, 1797, and December 31, 1810, which showed that it had spent 30,629.45 pesos on hunting down runaway slaves and noted that a part of those expenses had gone for pursuing rebellious Indians (ANC, RC/JF, leg. 141, no. 6,917).

This information, along with various reports concerning the existence of rebellious Indians in Cuba at the beginning of the nineteenth century, leads to the inference that there was some mixing of Indians and "Mexican" Indians with black runaways, deserters, and others who had been marginalized from that society in the woods and on the roads. All this merits a separate study, since it is one of the social problems that had the greatest reverberations in those years. Moreover, it may have concerned an ethnic group (possibly Apache) with warlike traditions whose members were brought from North America as slaves.

With respect to slave resistance, a special meeting of the *cabildo* of Santiago de Cuba was held on May 28, 1805, to create a company that would be in charge of hunting down the runaway slaves in the region, who "overran the countryside" and were wreaking havoc on the plantations near the city of Santiago de Cuba (Bacardí Moreau 1925, I, 53). Early in 1808, Bernardino Espinoza was commissioned to go after runaway slaves, both vagabonds and those living in settlements (ANC, RC/JF, leg. 141, no. 6,917). In April of that year, a group of plantation owners presented a document to the Santiago de Cuba authorities that said, "We, the undersigned plantation owners of this jurisdiction, are suffering from the ills caused to agriculture by the continual flight of slave workers because there are not any standing slavehunting militias that make them afraid" (leg. 12, no. 45), and it added that at least one slave had run away from every plantation.

This petition expressed the strong feelings and concern of the owners, who saw that ever more slaves were running away and knew that there were not any full-time slavehunting militias for hunting them down. Therefore, the signatories of the complaint proposed to the *cabildo* that it create a slavehunting militia "with fifty useful, expert men" who would "overcome these difficulties in two months of activity." They stated further, "If the copper workers, who are the Spartans of this area, are chosen, we expect that, if not exterminated, they will be contained, and we will achieve some temporary peace" (ANC, RC/JF, leg. 12, no. 45).

These criteria bring out the nature of the problem in that historical period. The proposal did not suggest the creation of permanent bands but requested that a large slavehunting militia composed of fifty men engage in operations for a period of two months, which shows how well they understood the specific conditions of the region, in which small bands of six slavehunters, such as those used in the western region, would not have been able to do very much against the groups of runaways hiding in the eastern mountains.

Reports such as the one just mentioned, related to the creation of slavehunting militias, indicate the existence of a social phenomenon that appeared with some regularity but had not yet reached its peak. Proof of this is that in 1811 the *cabildo* turned down a proposal for creating a police board for slaves, saying that, at that time, everything was quiet in Santiago de Cuba and the surrounding area (Bacardí Moreau 1925, II, 75). The following year, however—in August 1812—news of a settlement of runaway slaves in the mountains in the Tiguabos area reached the *cabildo*.

Up until then, the El Portillo runaway slave settlement (1747) was the only one whose existence had been specifically noted, along with some vague references to two others in the Mayarí and Moa regions. The documents studied contain no reports that make it possible to locate or describe any other runaway slave settlements in as great detail as the El Portillo one. The news of the settlement in the Tiguabos area initiated a period of a more or less systematic search for and continued attacks on such settlements. Many references were made to the Tiguabos settlement, even in later years, but lack of data concerning its characteristics makes it impossible to assess its importance exactly. There is a drawing showing dwellings of different sizes that traditionally has been said to refer to that settlement, and it provides grounds for considering Tiguabos to be one of the most important runaway slave settlements in the eastern region. However, lack of proof that the drawing really was of the Tiguabos settlement makes it impossible to view that conclusion as more than a hypothesis (ANC, CCG, leg. 30-A, no. 60).

These references, however, show the importance that the town of Tiguabos was gaining in the system of repression against the eastern runaway slave settlements. Compared with many other towns in the same jurisdiction, Tiguabos was not very developed, but it was strategically located. It was in the exact center of the region, which made it possible to set out from it in various directions and reach the Mayarí, Moa, and Baracoa mountain regions quickly.

Table 6 presents data taken from the 1811 census of the town of Tiguabos (ANC, GG, leg. 392, no. 18,623), showing the characteristics of the population.[3] Of the 602 men and women living in the area, those classified as white Spaniards (as Cuba was considered to be a province of Spain) constituted the largest group. However, they owned only 23 percent of the slaves, whereas the 45 whites of French origin owned 77 percent of the slaves. This highlights the repercussions that the Franco-Haitian immigration had in the Tiguabos area and in the development of slave plantations.

Table 6. Population of Tiguabos, 1811

CATEGORY	NUMBER OF INHABITANTS	PERCENTAGE
White Spaniards	179	29.73
White French	45	7.48
Free blacks and mulattoes (Spanish)	123	20.43
Free blacks and mulattoes (French)	28	4.66
"Spanish" slaves	52	8.64
"French" slaves	175	29.07
Total	602	

Source: Based on data from the Tiguabos census (ANC, GG, leg. 392, no. 18,623).

The vast majority of the plantation owners of French origin grew coffee, and they had purchased slaves in the eastern markets to augment the few they had brought with them.[4]

The influence that the Franco-Haitian immigration had on slave rebellions and on the number of slaves who ran away and lived in settlements in the eastern region was not determined by the ideology and ideas of emancipation; rather, the key aspect was the growing importance of plantations and the sharp increase in the number of slaves—real-life aspects that facilitated the development of the contradictions that led to a rise in slave resistance.

The example of Tiguabos is illustrative of the process that also took place in many other areas in the region, but that territorial division, which had grown out of an old Indian settlement, played an important role in the history of the attacks on the eastern runaway slave settlements. Groups of descendants of Indians lived there—individuals who, because they lived in conditions of extreme poverty, with no land or moneymaking skills, became one of the human resources employed most frequently in the militias of slavehunters. In the mid-nineteenth century, the slavehunting militia of "Indians" from Tiguabos headed by Miguel Pérez became famous.

As the nineteenth century advanced, little or no attention was paid to

Table 7. Population of the Eastern Region, 1811

JURISDICTION	WHITES	FREE MULATTOES	FREE BLACKS	MULATTO SLAVES	BLACK SLAVES	TOTAL
Santiago de Cuba	9,121	5,684	486	2,518	6,318	24,127
Bayamo	14,498	13,832	7,021	7,131	5,502	47,984
Holguín	8,534	2,996	1,546	1,634	2,140	16,850
Baracoa	2,060	995	324	53	611	4,043
Total	34,213	23,507	9,377	11,336	14,571	93,004

Source: Based on data from the census, not counting Las Tunas, though it was administered by Santiago de Cuba (ANC, RC/JF, leg. 184, no. 8,329).

the development of Tiguabos—a state of affairs unlike that of the other new towns, such as Saltadero, which had been founded a little to the southeast, near the bay. In 1843, the seat of government was moved to Saltadero—whose official name was Santa Catalina del Saltadero (Rousset 1918, III, 201). Later, in 1860, it became known as Guantánamo. However, Tiguabos still remained important as a starting point for expeditions against the runaways living in settlements.

Despite the advances made in terms of demographic growth and in many areas of the economy, the eastern region continued to have the lowest population density and the most uncultivated land. The 1811 census shows the extent of its demographic growth (see Table 7).[5]

Between the census of 1792 and that of 1811, the population in the eastern region increased by 44,236 inhabitants, owing to increases in both the free and slave populations. The number of slaves rose from 14,184 to 25,907 and the number of whites from 19,977 to 34,213—the latter growth mainly in Bayamo. The number of slaves in Santiago de Cuba and Baracoa did not increase very much, but the number of slaves rose considerably in Holguín—from 753 to 3,774. For nearly twenty years, the number of free blacks and mulattoes remained nearly static in such places as Santiago de Cuba and Baracoa (in the latter, it rose from 1,314 to 1,319), but the number of free blacks and mulattoes in Bayamo nearly quadrupled (rising from 5,725 to 20,853). The considerable increase in the number of slaves reflected the development of slave plantations (development that, however, was always less than in the western part of the island) and the contradictions of the unequal development generated by that system within the region.

The growth in the number of free blacks and mulattoes in some places is explained by the continuation of cattle raising, in which the process of legal emancipation was less restricted.

The demographic processes that took place during the first twenty years of the upsurge in slave plantations in Cuba brought out the specific regional characteristics of the easternmost part of the territory. According to the figures, Bayamo had a situation that was more consistent with the development of the general economy during that period, which was linked to the boom in the sugar industry in its area. But, independent of those movements and variations in the internal process of the development of the economy in that region, in the latter half of the nineteenth century the easternmost part of the island to some extent shook off the lethargy imposed by a consumer economy, as corroborated by its demographic composition. This explains the increase in slave resistance that occurred beginning in the first few years of the second decade of the nineteenth century, including the main form it took in that territory: runaway slave settlements.

The second decade of that century was a stage that was qualitatively different from all preceding ones, both because of the considerable increase in the number of events related to the slaves' rebelliousness and because of the extremely dangerous levels the issue reached for the slave owners. All this had its most eloquent manifestation in the creation of a regional plan for tackling the problem.

Between 1811 and 1815, important events took place that led to an intensification of the struggle against runaway slave settlements in the next five years. Under the administration of Governor Antonio Mozo de la Torre, a large "armed contingent" (Jerez de Villarreal 1960, 106) was formed in 1814 that was assigned the task of destroying several runaway slave settlements in the mountains east of Santiago de Cuba—that is, in the Gran Piedra mountain range, one of the areas in which French coffee plantations had been established.

Up until then, incidents had pointed to the existence of *palenques* west of Santiago de Cuba and in the mountains of the Mayarí, Moa, and Baracoa areas. These mountain ranges were included in this study because they were the site of a system of runaway slave settlements that were always concentrated in the highest, least populated areas in the eastern part of the island.

That same year, 1814, representatives of the eastern plantation owners in the *cabildo* of Santiago de Cuba drew up and passed a set of regulations that prescribed special measures for that region (ANC, AP, leg. 297, no. 109, contains a copy of the regulations). Thus, a regional strategy was created against the danger posed by the runaway slave settlements. The publication of those regulations, which were in force in that region only, reflected the specific characteristics and worrisome levels of the problem in those territories.

In the other jurisdictions of the island, bands of slavehunters operated under the Havana regulations, which were reprinted several times in the first half of the nineteenth century. But, in the eastern region, those regulations seem not to have been effective. Why was this?

The Regulations of 1796 (Real Consulado/Junta de Fomento 1796) placed the greatest emphasis on the repressive system against vagabond runaway slaves, who were described as a plague that was overrunning the countryside in the western region. Under those regulations, all the heads of bands of slavehunters in the areas that contained runaway slave settlements—which could be attacked only with authorization by the captain general—made monthly tours of inspection through those areas. Thus, that document, which was issued just a few years before the slave trade was outlawed, did not provide any real answer to the complexities of the problem in the eastern region, where access to the places where the *palenques* were located was much more difficult than in the western region—because of the distances involved, the mountains to be climbed, and the general lack of knowledge of the area.

Therefore, the authorities and plantation owners in the eastern region, who were concerned by the growing alarm of the whites in the area and by recurring reports of the presence of groups of runaway slaves in the most isolated areas, established a different system for hunting them down. The main differences were that the bands of six men were discarded and slavehunting militias of twenty-five men each carried out the operations. These slavehunting militias were formed only when a raid was about to be made in a given area, and each was headed by a high-ranking officer and a lieutenant. A commission of plantation owners saw to it that each slavehunting militia kept a diary of operations.

Each member of the slavehunting militia was armed with a machete, pistol, and cudgel, and one out of every six men also had a blunderbuss. The leader was paid thirty pesos a month, the lieutenant twenty-four, and each of the other members of the slavehunting militia fifteen. The Havana regulations had not established any fixed sums in this regard.

This proves that, in the eastern region, runaway slave settlements were the main target of the repression. Therefore, it is necessary to present the slavehunting militias' organizational details. All the runaways who were captured alive were sent to the Santiago de Cuba city jail and held there subject to the orders of the governor, accompanied by a document. Those owners who had made a monetary contribution to the commission could recover their slaves at no additional cost, but the ones who had not made a contribution had to reimburse the authorities for the expenses of their capture and also pay a fee for their imprisonment. Runaways who had headed settlements were to be sold abroad.[6]

The slavehunting militias had to turn in periodic reports of their operations from wherever they were, using people living in the area or other emissaries. When the operations were over, each slavehunting militia had to turn in a diary of operations recording where it had gone and everything that had happened. The complexity of their journeys and of the operations in distant mountainous areas led to differences between these diaries of operations and the ones that were kept in the western region to sum up the monthly operations of the bands, whose members turned in their reports and collected their pay on the last day of each month.

As for payment for the captured runaways, whereas payment in the western region was based simply on capturing runaways alive, in the eastern region it was also based on how far away the runaways were when they were captured. Thus, four pesos were paid for each runaway captured less than four leagues (around ten and a half miles) away, ten pesos for each one captured between four and ten leagues (between ten and a half and twenty-six miles) away, and twenty pesos for each one captured between ten and twenty leagues (twenty-six and fifty-two miles) away. The bounty for each one captured at a distance greater than that was thirty pesos. This was a great incentive for members of the slavehunting militias, who combed the most isolated areas, trying to take prisoners alive—they were not paid anything for dead ones.

To carry out those operations, each slavehunting militia split into three pickets of men who combed the areas around the zone of operations. This form of operation was dictated by the type of terrain and by the military nature of these activities.

These aspects show some of the differences between the regulations issued by the Royal Consulate in Havana, which were in effect for the western and central regions, and the regulations that the Commission of Eastern Plantation Owners drew up. They reflect the differences between the main forms of slave resistance in each region. The two sets of regulations had the same purpose, but their details reflected the specific regional aspects of the problem.

In the eastern district, it has been proved that the system established by those regulations remained in effect—with some changes introduced by other regulations that were issued in 1832—up to 1850 and possibly until slavery was abolished.

Along with those regulations, the members of the *cabildo* of Santiago de Cuba discussed who was to be appointed to head the first slavehunting militia and finally chose Antonio Mustelier and Rafael Cabrera. This was for a column that would operate in certain, defined areas. From this, it may be understood that, in line with the manifestations of the problem, they had not yet decided—nor does it appear that it was necessary—to have several slavehunting militias operating at the same time.

Even though I have not found any reports referring to the operations of Mustelier and Cabrera's slavehunting militia, it may be inferred that the operations were carried out near Santiago de Cuba—that is, in the Gran Piedra mountain range, where many of the incidents mentioned were concentrated. In February 1814, the same month in which the regulations were drawn up, reports came in concerning the existence of runaway slave settlements in the Mayarí Mountains and in the Toa River area. The statement presented to the *cabildo* mentioned "incursions that the runaway blacks who [had] settled around thirteen leagues [thirty-four miles] to the windward of here [had] begun to make in the plantations, pillaging them, mistreating their owners and managers with whips, and committing other abuses" (ANC, AP, leg. 109, no. 34).

On the 22nd of that month, the captain of the slavehunting militia from Mayarí informed the departmental authorities that a group of around twenty runaway slaves who lived in a settlement had attacked the Benga el Sábalo plantation, which belonged to Esteban Contreras; stolen all the furniture; and killed some animals.[7] As a result, the slavehunting militias worked more intensively. At midnight on February 23, another group of runaway slaves who were in the mountains near the Sigua plantation (east of Santiago de Cuba) attacked the houses on the Limones plantation, set fire to them, and, as the records state, "committed several murders" (Bacardí Moreau 1925, II, 99).

This considerably alarmed the plantation owners and authorities of Santiago de Cuba—partly because the plantation was relatively close to the city. The local heads of the Holy Brotherhood asked the top authorities of the department for weapons and supplies with which to launch an immediate attack on the runways.

Thus, in late 1814 and early 1815, there were precise reports about the runaway slave settlements in the Gran Piedra mountain range and in the Mayarí and Toa areas. In February 1815, Felipe Quintero was chosen to head a slavehunting militia that would operate against the runaways who had settled in the mountains east of Santiago de Cuba, and Captain Alfonso Martínez, who had been transferred from Havana for the purpose, was put in charge of attacking the runaway slave settlements in the northern mountains, especially in the Moa area, where a large *palenque* had been reported. This plan constituted an important advance in terms of consolidating the repressive system in the eastern region, even though it did not call for simultaneous operations in different areas.

Two important expeditions, then, were organized to destroy two runaway slave settlements that posed a threat to the peace of the plantations. The first operation, headed by Felipe Quintero, with Esteban Balangué as second in command, was carried out between February 20 and March 30, with the slavehunting militia advancing into the Gran Piedra Mountains as far as the banks of the Caonao River.

Felipe Quintero's diary of operations (ANC, AP, leg. 109, no. 54) was the earliest one that I have found. In it, he recorded all the operations that were carried out in this expedition under his command. The diary is one of the first documents that contains a wealth of information for studies of the system of runaway slave settlements in the eastern region and of the repressive apparatus that was created to crush them.

Runaway Slave Settlements East of Santiago de Cuba

The militia of forty-one slavehunters headed by Felipe Quintero combed the mountains east of Santiago de Cuba for thirty-nine days. The scene of the operations was what is now known as the Gran Piedra mountain range, which extends for a little more than twenty-one miles in an easterly direction from Santiago de Cuba to the Guantánamo Basin. The highest peak in the range, now known as the Gran Piedra, is a little more than four thousand feet above sea level. In that era, there were many coffee plantations on the sides of some of those mountains, but most of the mountains were uninhabited.

Felipe Quintero, who was familiar with the area—as may be inferred from the information recorded in his diary—noted by name the places where some runaway slave settlements that had already been attacked had stood. Almost certainly, he had taken part in the earlier raids. The slavehunters left the city of Santiago de Cuba at midnight on February 20, heading east, toward the Candelaria coffee plantation, which was one of the nearest points in their long journey to attack the San Andrés *palenque*.[8] By February 22, they had reached the Providencia coffee plantation, which was owned by Esteban Balangué, second in command of the operation.[9] Calculations made concerning this journey—in which distances, time, and the conditions of the terrain were among the factors considered—show that the members of the slavehunting militia had walked nearly 160 miles. From there, complying with the regulations that were in effect, they sent a report on the state of operations to the city of Santiago de Cuba (see fig. 2).

Two runaway slaves—Batista Bayona and his wife, who had first fled

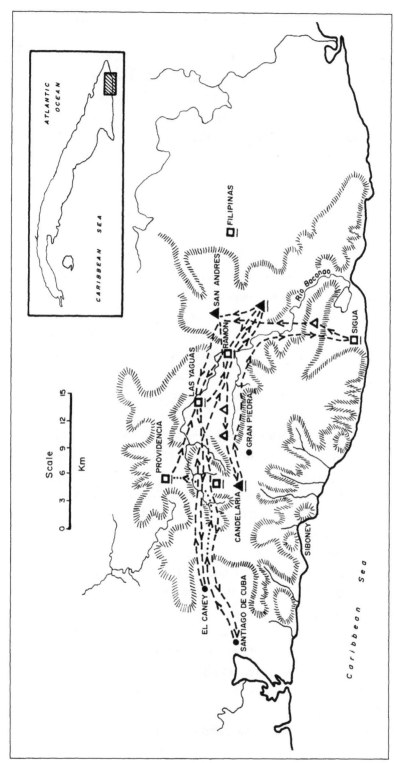

Figure 2. Operations carried out by Felipe Quintero's slavehunting militia in the Gran Piedra range, east of Santiago de Cuba. The members of the slavehunting militia left the city heading eastward; went to the Providencia and Las Yaguas plantations; attacked the La Cueva and San Andrés runaway slave settlements; checked on the La Esperanza and Guadalupe settlements, which had been discovered and attacked in the past; and attacked the Candelaria settlement. From there, they visited the Sigua plantation and then went north to inspect the Palenque de los Vivís. After leaving there, they returned to the San Andrés settlement and to the Las Yaguas and Candelaria plantations.

from the coffee plantation and then deserted from the San Andrés settlement, which was to be attacked—turned themselves in at the plantation.
Bayona also provided information that led to an attack on a previously
unknown runaway slave settlement called La Cueva, which was headed
by Cayetano Solórzano (see Appendix 2). Bayona said that, when the
head of the runaways living in the San Andrés settlement heard of the
operations that the slavehunting militia was carrying out, he left twenty
women in the settlement with six men to protect them, while he and the
others scattered, possibly to draw the attention of the attacking forces.[10]
This terrified Bayona—who, along with his wife, betrayed the others, for
they turned themselves in and provided information about where both
this settlement and the La Cueva settlement were. Bayona also served as a
guide in the subsequent operations. Quintero then headed east, but he
left twenty men at the plantation, fearing that the runaways from the
settlement would attack it.

Quintero and his militia walked toward the woods on the Filipinas
plantation, passing Francisco Novias Padillo's coffee plantation at the foot
of El Pilón Hill, where they received reports that runaways from the
settlement had attacked two plantations the night before: one owned by
Ana Mayo and the other by Emilio Magdonado.[11] Then they continued on
their way, going by other coffee plantations they knew, always through
"places that were almost impassable, because of the many streams" (ANC,
AP, leg. 109, no. 34).

On the 25th, the slavehunters reached the foot of the hill on which the
La Cueva *palenque* was located.[12] They called a halt there so as not to be
discovered and began the attack at 3:00 A.M. on February 26.[13] They
had left Santiago de Cuba only five days earlier and had already arrived at
one runaway slave settlement—which, even though it was not the one
they were looking for, still proved profitable. The attack on that settlement must have caught the runaways off guard, because two of them
were killed; the others tried to break through the encirclement, but seventeen were captured. The members of the slavehunting militia seized
large quantities of the runaways' supplies—sheets, blankets, mosquito
nets, shirts, blouses, breeches, petticoats, tunics, jackets, mattresses, tin
pitchers, and bottles of lard—put the fifty rude huts to the torch, and
destroyed the crops (ANC, RC/JF, leg. 141, no. 6,913). Of all the runaway

slave settlements that were attacked and are studied here, this was the one at which the most runaways were captured alive, almost certainly because they had been caught off guard, in the middle of the night.

After the attack, the slavehunting militia headed northwest, toward the Las Yaguas plantation, near the Ramón plantation—place-names that are still used. There, at Las Yaguas, the slavehunters met a picket of cavalry and another of infantry headed by Antonio María Mancebo and were ordered to go back to Santiago de Cuba. However, they were still high on the success of their attack on the La Cueva settlement and wanted to go on and attack the San Andrés settlement, which was the main target of the raid; therefore they went to the town of El Caney, near Santiago de Cuba, from where they wrote to the authorities, requesting authorization to continue the operation. Along the way, some of the slavehunters protested against guarding the coffee plantations, arguing that they had come to attack runaway slave settlements, not stand guard. In fact, their discontent was due to their not having received any pay. These disagreements among members of the slavehunting militia ended when several of them—whom the others considered deserters—quit and went home.

On March 13, the slavehunters set out again for the San Andrés settlement, revisiting the site of the La Cueva settlement to check that the runaways had not started to rebuild. After that, they went on and, when they finally reached their goal, found the settlement completely abandoned—which, as may be seen in nearly all the cases studied, was a constant in the runaways' defense tactics. At that runaway slave settlement, which was slightly to the north of La Cueva, the slavehunters did not record the number of huts, but three aspects indicate that the *palenque's* dimensions were similar to those of La Cueva: first, the settlement had "abundant crops"; second, the members of the attacking militia left eight huts standing, in which twenty slavehunters camped; and, third, the runaways who lived in this settlement were the ones who had attacked the San Andrés plantation, which proves that it could not have been a very small group.

After that attack, the slavehunters went westward, toward the Candelaria plantation. On the way, they passed several runaway slave settlements about which they recorded very little information in the diary, so the locations they assigned them are inferred. Those settlements were

La Esperanza—where the members of the slavehunting militia also destroyed a banana plantation that had between two hundred and three hundred plants, plus sweet potatoes, beans, and other crops—and the Guadalupe settlement, which they checked without incident. Last, on a hill near the Candelaria plantation, they found a runaway slave settlement that they called by the same name as the plantation. They attacked this last settlement at dawn on March 20 and managed to capture two of the runaways and burn between thirty-five and forty huts, as Quintero noted in his diary.

After this, they headed for the Sigua plantation, on the banks of the Baconao River, toward the southern coast, to replenish their food supplies. They stayed there for three days because fourteen members of the militia were sick. On March 25, they left the Sigua plantation, going north along the Baconao River. They passed a runaway slave settlement they already knew about and had attacked earlier, called the Palenque de los Vivís.[14] Its location on the drawing is inferred, since the diary does not offer any information in this regard. The slavehunters went by the San Andrés runaway slave settlement again, where they spent the night in the same huts they had left standing after their attack. From there, they went toward Providencia, where they had agreed to take on new men to replace the slavehunters who were sick, but they halted at the Las Yaguas plantation. While there, they received orders to withdraw to the city of Santiago de Cuba, and the orders were confirmed on March 30. On April 5, Quintero turned in the written document and reported to the authorities on the results of the operations.

The final results of the expedition included the capture of nineteen runaways who had been living in settlements; the deaths of two; and attacks on a total of six runaway slave settlements, only two of which had been known and attacked previously. Abundant crops were destroyed, and close to a hundred huts were burned. The operations had been successful for the slave owners' interests. Unfortunately, Quintero's diary is the only one that has been found to date that records operations in this area east of Santiago de Cuba, though the existence of other, similar expeditions may be inferred, since other documents contain references to them, especially to activities that took place before these operations.

Thus, the existence of at least six runaway slave settlements in the mountain range east of Santiago de Cuba and of an extensive communications network among them—good enough so they knew that a slave-hunting militia had been sent against them—is proved. The runaways living in only one of the settlements were caught off guard, because they were attacked in the middle of the night and because the slavehunting militia was helped by a traitor, one of the runaways who had lived in another settlement, who served as its guide. The tactic of falling back before slavehunting militias arrived prevailed throughout the area.

Several months later, another combing operation was mounted, this time against the runaway slave settlements in the mountain range in the northern part of the eastern territory. In that operation, another *palenque* was found—the one that traditionally has been considered the most important one in Cuba.

Runaway Slave Settlements in the Northern Mountain Ranges

Between 1811 and 1816, there was a great upsurge in runaway slave settlements as the main form of slave resistance in the eastern region of Cuba, but between 1816 and 1821, there was a veritable synchronization of events and incidents that showed how important that kind of recourse had become, and this led the slave owners to take special measures.

Important references were made in that period to the existence of several runaway slave settlements—such as Bumba, Maluala, and El Frijol— and other authors have consulted these references, though only partially. Therefore, it is not necessary to analyze them, except for El Frijol, as it is considered to have been the largest runaway slave settlement in the history of Cuba

Official reports acknowledged that groups of runaway slaves had been living in settlements in the mountain ranges in the northern part of the region ever since 1747. In October 1815, at the time of the incidents described earlier, the authorities in Santiago de Cuba asked Second Sergeant Alfonso Martínez, alias "Death," and First Corporal Francisco Roch, both of the Regiment of Havana, to go into those mountains and destroy a *palenque* known as the Moa settlement (because it was in the same mountains as the Moa plantation), which had become rather notorious.

There are references—not corroborated by any documents—to some operations against runaway slaves living in settlements in the northern areas and to an attack on the runaway slave settlement called Limones, some of whose inhabitants had managed to escape and had taken refuge in the Mayarí woods. There are also references to the operations carried out by a slavehunting militia of fifty men, which constituted the first news of the existence of a large, unidentified runaway slave settlement in the area (Bacardí Moreau 1925, II, 106). The most comprehensive reports I have found, however, refer to the attack that Second Sergeant Alfonso Martínez directed on October 16, 1815—the details of which he himself reported. It concerned the "Moa" runaway slave settlement, which the runaways called El Frijol, because it was in the mountains of that name, between the Jaguaní and Toa Rivers (see fig. 3).

The first attack on that runaway slave settlement has not been included in earlier studies. The attacking militia, consisting of twenty-eight men, left the town of Sagua, where a reinforcement of thirteen slavehunters joined it (ANC, AP, leg. 109, no. 34). They headed east, toward the head-waters of the Jaguaní River, where it was supposed the renowned settlement was located, but along the way they came across three runaway slaves carrying heavy loads of bananas. Even though the runaways fled immediately, the slavehunters managed to capture one of them, who was badly wounded. On being interrogated, the prisoner provided information of crucial importance that sealed the settlement's fate.

The captured man had run away from the Moa plantation. He said that the runaway slave settlement where he lived was called El Frijol (ANC, ME, leg. 4,070, no. A-i) and had a total of twenty-five inhabitants armed with machetes, knives, and five "nearly useless" shotguns. Thanks to this information, which his captors extracted from him, the slavehunters managed to locate the settlement in the mountain range.

Thus, they set out in the right direction and, after several days, ran into two ambushes set by the runaways, who had been warned. In the first ambush, one of the members of the slavehunting militia, José Ignacio Pavón, was killed, and three others received bullet wounds: "Jerbacio" Laborda in the head, Juan González in the thigh, and Santiago Domínguez in the head and arm.

This information is very important concerning the runaways' defense

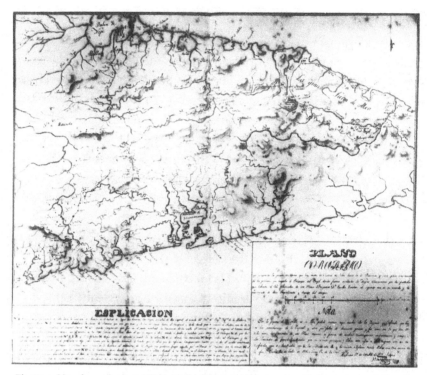

Figure 3. *Map drawn by Juan Pío de la Cruz in 1816, showing the region between Santiago de Cuba and Baracoa. The route and campsites of the troops that attacked the El Frijol runaway slave settlement and the site of the settlement are marked on it. (Archivo Histórico Militar de España, Fondo América Central, Cuba, no. 12,462)*

tactics. The sample studied shows that only three runaway slave settlements in the eastern region of the island put up total resistance to attack: El Frijol, in 1815; Bayamito, in 1831; and Vereda de San Juan, in 1849. The runaways at El Frijol responded to and beat back that first attack, but they did not manage to do the same against the attacks made on them in subsequent years. It should also be emphasized that, of all the runaway slave settlements studied here, in only two cases did the slavehunters have to withdraw without achieving their goal: the first was this attack on El Frijol in 1815, and the second was the attack on the Guardamujeres settlement, in 1848. In all other cases, the slavehunters managed to break into the settlements and destroy them.

Throughout the history of runaway slave settlements in Cuba, the only case in which the runaways successfully beat back the slavehunters' attack was this one, the attack made on El Frijol in 1815. (Even though the runaways living in the Bayamito and Vereda de San Juan settlements put up resistance, they were destroyed.) In response, the authorities in the eastern region launched a troop of four hundred men—slavehunters, soldiers, and militiamen—against that settlement the next year. This may have been one of the experiences assimilated most rapidly by the runaways living in settlements in the eastern region. In the face of resistance such as this, the repressive forces used extraordinary resources that enabled them to demolish the settlement. After this attack, the cruel and tireless persecution to which the runaways in that settlement were subjected for four years determined the defense tactics that runaways living in settlements in those areas used later on—tactics that mainly consisted of abandoning the settlement before their enemies arrived.

Following the initial confrontation at the El Frijol settlement, the slavehunters kept advancing despite their losses and fell into a second ambush, in which five other members of the slavehunting militia were wounded: Pedro Ramírez and Víctor Nazario received bullet wounds, and José Francisco Castillo, Pedro González, and Pascual Osorio were wounded with spears. (The head of the militia later sent two of the spears back to the city.) After the two ambushes, the slavehunters caught sight of the settlement and waged a supposedly unequal battle, which Alfonso Martínez described "I saw again that three divisions were coming to attack me to the sound of drum beats and that there was loud shouting and singing with drums inside the settlement, which showed that there must be around 200 of them, not counting the three divisions already mentioned, so I gave instructions for a retreat, since the men asked me to. . . . After having left, I made the black confess, asking him why he had deceived me, and he said it was true that there were more than thirty blacks; that the captain, who was from Havana, was named Sebastián; and that there were thirty-two blacks, a sugar mill, . . . a mango tree, some pigs, a large field of sugarcane, a banana plantation that had lost all its bananas, and four tobacco houses" (AHSC, GP, leg. 554, no. 2).

Two aspects of Captain Alfonso Martínez's description should be analyzed. The first is related to the tribal nature of the defense mounted by the runaways who lived in the El Frijol settlement. The report clearly states that they marched against the attackers in divisions (groups) to the sound of drums and to much shouting. This is a unique form of battle that was not used in the defense of any of the other runaway slave settlements or in clashes between runaways and slavehunters. It shows a strong presence of African elements in the defense tactics used at El Frijol, which may have been responsible for the slavehunters' resounding defeat, but this is only hypothetical. What is certain is that all later examples showed a radical change in defense tactics: the runaways withdrawing when faced with imminent attack and then going back later to live in the settlement again.

The second aspect is related to the supposed existence of a vastly superior force of runaways. On this occasion, Alfonso Martínez was forced to withdraw without achieving his objective. By the time of the attack, one member of the slavehunting militia had been killed and eight wounded, several of them by bullets, and Martínez came up against unexpected, organized resistance. It is important to note that his men asked him to withdraw. All this made him think—or led him to exaggerate, for the same reasons—that there were more than two hundred runaways in the settlement, as noted in his report.

In the first version extracted from the captured runaway from the settlement, the victim said that twenty-five runaways lived there, and Martínez calculated that there were two hundred. After his force withdrew, the head of the expedition rebuked the prisoner for having deceived him, and the runaway answered that there were more than thirty men and thirty-two women. The prisoner who was interrogated never spoke of two hundred runaways living in the settlement; it was Alfonso Martínez who wanted to believe that there were so many—first, because it justified his defeat, and second, because he wanted to get a larger force, which is what happened the following year, when he attacked the runaway slave settlement again, this time with four hundred men, most of whom were soldiers.

It is understandable that the head of the slavehunting militia would say this and that the colonial authorities would accept it, but it is inexplicable that studies made in Cuba would repeat that two hundred or even three hundred runaways slaves were living in that settlement. Alfonso Martínez stated in his report that two hundred men and thirty bulldogs would be needed to enter the settlement, which they could reach by setting out from Baracoa and going by canoe—first up the Toa River and then up the Jaguaní. That operation was carried out between March 18 and June 2 the following year.

According to the report on the operations carried out in 1816, the installations and resources the attackers found at the El Frijol *palenque* included twenty-two huts forty-four feet long; thirteen huts forty-four feet wide; twelve thousand banana plants; a rudimentary, hand-operated sugar press; and five hundred fan-palm-fiber hammocks (AHSC, Administración regional, Cimmarones, leg. 1, no. 7). Some initial analyses of this information can be made. In all, there were thirty-five huts—a figure that other authors have accepted without evaluation. It is hardly believable that two hundred or three hundred runaways, as some authors state, fit in thirty-five huts. Moreover, the file on the case contains another list that corrects some of the initial figures. If the analysis is made on the basis of the first report, which states that there were 500 hammocks, it is easy to deduce that Martínez's figures were not large enough, but, if attention is paid to the second list, which states that there were 120, not 500, things change considerably.

Martínez's estimate was not the only source of errors in calculating how many runaways were living in the El Frijol settlement. A communiqué from Eusebio Escudero, governor of Santiago de Cuba, spoke of around three hundred runaways living there (ANC, RC/JF, leg. 141, no. 6,935). However, that same official denied those initial calculations when, in another communiqué that he signed, he stated that there were barely fifty (leg. 25, no. 1,364). In addition are the statements made by some of the runaways who were captured in the second attack to the effect that, "with some variations, the runaway slave settlement called El Frijol, which is situated in the highest part of the Moa Mountain Range in the territory of Baracoa, had between seventy and a hundred blacks" (AHSC, GP, leg. 554, no. 2).

The analysis and explanation of the number of runaways living in the El Frijol settlement are necessary, not only to show the importance of subjecting sources to critical examination but also, and above all, because numbers have much to do with the methods and tactics of that form of slave resistance. A human settlement trying to survive despite continual attack by enemy forces could not afford the luxury of creating towns of three hundred inhabitants in the conditions that prevailed in Cuba in the nineteenth century. That would have violated the principles of peace and security, especially in Cuba, where the repressive system that had been created against those settlements assumed particularly intense and varied forms during that century.

Some other aspects of the commonly accepted reports on that runaway slave settlement should also be subjected to critical analysis—for example, the "sugar mill." The first runaway who was captured in 1815 said that there was "a sugar mill," but the first inventory made after the 1816 attack noted that there was a rudimentary, hand-operated sugarcane press. These contradictions in terms in the colonial documents have led to romantic approaches and to far from felicitous repetitions that have given rise to the supposed existence of a highly developed sugar mill in the settlement—when, in fact, it was a rudimentary, hand-powered apparatus made of several tree trunks that was used to press the sugarcane and extract the juice, which the runaways either drank or used to sweeten their food.

Another aspect worthy of reflection is that of the twelve thousand banana plants. As in the case of the hammocks—in which the 500 of the initial estimate turned out to be 120 when they were counted—the original estimate was surely far too high, but, unfortunately, the later report did not contain any information on how many banana plants there really were. Some basic calculations lead to a more realistic view of things, however. Twelve thousand banana plants, each one occupying at least forty-three square feet (the minimum space required for this kind of plant), would mean a plantation nearly two-hundredths of a square mile in size if planted together. If planted in small plots or along the banks of streams, the area covered by the banana plants would have attained fantastic dimensions.

Therefore, several questions arise. Could a runaway slave settlement be so large? Would not that violate the most elementary principle of its own survival? In view of these questions, it is not necessary to be familiar with the terrain in the area where the runaway slave settlement was located or to calculate its supposed extension on a scale map to show the area covered. A historian cannot accept the figures of two hundred or three hundred runaways, five hundred hammocks, and twelve thousand ba-nana plants because they contradict the principles that governed that kind of settlement in the prevailing historical conditions. Moreover, the documents themselves disproved them.

Like the aspects just noted, the affirmation that the runaways living in the El Frijol settlement engaged in considerable trade with Jamaica and Haiti (Danger 1977, 44; Franco 1973, 104) does not hold up under even the most basic historical analysis. The information was contained in a docu-ment issued by the colonial authorities that asked for support in attacking the runaway slave settlement—which explains why the authorities in-cluded this claim: they were exaggerating the real level of the problem and the threat it constituted in order to get the help they wanted.

The document claimed that the trade was carried out by an individual who had a small boat on the coast near Moa. Thus, the runaways' prod-ucts would first have to be taken through the mountains, where there were no paths, so they would have to be carried along the banks of rivers and streams, a land route scores of miles long; after that the boat would have to skirt the whole coast of the eastern region, since, to get to Haiti and Jamaica, it would have to leave Cuba from the northern coast.

Trade of this kind presupposes supplies of products of interest to both parties. If that trade existed and the main interest of the runaway slaves living in the settlement was to obtain weapons, as all the documents of that era seem to indicate, the runaways living in the El Frijol settlement must have had a veritable arsenal at the time of the attack, yet they had only five shotguns. Moreover, the people in Haiti and Jamaica could not have been very interested in the bananas and root vegetables from the settlement, because those items were both very abundant and inexpen-sive on any market in the Caribbean. If they were interested in obtaining honey and beeswax, it is highly unlikely that there was enough of those products at the runaway slave settlement to sustain any extensive trade.

The concept of trade presupposes a surplus of the resources required for subsistence, agricultural or industrial production (or both) that cre-ates a surplus that is used for trade with a commonly accepted means of circulation. Could the runaway slaves living at the El Frijol settlement produce anything with which to trade? Did they obtain enough from the wild bees' hives? Acceptance of these suppositions as truths shows the absence of a critical approach toward sources and a desire to exaggerate the value and importance of that topic.

The reconstruction of historical events requires that we seek the reality that is hidden in the tangle of contradictory information from the era. Doing this does not detract from the historical merit of the runaways who lived in those settlements; to the contrary, it acknowledges their rightful place in history. Moreover, none of the information and lists found in the runaway slave settlement contained any mention of the possibility of that trade.

The colonial authorities' documents that gave the total number of runaways living in the El Frijol settlement at the time of the second attack kept reducing that number—a fact that, curiously, was not mentioned in any previous studies. According to the authorities' public statements, the immediate result of the attack was the capture of 5 runaways who had been living in the settlement, but between March 28, 1816, when the second attack was made, and May 14 of that same year, a total of 89 runaways who had been living in the settlement turned themselves in voluntarily as a result of the attack made on the El Frijol settlement and of the campaign carried out by several bands of slavehunters, who kept operating in the area, and the number of runaways who were captured rose to more than 14, not counting those who were captured in other parts of the same area. By May 30, a total of 114 runaway slaves had been accounted for.

The El Frijol runaway slave settlement, which was attacked four times between 1815 and 1819, was one of the most famous of those settlements in Cuba in the nineteenth century. The authorities themselves exaggerated its importance—first of all, because they wanted to portray it as posing a danger, and, second, because they wanted to inflate the importance of the repressive activities they launched against it. Even though Franco (1974), Danger (1977), and Sánchez Guerra, Guilarte Abreu, and Dranquet Rodríguez (1986) considered it the most important of the runaway slave settlements because it constituted an economic unit, that was no reason for differentiating it from the others, since every runaway slave settlement constituted a subsistence economic unit. In Cuba, the concept of *palenque* implies the existence of an economy that goes beyond the levels of mere appropriation and enters production levels. Nor was that runaway slave settlement the most important one in terms of its size and activities. The analysis of other such settlements will bring this out.

The eastern authorities' interests and fears led them not only to attack the runaway slave settlements but to seek other solutions, as well. Since the attacks and the maintenance of slavehunting militias were really temporary, partial remedies for a social phenomenon engendered by slavery that had been increasing in a way that was dangerous to the slave regime, more stable solutions were studied.

Eusebio Escudero, governor of Santiago de Cuba, wrote to the captain general very realistically on May 11, 1816: "No matter how great the efforts we make to capture these renegade blacks and no matter how far the slavehunting militias spread from the Mayarí woods to the easternmost end of the island, it will never be possible to prevent some of them from being overlooked in these isolated, uninhabited woods or, with the passage of time, for them to gather together again" (ANC, RC/JF, leg. 25, no. 1,364).

A plan was devised for having whites settle in the high mountains of the northern range in the territory, mainly in the El Frijol Mountains, between the Jaguaní and Toa Rivers. Since nobody owned the area where the runaway slave settlement was located and it was considered to belong to the Crown, it was to be given to between fifteen and twenty industrious families of French and Spanish descent, who were to engage in agriculture there. A very rough map was drawn, and the sites of the El Frijol runaway slave settlement and the nearest populated areas were marked on it. The map—which included rural properties but not towns—showed four large plantations: El Bruto, Moa, and two others whose names were not recorded, all at considerable distances from one another (Franco 1973).

No information has been found to explain why that plan failed, but it was hardly likely that any families would want to engage in agricultural pursuits in that area, where there were no means of communication and from which the transport of crops would be very difficult and expensive; in addition, the area itself was notorious as a favorite haunt of runaway slaves.

During the same month in which the second attack on the El Frijol settlement was made, a group of twenty-five slaves who had rebelled attacked a plantation in the Mayarí Mountains. One of them who was captured stated that most of them came from Arroyito, Songo, and Sagua; one was from Baracoa; and another was from Havana. They were headed by a "French black" named Manuel, and they were armed with four guns and four "liters of gunpowder." Their settlement was on a mountain near the Micara plantation (in what is now Mayarí Arriba) and was protected by stakes, with only two means of access. The members of this group also attacked a farmer's thatched-roof hut in Sabanilla and set it on fire because the people living there refused to open the door so they could take the things they wanted. Unfortunately, the available documents do not contain any information on what finally happened to this turbulent group.

Apart from the project of promoting settlement by whites as a more effective solution for the problem—a project that never progressed beyond the stage of intentions—Governor Eusebio Escudero came up with another plan, which bears his name. On September 1, 1817, Escudero ordered that a file be kept that would sum up the problem of the eastern runaway slave settlements and analyze the threat they posed. Using it, he drew up a plan that was supposed to put an end to one of the problems that had filled most of his time since taking office.

The plan began with a report in which the concept of runaway slave settlement was defined; the existence of some of them that had been discovered in previous years, such as the ones in the Sierra Maestra and in Limones, Sagua, Tiguabos, and Caujerí, was noted; and, especially, data on the El Frijol settlement were included. The report stated that the authorities had known of this last settlement for the past seventy years, which agreed with the *cabildo* of Santiago de Cuba's records for 1747 (ANC, RC/JF, leg. 141, no. 6,935). In his document, Escudero said that there were around three hundred runaway slaves living in those mountains. Even though he stated clearly that this was a general figure for all the runaways living in settlements in those mountain ranges, it may have been understood to refer only to the runaways living in the El Frijol settlement—and, therefore, may have been the origin of the exaggerated figures some authors have used in this regard.

Later, Escudero proposed a plan for granting freedom to runaway slaves who lived in settlements if all the runaways in any one settlement turned themselves in and then helped to catch the runaways living in other settlements who refused to surrender. For this purpose, Escudero created the term "reformed fugitive," which was the keystone of his project. Even though the plan was criticized because it was dangerous to depend on runaways who had lived in those settlements, it was applied to the runaways from the Maluala settlement. This gave rise to a series of incidents that Franco (1973) has described and ended in resounding failure.

That plan was based on an old method that the colonial authorities had resorted to in other places in the Americas, such as Panama and Cartagena, where the phenomenon of runaway slave settlements had been a problem since the previous century. However, like the project promoting settlement by whites, the attempts to destroy the *palenques* by means of this plan served only to show the wealthy sectors in colonial society how useless such efforts were against this kind of resistance.

Eastern *Palenques* in the Period
of Slave Plantation Expansion

A fter the second decade of the nineteenth century, the main form of slave resistance in the eastern part of the island—the creation of runaway slave settlements—was a consolidated, relatively stable recourse of rebellious slaves. The royal order that the Spanish monarch signed in Madrid on June 24, 1820, shows the level and nature of the problem, which had already gone beyond the stage of isolated, happenstance manifestations. In it, he ordered that attacks on the *palenques* in the region be continued, because he was afraid that the runaways living in the settlements might form links with the black Republic of Haiti. The accompanying letter that the captain general sent to the governor of Santiago de Cuba along with the king's order states, among other things, "The king has been informed of what you said about the meetings held by vagabond blacks which began to be observed near Santiago de Cuba in September 1814 and about the provisions that Governor Eusebio Escudero has adopted for attacking them and freeing the plantations of the ills to which they are exposed. He has ordered that you concentrate on the destruction of the runaway slave settlements and that you strive to find and cut off the means that may facilitate direct or indirect communication between them and the French part of the island of Santo Domingo" (ANC, AP, leg. III, no. 122).

This royal order was circulated quite a long time after the outbreak of the Haitian revolution, but the existence and notoriety of the runaway slave settlements made the whites fear that the black republic might give the runaways assistance. However, this fear was based more on the ripening of internal contradictions—reflected in the strength with which the recourse of fleeing and living in a *palenque* had caught on—than on the external phenomenon of possible, though far from feasible, help from abroad.

Between 1820 (the year in which the royal order was promulgated) and 1828 (the year in which another slavehunting militia went out whose diary of operations has been preserved), many events took place that showed the continuation of and increase in that form of slave resistance. In October 1820, Pedro Collado was named as captain of a militia of slavehunters (Bacardí Moreau 1925, 2:149). In July 1821, a slavehunter named Vicente Jardines claimed payment of seven hundred pesos for some operations he had carried out against runaways living in settlements (2:170). And, in May 1822, the existence of a band of thirteen runaway slaves who were said to be well armed and looking for a *palenque* in which to take refuge was denounced (they had been seen on the Toa plantation) (2:185). A month later, two slavehunting militias were authorized to set out, to operate in the Mayarí and Sagua mountain ranges. In October of that same year, the *cabildo* of Santiago de Cuba received complaints about the behavior of two slavehunters who were members of the militia operating under the command of Captain Esteban Ulloa (2:191), who was also criticized by the newspaper *El Dominguillo* and forced to resign his command (2:196). In February 1823, a new slavehunting militia was created in Santiago de Cuba to go after "runaways and evildoers" (2:199), and on February 24, the Board of Plantation Owners of Santiago de Cuba resolved to levy a tax of four pesos for every slave over ten years old, to defray the expenses of the pursuit of runaway slaves (2:199). The next month, the mayor of Tiguabos presented a proposal to the *cabildo* of Santiago de Cuba that a slavehunting militia attack several runaway slave settlements in the El Frijol Mountains, Santa Cruz, and Moa. The proposal particularly called attention to a runaway slave settlement on the Moa headlands. In reply, a band was formed that left Santiago de Cuba and joined the militia of slavehunters from Tiguabos. After a combing operation in the rough terrain around Moa and in the El Frijol Mountains, they returned without any notable results (2:203). In June, it was reported that another small band of runaways—three of them—had been located on the Limoncito plantation, near Tiguabos (2:210).

Nearly a year later, in May 1824, a band of slavehunters headed by Captain José Lora attacked a runaway slave settlement in the Partido de Santa Catalina area (Bacardí Moreau 1925, 2:219).[1] In December 1827, the head of the slavehunting militia from Sevilla (west of Santiago de Cuba) sent a report to the governor stating that there was a settlement of forty runaway slaves at Alto de Aguadores, a little more than two and a half miles from the city (2:210).

All these reports, placed in chronological order, show that there was an extensive system of runaway slave settlements in the various mountain ranges in the region and that slavehunting militias and bands of slavehunters were created more frequently than ever before.

In addition to the development of runaway slave settlements, incidents related to other forms of resistance and rebellion took place, but the authorities never considered them to be as serious as the proliferation of settlements. One of the most important incidents was the flight of a "large number" of slaves from Manuel Justiz Ferrer's sugar mill (Callejas 1911, 122) and the crushing of a supposed uprising of slaves headed by Vicente Pérez, Marcos, and Salino—all slaves—and Tomás Ferrer, a free black. The plan was to have extended through El Caney and Bayamo and then to other settlements. In July 1825, nine blacks were hanged for having rebelled and killed the overseer on the Somanta plantation (Bacardí Moreau 1925, 2:225) Nearly all the uprisings were put down immediately and bloodily. One of the things that almost always put an end to those attempts was the presence of informers among the participants or other slaves who knew of the plans. This was the worst danger confronting this form of slave rebellion. Large-scale participation by the slaves was required to carry out an uprising or violent emancipation, which made this form of rebellion very vulnerable, because the system corrupted many of them—especially those who had ties with their masters.

An increase was also recorded in the number of slaves who ran away and became vagabonds, but it was restricted by its own limitations. In 1824, a depot for holding vagabond runaway slaves who were captured was built in Bayamo (ANC, RC/JF, leg. 44, no. 1,932; leg. 144, no. 7,000) The other jurisdictions in eastern Cuba maintained the procedure of keeping them in jails until their owners claimed them. If their owners did not do this, the runaways were sent to the main depot in El Cerro, in Havana.

Regarding the runaway slave settlements, the diary of operations kept by Ignacio Leyte Vidal, commandant of the slavehunting militia that operated in the Mayarí Mountains in 1828, contains so much information that a more detailed analysis of the matter can be made. The diary in question has enabled researchers to trace the route the slavehunting militia took in the mountains, define its areas of operations, and make an estimate of the areas occupied by the runaway slave settlements.

Runaway Slave Settlements in the Mayarí Mountains

One year before the attack headed by Leyte Vidal took place in Mayarí, the island had been divided into new territories for administrative purposes. Three departments were created—Western, Central, and Eastern. The Eastern Department was subdivided into four sections, with the city of Santiago de Cuba as departmental capital. The top government officials continued to live there, but the heads of the army lived in the various districts and presided over the town halls, to which the commandants and captains of the slavehunting militias reported. This division reflected the development in the realm of colonial administration that the island had achieved at that time. But, despite advances, some of which have already been mentioned, the eastern region still had large uninhabited areas that served as a refuge for runaway slaves. Describing the characteristics of the geography in the eastern region, the 1827 census stated, "Except for some isolated points in which scientific observations have been made, all the rest is completely unknown. Its lack of population; the immense

Figure 4. *The Cristal mountain range, where the Guarda Basura, La Ceiba, Bumba, Maluala, and other runaway slave settlements were located. It was the scene of the operations carried out by Ignacio Leyte Vidal's slavehunting militia in the 1820s. (Photo: R. Bombino)*

forests that still cover most of its area; and the nature of its mountain ranges, especially in the eastern part, which are so rugged that most of them are inaccessible, are largely responsible for this" (Comisión de Estadísticas 1829, 5).

This was the general situation in the region, especially in the area of operations of the slavehunting militia headed by Ignacio Leyte Vidal, in the Cristal mountain range, south of the town of Mayarí. At that time, the area contained many tobacco plantations but only a few, very isolated plantations of other kinds, all of which were concentrated near the rivers, so there were large expanses of terrain higher up that were unknown and that served as refuges for many runaway slaves (see fig. 4).

The town of Mayarí grew out of a tiny hamlet called La Caridad de Mayarí, built on the spot where a group of Indians from the surrounding area had gathered in 1557. All the documents from the colonial period describe it as a very poor town, with houses made of fan-palm fronds, on the banks of the Mayarí River. When Bishop Morell de Santa Cruz made

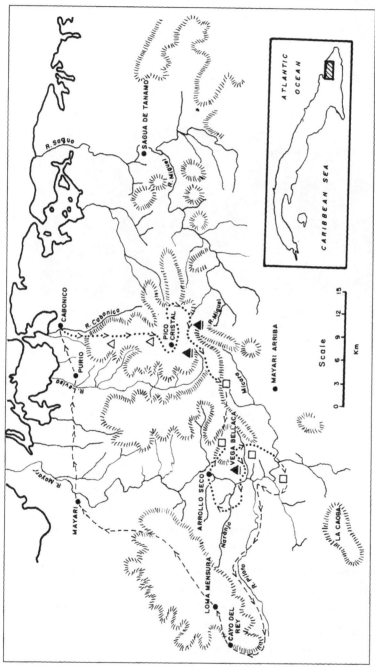

Figure 5. *Operations of Ignacio Leyte Vidal's slavehunting militia in the Mayarí Mountains in 1828. The members of this slavehunting militia set out eastward from Mayarí; went to Purio and Cabonico; and then went south, up the mountains. They checked on the Carga Basura and La Ceiba runaway slave settlements, which had already been discovered and attacked; skirted Cristal Peak; and, at a branch of the Miguel River, found and attacked a runaway slave settlement that they called by the name of the river. After this, they attacked the Río Levisa settlement, went to the Micara and Vega Bellaca plantations, attacked the Río Yaguasí palenque, went to the Seco Stream and the Piloto River, climbed Mensura Hill at Cayo del Rey, and then descended to the town of Mayarí.*

an ecclesiastical visit to it in the mid-eighteenth century, he noted that it had around three hundred inhabitants, who grew tobacco. Except for the site of the town, nearly all the territory was wooded; cedar, mahogany, sabicu, and pine trees abounded. Because of the prevailing economy, the slave population there was always small, but Mayarí had rugged mountains with large rivers and many streams, so it offered a safe refuge to the slaves who ran away from other places.

References to runaway slave settlements in those mountains began to appear in colonial documents in the mid-eighteenth century. Many notorious incidents related to the *palenques* took place in those mountains. The year before Leyte Vidal's operations against the runaways living in those settlements, the population of Mayarí was 667—198 whites, 401 free blacks, and 68 slaves. To the west, the closest town was Holguín. Only 15 percent of its population consisted of slaves, and its economy was mainly based on cattle raising. To the east, the nearest town was Sagua, which had only 376 inhabitants—155 whites, 174 free blacks, and 47 slaves. Sagua's economy was based on lumber and tobacco—there were sixty-eight tobacco plantations. Farther to the east, Baracoa had 2,690 inhabitants—921 whites, 1,111 free blacks, and 658 slaves (Comisión de Estadísticas 1829, 87). It had a local economy.

In view of these figures on the slave population and kind of economy that prevailed in the towns along the northern coast of the Eastern Department, it may be supposed that most of the runaway slaves who sought refuge in those mountains did not come from the surrounding area. Some of the runaways who were captured had escaped from the nearby towns and plantations, but most had fled from the central and southern parts of the department, mainly Santiago de Cuba.

The thirty members of Leyte Vidal's slavehunting militia set out from the town of Mayarí on April 20, 1828, heading east. After crossing some nearly flat terrain, they reached Hato de Cabonico (not to be found among current place-names), which was between El Purio and El Quemado. This must have been a distance of between fifteen and sixteen miles. Considering the distance, the time it took to cover it, and the diary entries (in which Leyte Vidal said that the group advanced on foot), we can be quite exact in reconstructing their route, the stretches covered each day, and the areas where the runaway slave settlements were found (see fig. 5).

The notes corresponding to April 24 said that the food was carried on the men's backs "because there was no way for beasts to get through." On April 28, when they reached the Micara plantation, Leyte Vidal wrote, "We went down to it along a stony stream. The descent was very difficult, and we had to hang on to vines" (ANC, GG, leg. 584, no. 28,861). Because of these characteristics of the terrain, the operations lasted for twenty-four days, not counting six days for resting and waiting for the rain to let up. The members of the slavehunting militia must have covered a total distance of around ninety miles. They attacked three runaway slave settlements that had been previously unknown to them and checked two that had been attacked in the course of earlier operations. All this shows that this was not the first time the slavehunting militia had gone into those mountains.

The two *palenques* that the members of the slavehunting militia had already known about and that they checked were the Guarda Basura and La Ceiba, whose locations on the map showing their route have been inferred, based on the calculations of distance and the route followed that appear in the diary.[2] The first was half a day's walk from Cabonico, going toward Cristal Peak. The members of the slavehunting militia found a recently built hut in that settlement, which had been attacked earlier, and destroyed the crops. This situation was repeated over and over again in the case of settlements that had been attacked earlier. It shows that the runaways who had lived in those settlements kept going back to them after they had been destroyed, mainly using them as places to fall back on and for provisions. In them, any runaway slave could seek temporary refuge and some food—yams, taro, and bananas, since they were plants that would grow back after being cut down.

Later, the members of the militia skirted Cristal Peak and crossed the Miguel River, where they found the first runaway slave settlement that was new to them. Unable to discover what name its inhabitants had given it, they called it the Río Miguel settlement. It had seven huts with two beds each—a total of fourteen—which surely coincided with the number of inhabitants. The slavehunters searched for traces of the runaways and guessed that they had three guns and few crops. The day after arriving at the settlement, which had been abandoned before they got there, they set out toward the Levisa River and, after a six-hour walk, found another runaway slave settlement, which had also been abandoned when its inhabitants heard that the militia was nearby. They had no way of learning the name of this one, either, and called it the Río Levisa settlement. It had nine huts, some of which had four beds, and they calculated that it had around twenty-five inhabitants. The attackers destroyed the crops—which they reported as abundant, with a variety of fruits. They also noted that tallow had been melted and sugarcane had been cut there not long before.

After five days of hard walking and after having crossed the Yaguasi Arriba River, they reached another runaway slave settlement, about which it seems that they had heard, because they had searched for it persistently. This place—which they recorded in the diary as the Río Yaguasi settlement—had only five old huts and few crops, so the slavehunters considered it a way station that the runaways used when making trips to the south. The diary entry for May 7 recorded an item of great interest: another slavehunting militia had left the town of Sagua and was engaged in operations near where Leyte Vidal's group was operating.

This reference was the first historical mention that has been found of simultaneous operations by several slavehunting militias in areas that were relatively near each other. This tactic was typical of the large-scale raids that were carried out in the 1840s, so it may be supposed that it was used since the 1820s, though not in a generalized way.

This kind of operation presupposes a degree of organizational development and planning at the departmental level and indicates a higher level of skill in the repressive system used against the runaways living in settlements, since it kept the slaves who had rebelled from escaping by simply moving from one mountain area to another. Several bands of slavehunters who set out from different points had been used against the El Portillo (in 1747) and El Frijol (in 1816) runaway slave settlements, but all of them had had the same goal: the settlement that they wanted to destroy. This new variant constituted a step forward in the system of repression, corresponding to greater knowledge of the tactics used by the runaways living in settlements.

The slavehunting militia headed by Leyte Vidal continued its long trek through the Mayarí Mountains. The slavehunters passed the Naranjo and Seco Streams, the Piloto River, and Mensura Hill before going back to their starting point.[3]

In terms of runaway slave settlements that were destroyed, the balance sheet of the operations had been favorable, but this was not so with respect to the capture of runaways, since the slavehunting militia returned without having captured any slaves at all. The tactic of falling back that the runaways living in the settlements used had proved to be effective, as had their system of lookouts, because, in all the cases cited above, the settlements had been abandoned before the militia arrived.

Four months after the operations that Leyte Vidal had directed in the Mayarí area, the town magistrate of Santiago de Cuba issued a request for assistance in weapons and money for continuing to attack runaway slave settlements, arguing, "For some time, they have been spreading in various parts of the jurisdiction" (ANC, RC/JF, leg. 150, no. 7,442). According to that colonial authority, reliable reports had been received that there were several runaway slave settlements, some of which had been attacked shortly before. He added that a member of one of the slavehunting militias had been wounded in one of the clashes.[4]

The new political-administrative division facilitated coordination among local government bodies and the Board of Plantation Owners of the Eastern Department, which was in charge of financing operations against the runaways living in settlements. In the Eastern Department, the 1820s ended with a series of alarming events in the sphere of slave resistance. Attention continued to be focused on the mountains in the Mayarí area. On June 26, 1830, Antonio de León, the military commandant of that territorial division, presented the governor of the department with a disturbing report, in which the following aspects were emphasized: the mountains between Mayarí and Baracoa were "full of runaway blacks" (ANC, AP, leg. 111, no. 122), but, contrary to what might be supposed, no damage had been done to the neighboring plantations. Mention was even made of an incident in which a cowhand who had fallen into a ditch filled with sharpened stakes that surrounded a *palenque* had been rescued and sent back by a group of around fifty runaway slaves.

This information confirmed that the mountain ranges in the Mayarí, Sagua, and Baracoa areas had become favorite places in which runaway slaves established settlements but that—unlike the runaways who had alarmed the plantation owners and authorities in the previous decade— they did not engage in any attacks or thefts. Nine days after this report was received, de León set out on an exploratory expedition through those mountains to attack the runaway slave settlements. On July 4, as a preliminary measure, he had sent a picket of men to the Arriba River to ensure that nobody would cross the river to warn the runaways living in the settlements. Early on the afternoon of July 5, a cannon was shot off in the town as a signal for the inhabitants to gather together. He then selected fifty of the men who had responded to the call, and they set out at three o'clock. They spent the night at the Frío River and then went to the Naranjo Stream. On July 7, they went up the Frío River "in the water" (ANC, RC/JF, leg. 125, no. 42) until they caught sight of a runaway slave settlement that they thought was a little more than five miles from El Naranjo, and they went closer to it "until [they] could clearly hear everything the blacks were saying." When they were very close to the place, de León ordered Ignacio Leyte Vidal, the lieutenant of the slavehunting militia, to take thirty men and attack the settlement from the other side, so as to keep the runaways from escaping. After waiting long enough for Leyte Vidal's group to get in position, de León decided to attack, but, on drawing even closer, he came up against "a great slope pitted with trenches and stakes" (ANC, RC/JF, leg. 125, no. 42), with two very narrow, twisting paths. They continued to approach the settlement until, at a bend in the path, a runaway from the settlement attacked them with a machete.

The slavehunter who was in front fired his blunderbuss. The recoil threw him to his knees, injuring him. At the same time, the runaway fled, leaving a trail of blood, which made it possible for the slavehunters to follow him and capture him alive. The rest of the runaways fled "on the other side, leaping down precipices that have to be seen to be believed." When the members of the slavehunting militia reached the top of the hill, they found only "signs of flight in the bits of clothing and hair that were hanging on thorns" (ANC, RC/JF, leg. 125, no. 42). The group of slavehunters under Leyte Vidal's command returned without having reached the other side of the settlement.

When the slavehunters examined the settlement, they found seventeen new huts widely separated from one another on the hill, with a total of thirty beds. After this, they pretended to withdraw and managed to capture another of the runaways from the settlement when, thinking that the attackers had gone away, he was returning to it. According to the statements of the two captured runaways, it was the Bumba *palenque*, which was "related to" the Maluala settlement, on the Levisa River. Sixty runaway slaves, half of them women, lived in the two settlements, which were also connected with three other runaway slave settlements, all of them small, called El Rincón, Tibisial, and La Palma. The defense system of this group of small runaway slave settlements that maintained contact with one another included trenches with sharpened stakes, with the huts scattered at some distance from one another, and the presence of lookouts—though, as has been seen in the case of the Bumba settlement, this last recourse seems to have failed.

After the expedition, de León proposed a break in the operations and wrote the military and political governor of Santiago de Cuba to this effect, saying that he did not think it was a good time to go out again, because the blacks were "incited." He concluded, "It would be better to wait a month or two, until they have calmed down and there is other news of them" (ANC, RC/JF, leg. 125, no. 40).

This proposal seems to have been accepted, because no other slave-hunting militias were formed in Mayarí until September 7. That one was composed of fifty-two men, with Joseph Angel Soría as first commandant and Joseph Ramón León as second, "both of proved courage and determined" (ANC, RC/JF, leg. 125, no. 43). The slavehunters set out for the mountains along the road to the Benga el Sábalo plantation and spent the night at the Seco Stream. Then they crossed the Naranjo Stream and went up the Frío River until they arrived at the ruins of the Bumba *palenque*. There, they split into two groups; one combed the hills near the Micara plantation, and the other headed toward the El Rincón, Tibisial, and La Palma settlements. They were to join forces at the place known as Pinal. Their plans also included attacking the Maluala runaway slave settlement and checking on the La Ceiba and Guarda Basura settlements, which they already knew about, and one on the Miguel River that Leyte Vidal had attacked in 1828.

According to a report from the Mayarí authorities dated October 4 (ANC, RC/JF, leg. 125, no. 44), the members of the slavehunting militia returned a few days after setting out, renewed their efforts on September 22, and returned again on the 30th. The information that accompanied the report sent from Mayarí does not indicate that they had managed to attack the Maluala settlement or any of the others. It only mentions that they burned some new huts that the blacks had built at the Bumba *palenque,* which had already been attacked.

Tightening of the Eastern Repressive System

While this was going on in the mountains in the northern part of the department, other interesting events were taking place in the mountain ranges to the south. The head of the Santiago de Cuba branch of the Holy Brotherhood commissioned a slavehunter named Tomás Coll, of the same city, and a band of men he had chosen to do "whatever [was] necessary" (ANC, Gobierno Superior Civil [hereafter cited as GSC], leg. 1,676, no. 83,860) in the countryside around Santiago de Cuba to maintain constant harassment of runaway slaves, deserters from the army and navy, and other individuals described as wrongdoers. In those years, it became common practice to grant extensive powers to bands of slavehunters.

More or less at the same time—in the 1830s—similar powers were granted to the bands of slavehunters headed by José Rafael Parrado, in Puerto Príncipe, and José Pérez Sánchez, in the Vuelta Abajo region, in the western part of the island.[5] The nature of the commission given to Tomás Coll indicates that he was mainly to go after vagabond runaway slaves rather than runaways living in settlements—against whom, as has been seen, large slavehunting militias were mobilized.

On March 19, 1831, the governor of Santiago de Cuba made a study of the current situation, which he described as dangerous, and of the runaway slaves' "establishment of formal homes and work," which he termed "scandalous." He particularly called attention to the runaway slave settlement called Bayamito, which a militia of forty slavehunters headed by a commandant and a lieutenant had attacked early in 1831. In the settlement, the attacking force had found forty-five "houses," in which 160 blacks lived.[6] The report included a new element in the analysis of runaway slave settlements, for it used the term "house" rather than "hut," as had been customary up until then. This element would be repeated later on in some of the diaries of operations that were studied. The possibility that this Santiago de Cuba official used the term out of carelessness can be ruled out because the same document states that each of the dwellings had a "living room and bedroom" (ANC, RC/JF, leg. 150, no. 7,462). This, along with other elements discussed later, makes it possible to say that not all the dwellings in the runaway slave settlements in the eastern region consisted of primitive huts made of royal palm fibers and fronds. The existence of houses with living rooms and bedrooms, even though made of the same materials as the huts, presupposes greater mastery of building techniques and an interest in comfort and family life. Moreover, all subsequent references that slavehunters made to "houses" invariably referred to highly developed settlements.

The Bayamito settlement, near the river of the same name in the Sierra Maestra—about which neither collateral information nor the diary of operations of the militia that attacked it has been found—must have had the same level of development as the El Frijol, Maluala, El Cedro, Todos Tenemos, and Calunga settlements, some of which are discussed individually later on. This opinion is based not only on the number and kind of dwellings but also on the fact that, in the mention he made of it, the governor of Santiago de Cuba said that the runaways living there had fought off the attack vigorously with firearms for two hours. He also said that four of the runaways in the settlement were killed, four others were captured alive, and the rest were scattered into the rugged mountains. The Bayamito settlement (1831) was the second large *palenque* in the eastern region whose inhabitants put up total resistance to attack; the first had been El Frijol, during the attack made on it in 1815.

A militia of forty slavehunters was formed to hunt down the runaways from the settlement who had fled. For a month, Commandant Félix Ruiz and the other members of the militia combed the mountains near Bayamito. At the same time, another slavehunting militia, headed by Cecilio Jardines, was formed in the mountain ranges to the north. During their operations, the members of this second militia captured a total of fourteen runaway slaves, six of them women. The slavehunters were dealt some losses—three men with serious wounds.

The two militias carried out their operations simultaneously, which shows how consolidated the repressive system in the eastern region had become.

In his evaluation of these last experiences, the governor of Santiago de Cuba said that they were important for developing regional tactics and strategies. He pointed out that if attacks on runaway slave settlements were to be successful, they would have to "be made with a heavy and active hand so as to destroy assemblies of such size that the weak efforts of the bands should not be risked; rather, *a military expedition should be employed to annihilate, destroy, and uproot them*" (ANC, RC/JF, leg. 150, no. 7,462).[7] This criterion expressed the main aim of the system, which responded directly to the principal form of slave resistance that worried the authorities and slave owners.

Far from declining, runaway slave settlements were growing in number, and some reached unusual levels of development. The authorities and slave owners realized that they would have to do more than send out small bands of slavehunters if they were to destroy them.

On December 3, 1831, the governor of Santiago de Cuba sent an official communiqué to the printing house of the Royal Consulate, and it was printed and distributed on December 24 as a supplement to the *Noticiero Comercial* (Trade News) of Santiago de Cuba. Among other things, it said, "May this government always remain alert in the prosperity of Providence . . . to wipe out those brigand runaway slaves, hunting them down to the point of wiping out the last of their refuges and turning them over to their owners, to whom they belong, or to the magistrate, whenever one of those punished by law is guilty of too many crimes, as a warning to others of their class and condition" (ANC, RC/JF, leg. 151, no. 7,462).

This document was circulated as a separate page, along with an official order stating that every slave owner was obligated to turn in a list of all the slaves he owned who had run away during the past ten years. Everything seems to indicate that this measure was not complied with on a regular basis, since the earliest complete list that has been found— discussed later on—was dated 1841. Moreover, the Board of Plantation Owners complained repeatedly that the owners were not complying with the order.

In a letter to the captain general dated December 30, 1831, the governor of Santiago de Cuba assured him that the matter had been attended to zealously and that it was "one of the concerns to which this government [had] devoted the most attention" (ANC, RC/JF, leg. 151, no. 7,462). After describing some experiences in hunting down runaways who lived in settlements, the governor proposed that a slavehunting militia of fifty men be created in each territorial division and that they divide up the areas of operations. To give weight to his proposal, the governor said that there were runaway slave settlements in the Baracoa, Bayamo, Holguín, Manzanillo, and Jiguaní areas. He considered all of them except Holguín to be important points for future operations. No evidence has been found that the recommendations sent to the captain general were given an immediate affirmative reply, but it has been shown that all the suggestions were applied, even if gradually, since all of them were adopted in future operations.

Historian Jerez de Villarreal (1960) stated that important mobilizations against the eastern runaway slave settlements took place in 1832 and 1833, though he did not say on what evidence his statement was based. However, documents written by the colonial authorities seem to bear this out. On January 4, 1832, Juan Serrano, head of the Santiago de Cuba branch of the Holy Brotherhood, commissioned Pedro Mederos, of the same city, to attack the many runaway slaves. On February 14 of that same year, Juan de Moya y Morejón, the military and political governor, held a meeting with representatives of the wealthiest plantation owners and formed a commission that would be in charge of creating a permanent fund for meeting the expenses of the continual attacks that were to be made on runaways living in settlements.

This marked an important milestone in tightening the mechanisms of the repressive system. Just as had been done eighteen years earlier, a new, updated document was drawn up in the city of Santiago de Cuba to replace the February 15, 1814, regulations. The new regulations were printed that same year (Comisión de la Junta de Hacendados de Santiago de Cuba 1832).

The Commission of Eastern Plantation Owners acted with the authorization of the captain general of the island, who approved the easterners' initiatives. Under the new regulations, the commission was empowered to

1. determine what resources were needed,

2. decide on and adopt fund-raising measures,

3. appoint who was to be in charge of collecting and managing the funds,

4. decide how many slavehunting militias were needed for operations,

5. decide on the number and kind of weapons the members of the militias should carry,

6. have access to official documents that recorded the existence of runaway slave settlements,

7. propose measures for making the "police" more effective in the countryside, and

8. take a census of the slave population in each territorial division in the eastern region.

The uneasiness in the region caused by the existence of permanent *palenques* had also become a generalized concern among the authorities of the island. According to the initial statements of the Commission of Eastern Plantation Owners, the situation had become dangerous in those years: "The number of runaway blacks is growing so much that it demands attention. They venture to commit infractions of the law, seizing or taking others with them, pillaging plantations, and pitilessly mistreating whoever falls into their hands" (Comisión de la Junta de Hacendados de Santiago de Cuba 1832, 3).

In view of these arguments, during a meeting held in Havana on June 8, 1832, the Board of Government of the Royal Consulate, headed by the captain general, approved the proposals and measures of the eastern plantation owners, whose work it described as "very important for safety and peace," since it concerned the destruction of the runaway slave settlements, which were "not only increasing in number but . . . also growing in daring and determination" (ANC, AP, leg. 131, no. 11).

The regulations of the Commission of Eastern Plantation Owners demonstrate the importance the topic had acquired in the 1830s. It was no longer a matter of isolated information from various territorial divisions and areas. A group of well-informed plantation owners had formed a commission and set the goal of wiping out the clandestine hamlets that runaway slaves had founded in the eastern region, both because they constituted an incentive for other slaves to run away and because the boldness of their activities posed a real threat.

One of the first measures the commission adopted was to collect two reals from each slave owner for every slave he had over twelve years old, whether rural or urban. This measure was applied to the owners of plantations and other properties in the El Caney, El Cobre, Tiguabos, Guantánamo, Mayarí, Sagua, and Santiago de Cuba areas. In contrast, the owners in Bayamo, Holguín, Baracoa, Manzanillo, and Jiguaní assumed the costs of the slavehunting militias that were formed in their territories.

Since the plantation owners wanted not only to destroy the runaway slaves' rural settlements but also to prevent their gathering together again in the future, some of the funds were set aside to promote settlement by white families in the most isolated areas, "mainly those between Mayarí, Santiago de Cuba, and Baracoa, because they [were] the main stimulus to disorder by runaway blacks" (ANC, AP, leg. 131, no. 11). But, as had happened with the project that had been drawn up for the same purposes in 1816, this measure was never applied.

The Commission of Eastern Plantation Owners immediately created four militias for attacking the eastern runaway slave settlements. Each militia consisted of twenty-five soldiers, a sergeant, two corporals, and thirteen civilians (slavehunters) chosen by the commandant of each militia. The thirteen civilians included the guides, who were always cowhands who were familiar with the terrain. The pay was a hundred pesos for each commandant, twenty for each sergeant, twelve for each corporal, and eight for each soldier. Each civilian was to receive twenty pesos. These amounts were paid while the slavehunting militias were carrying out operations.

The commission stipulated that it would pay four pesos for every vagabond runaway slave who was captured. This was similar to the amount that, under the regulations of the Royal Consulate, had been paid ever since 1796. However, eight pesos would be paid for each runaway slave who lived in a settlement. Thus, an important difference was established between the monetary incentives in the eastern region and those that the Royal Consulate had established for the Central and Western Departments. It also changed the rate that had been set in the regulations that had been in effect in the eastern region since 1814. Two factors seem to have influenced this change. First, as shown in the various diaries of operations, in the Eastern Department, the bands of slavehunters and slavehunting militias captured more runaway slaves who lived in settlements than vagabond runaway slaves, which resulted in a quite stable income. The second factor was related to the conditions in the region: as already stated, the regulations of 1814 had established a form of payment that was linked to the distance between the place where the slavehunting militias set out and the site where the runaways who lived in settlements were captured. This method was used to stimulate the capture of groups that had settled far away, but there was no reason for it when slavehunting militias were set up to operate in each territory.

The rules that were established in 1832 were very simple and practical and reflected the fact that the system of repression had become generalized in that decade. This was because reports of runaway slave settlements came in from all the mountain areas in the department at the same time. With these regulations, the eastern system of mixed slavehunting militias (consisting of civilians and military men) became official, and it is important to bring out a substantial difference that existed between those slavehunting militias and the bands that were commissioned by the Royal Consulate.

Each band consisted of six men and was usually headed by a civilian who had specialized in hunting down runaway slaves. The members of those bands were usually unscrupulous, engaged in extortion and rape, and had frequent—and serious—arguments with plantation owners and slave owners because of the damage they did to the owners' property. In contrast, the eastern slavehunting militias—most of whose members were military men—consisted of more than twenty-five men each and were supported by the local authorities and plantation owners. The members of each slavehunting militia maintained military discipline, had a pre-established route for their operations (Comisión de la Junta de Hacendados de Santiago de Cuba 1832, 10), and had clearly defined goals that were confined to a short period of the year. In general, the members of the slavehunting militias obeyed the rules set by the owners. Therefore, none of the documents about the slavehunting militias that have been studied reported any incidents or disputes similar to the ones that abounded in the case of the bands of slavehunters.

During 1832, the Commission of Eastern Plantation Owners put the finishing touches on the eastern repressive system. Article 27 of the regulations (which applied only to that area) stated that several slavehunting militias should carry out their operations simultaneously for a period of three months, thus generalizing and consolidating some of the experiences gained in past years.

Even though they had asked for a new census, the members of the commission had to content themselves with the data of the 1827 one, which were the most reliable recent figures. Since they had received lists of runaway slaves from only thirty-six slave owners, they had to employ the new method of launching simultaneous attacks in various places without having all the information they had requested. Also in 1832, the first four slavehunting militias—or columns, as they were also called— were formed. They were commanded by the officers Pablo Francisco Caignet, Esteban Ulloa, Julián Ruiz, and Juan Campos.[8]

While this was going on, several incidents occurred that showed that the contradictions inherent to slavery were becoming more acute. The Río Arriba plantation, in Mayarí, which was owned by Tomás Asencio, was attacked and burned; in the Río Seco area, a little to the south, another plantation, owned by Benigno Hechevarría, was also attacked; and the La Sierra plantation was attacked and robbed. Of all the incidents that took place in the first few months of the year, the most alarming was the attack on the Santa Catalina plantation, where the runaway slaves hanged three of the people living there. After this last attack was reported, the authorities of Santiago de Cuba inspected the plantation and found the three bodies (Bacardí Moreau 1925, 2:263).

These events differed in an alarming way from all earlier attacks by runaway slaves. Up until then, they had mainly made attacks in order to seize the equipment and resources they needed for establishing a settlement in the mountains, to take the slaves from the plantation with them, or to free those slaves. When any of the inhabitants on the plantations that were attacked had been killed, it had been the result of a clash;

never before had the runaways killed anyone on purpose. This new turn changed everything.

After this, a group of slavehunters who must have been motivated by vengeance went to the plantation to kill those who might possibly have been given severe punishments when they were slaves. The hangings resulted in an intensification of efforts to hunt down runaways and the taking of special measures, such as creating a "court" in Santiago de Cuba that specialized in cases in which rebellious slaves were accused of crimes. Within a few months of its creation, this court had become notorious for the harshness of the punishments it imposed.

However, the attacks that were made against the runaways living in settlements in the mountains had little results. As Juan de Moya, governor of Santiago de Cuba, said in May 1832, "Unfortunately, the slavehunting militias used in this important service have done nothing more than arrive at the runaway slave settlements and destroy their houses and crops, which is not the main aim, because the blacks—who have, doubtless, been warned—abandon everything" (ANC, AP, leg. 131, no. 11). While the governor's report was on its way to the captain general, an armed band of runaway slaves went to the Peladero estate, around twenty-one miles from Tiguabos, and attacked and burned it. Some cowhands from Sagua who had been moving the cattle were nearby and witnessed the attack. Later, they confessed that they had hidden when they realized that there were a great many blacks. Two overseers—Carlos Jardines and a man called Tomás, known as "El Inglés" (the Englishman)—were killed in the attack. Another man, Vicente Jardines, managed to escape after being dealt two machete wounds in the head.

The cowhands from Sagua and Vicente Jardines reported the attack immediately. As a result, a slavehunting militia consisting of forty men under the command of Gabino Otamendi set out from Tiguabos at ten o'clock that night. The latest news they received before leaving was that the band of runaways was going through the Bayate plantation. They caught up with the runaways at Marcos Sánchez's plantation, in Jaragueca (around sixteen miles from the town of Tiguabos), the next day. Four of the runaways were killed and one captured alive in that first clash. The captured runaway, Agustín, was immediately identified as being the property of

Oñate, who lived in the same area. Later, the slavehunting militia lost the tracks of the others. Then, at around eight at night, the band of runaways made a surprise attack with firearms, seriously wounding José García López, a slavehunter, in the chest. The runaways withdrew again when the members of the slavehunting militia returned their fire.

Throughout the month of May, the slavehunters continued to hunt the runaways in the Sabanilla and Ti Arriba areas, going as far as Mayarí Arriba, but did not find them. The report that closed those incidents stated that, on May 31, the efforts made by the slavehunting militias were considered useless, since it was known that the band of runaways had taken refuge in the most rugged part of the Toa River area (ANC, AP, leg. 131, no. 11).

Because the attacks on runaway settlements and armed bands had been intensified, the regional authorities attributed the increased aggressiveness of the runaways living in settlements to the inattention given runaway slaves. They considered that the mountains surrounding the towns of Mayarí, Tiguabos, and Baracoa were the main areas harboring runaway slave settlements. Fears continued to be expressed concerning possible links between the runaways living in settlements in those areas and Haiti (ANC, AP, leg. 135, no. 15).

The special court that tried crimes by rebellious slaves continued to do its repressive work, which the owners praised highly. The punishments that were applied included the execution of three slaves who had taken part in an attack on a coffee plantation on May 27, 1835. After being garroted, the bodies of the three were quartered and their remains placed in iron cages for viewing.[9] On June 11 of that same year, two other runaway slaves were executed, and, in February 1838, so were several runaways who had lived in settlements and were captured in different places (Bacardí Moreau 1925, 2:281).

Throughout the 1830s, the official correspondence sent by the governor of the department made special note of hunting down runaways who lived in settlements. When Antonio María de la Torre became governor, it became immediately obvious that he was taking this matter very seriously. The correspondence he sent repeated that the most dangerous area was the mountain range near the Toa River. The increase in the number of runaway slave settlements and in the repressive measures during the first few years of the 1830s was analyzed as follows: "That was when the blacks especially terrified the inhabitants of this province, where they not only committed the most outrageous crimes but even dared to attack a plantation and kill its overseer ten and a half miles from this place. It was also when they were hunted down the most, with attacks in all directions, the destruction of their settlements and of the huts where they sought shelter, the killing of many, and the capture of a large number, who were taken to this city and tried" (ANC, RC/JF, leg. 142, no. 6,963).

The information the governor gave presented the slave owners' view of events and the level that the slaves' resistance had reached in that decade. Referring to the operations that had been undertaken against the runaways living in settlements, the governor of Santiago de Cuba said, "The forces of the provincial battalion and some slavehunting militias of fellow countrymen who served as guides carried out this simultaneous movement against all the points occupied by the runaway blacks," and, concerning what he himself had done, added, "Ever since I assumed command of this province, I have taken prompt, effective measures in all the territorial divisions to ensure that, wherever any of those blacks were, there should be no letup in hunting them down" (ANC, RC/JF, leg. 142, no. 6,963).

Therefore, it can be said that, in the 1830s—specifically, starting in 1832—one of the most important functions of the departmental government was to hunt down the runaway slaves who lived in settlements in the eastern mountains. The tension may have eased occasionally, but the struggle between the runaway slave settlements, as the main form of slave resistance in the eastern region, and the repressive system that was created to destroy them was one of the most important activities during those decades.

Far from being exceptions, the eastern slavehunting militias' diaries of operations that have been found—which are the main sources on which this book is based—are good examples, a small sample, of the documents reflecting one of the social constants of that period: slave resistance. There are sure to be many other diaries of operations that have not been found as yet; these will make it possible to expand this study.

Consolidation of Resistance and Repression

The 1840s showed a considerable upsurge in slave resistance as a result of the socioeconomic contradictions inherent to the period of greatest development of the slave plantation economy and the beginning of its crisis on the island. In this period, vagabond runaway slaves and armed bands of runaway slaves continued to be the most prevalent forms of slave resistance in the Vuelta Abajo region, in the west, but the most important slave uprisings in the history of Cuba took place in Matanzas, which had quickly become the center of sugar production on the island and the area where the most slaves were concentrated.

In the Eastern Department, runaway slave settlements continued to be the main form of slave resistance. Therefore, it was the scene of the most noted and important attacks that were made on the small, clandestine hamlets that the runaway slaves had founded.

The 1841 census (Comisión de Estadísticas 1842) offers some data that make it possible to measure the importance of the factors directly linked to this social phenomenon. Using the categories that were employed in that era for registering the population, Table 8 shows the differences between the island's three large regions.

According to the data of that census, even when the Eastern Department was at its greatest territorial size, it had a smaller population than either of the other two departments. Moreover, there were only a fifth as many slaves in the Eastern Department as in the western region. Even though the Eastern Department had fewer inhabitants and fewer slaves, as in earlier decades, it had more or less the same socioeconomic structure as the rest of the island. In 1841, slaves constituted 51 percent of the population in the western part of the island, 26 percent of the inhabitants in the central area, and 36 percent of the population in the eastern region. Therefore, considering this matter in terms of the regions in which the highest percentages of the total population were slaves, the situation was more acute in the west than in the eastern and central regions, but all the regions had large groups of slaves. The economic and demographic bases of the problem reached their highest expression in those years, though with different levels, and none of the old jurisdictions were exempt from the social manifestations generated by slavery.

Table 8. Population of Cuba, 1841

DEPARTMENT	WHITES	FREE MULATTOES	FREE BLACKS	MULATTO SLAVES	BLACK SLAVES	TOTAL
Western	244,023	25,280	41,183	5,885	315,389	631,760
Central	113,873	21,294	10,285	2,849	47,307	195,608
Eastern	60,395	41,480	13,316	2,240	62,825	180,256
Total	418,291	88,054	64,784	10,974	425,521	1,007,624

Source: Based on data from the 1841 census (Comisión de Estadísticas 1842).

Five years later, according to the 1846 census (Comisión de Estadísticas 1847), the Western Department had 560,492 inhabitants, 227,813 of whom—41 percent of the total—were slaves. It also had 735 sugar mills and 1,012 coffee plantations. In contrast, the Eastern Department had 177,427 inhabitants, 48,961 of whom—28 percent of the total—were slaves. It also had 303 sugar mills and 580 coffee plantations. Viewed another way, 21 percent of the 1,442 sugar mills and 35 percent of the 1,670 coffee plantations that existed on the island in 1846 were in the eastern region.

These figures show not only the differences between the two regions in terms of the level of development of slave plantations—which many researchers have emphasized and which can be explained as a result of the more benign regime of exploitation in the eastern region—but also the presence of quantitatively and socially significant elements, such as the thousands of slaves whose labor was exploited by hundreds of those productive units that supplied the capitalist market. Table 9 presents the figures on the slave population, sugar mills, and coffee plantations in the Eastern Department in 1846, showing the differences between the various jurisdictions in that department in terms of those aspects.

Thus, we see that Santiago de Cuba and its forty-six rural territorial divisions contained the largest percentage of the slaves in the department. The figures for the other jurisdictions are not significant compared with the figure for Santiago de Cuba, though the growth that had taken place in some of them should not be disregarded. If these data are compared with those of the 1827 census (ANC, GSC, leg. 1,676, no. 83,860), it can be seen that the number of slaves in Bayamo dropped from 10 percent

Table 9. Slaves, Sugar Mills, and Coffee Plantations in the Eastern Department, 1846

JURISDICTION	SLAVES		SUGAR MILLS	
	NUMBER	PERCENTAGE OF TOTAL IN THE DEPARTMENT	NUMBER	PERCENTAGE OF TOTAL IN THE DEPARTMENT
Santiago de Cuba and its forty-six territorial divisions	35,444	72.39	112	36.96
Bayamo	2,921	5.96	43	14.19
Holguín	2,961	6.04	80	26.40
Baracoa	1,489	3.04	10	3.30
Manzanillo	1,072	2.18	20	6.60
Jiguaní	677	1.38	27	8.91
Saltadero	4,397	8.98	11	3.63
Total	48,961		303	

Source: Based on data from the 1846 census (Comisión de Estadísticas 1847).

of the total in the department to 6 percent of that total, whereas the number of slaves in Holguín grew from 5 percent to 6 percent of the total. The percentage in Baracoa remained almost the same, declining from 4 to 3 percent of the total number of slaves in the department. The growth of Manzanillo was noteworthy: its slave population grew from a practically insignificant number in 1827 to 1,072 (with twenty sugar-production units). The rapid growth of Saltadero is also interesting: though not even entered individually in the 1827 census, it appeared in the 1846 census with 4,397 slaves, or almost 9 percent of the total slave population in the department. The number of coffee and cotton plantations in this last population center had grown considerably.

Sugarcane plantations were important to Santiago de Cuba's economy, and 37 percent of the sugar mills in the eastern region were in this jurisdiction. The next most important areas in this regard were Holguín, with 26 percent, and Bayamo, with 14 percent of the total for the region. The

COFFEE PLANTATIONS	
NUMBER	PERCENTAGE OF TOTAL IN THE DEPARTMENT
510	87.93
5	0.86
1	0.17
22	3.79
0	
0	
42	7.24
580	

figures on sugar mills for the other jurisdictions were not significant, but the forty-two coffee plantations in Saltadero and the twenty-two in Baracoa explain the growth of the slave population in the former and the maintenance of similar levels in the latter. Santiago de Cuba had 88 percent of the coffee plantations in the department.

Just as Havana and Matanzas had higher figures than the rest of the island in some socioeconomic indicators, Santiago de Cuba had higher figures than the rest of the Eastern Department. For example, during the first few years of the 1840s, nearly ten times as many runaway slaves were reported in Havana as in the Eastern Department, and within the latter, nearly ten times as many runaway slaves were reported in Santiago de Cuba as in the other jurisdictions.

In the eastern part of the island, the population was mainly concentrated in the urban centers and productive units, such as the sugar mills, coffee plantations, and mines, but most of the land was still uncultivated,

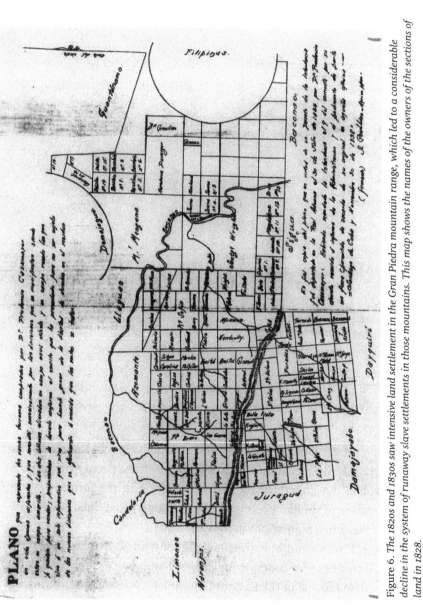

Figure 6. The 1820s and 1830s saw intensive land settlement in the Gran Piedra mountain range, which led to a considerable decline in the system of runaway slave settlements in those mountains. This map shows the names of the owners of the sections of land in 1828.

and there were vast expanses of natural pasture. Most of the territorial divisions and enclosures, which many of the documents used here referred to as plantations, were simply large areas of land with natural pasture and two or three huts in the middle.

The large mountain ranges, such as the part of the Sierra Maestra that ran from Cruz Cape to El Cobre, the famous El Frijol Mountains, and the mountains in the Mayarí and Sagua areas (these last to a lesser degree), remained practically uninhabited and unknown. In contrast, the part of the Sierra Maestra that extended from Santiago de Cuba to close to the Bay of Guantánamo (known as the Gran Piedra range)—which had been Esteban Quintero's area of operations in 1815—had a fairly large population by then, mainly on the coffee plantations. Even though some of the documents that recorded slave resistance in this area in that period may have been lost—or, at least, have not been found—it can be said that, in that decade, the runaways who lived in settlements in those mountains were not included in the large-scale attacks of 1842, 1848, and 1849, which are discussed in later chapters. Neither the diaries of operations related to those attacks nor the maps of the department contain any references to problems in that area. There are only a few, scattered reports of runaways and rebellions—nothing about runaway slave settlements.

The decline in the number of runaways living in settlements in those mountains was directly linked to the intensive process of settlement of the land that had taken place during the previous three decades. Early in 1838, a map was made of this subregion; it shows that the land had been divided up into various farms (see fig. 6)—and that runaway slaves had few possibilities of settling in the region (AHSC, GP, Planero 1, gaveta 8, plano 56).

In contrast, most of the mountain areas between Saltadero, Sagua, and Baracoa were uninhabited and unworked. Early in 1841, the governor of the Eastern Department sent the captain general a map of this subregion showing the area that was lawfully inhabited and the areas that runaway slaves had occupied (see fig. 7). The legend on that map read: "The extension or boundary of the Baracoa Jurisdiction is widest on the north-south axis, as shown on the back of the map. The cultivated part averages a little over five miles long, and the only ones going through the territory

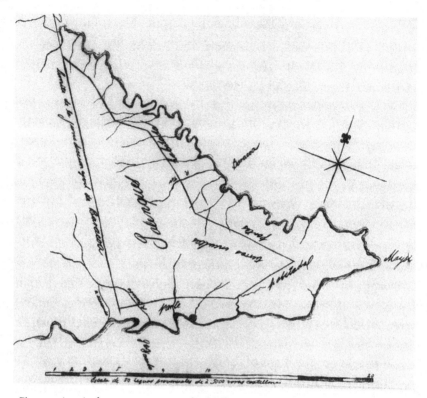

Figure 7. *Area in the easternmost part of Cuba that contained runaway slave settlements. The governor of Santiago de Cuba sent this map to the captain general along with the 1841 census of Baracoa. (ANC, GSC, leg. 3,668, no. 12,613)*

are runaway slaves, fear of whom makes it ever more necessary to prevent their use of it" (ANC, GSC, leg. 3,668, no. 12,613).

A close look at this map shows why the authorities of the department considered the El Frijol Mountains, which were bounded by the three towns just mentioned, to be occupied only by runaways living in settlements. According to a geography book that was published in 1866, many caves had been discovered in those mountains in which "a colony of runaway slaves had lived, isolated from society, for many years—up to 1842, when the colony was destroyed and the runaways captured by order of Captain-General Don Gerónimo Valdés" (Macías 1866). The information contained in this text is of historical value because it is a contemporary view of the facts, but it contains some inaccuracies.

The El Frijol Mountains, a range of low mountains separated from one another by deep clefts, were around nine miles across and sixteen miles long and lay between the Jaguaní and Toa Rivers. The mountain massif had a winding base, in which caves did not—as had been supposed—abound.[10] That supposition was due to lack of knowledge about the region in that period, for the notes and references made to it in the diaries of operations of the slavehunting militias were practically the only source of information. Those diaries recorded interesting data about the flora, fauna, place-names, population, houses, and even rainfall, but, in fact, they were read only by the local authorities and some members of the Commission of Eastern Plantation Owners and Royal Consulate.[11]

Very little was known about those mountain ranges in the first half of the nineteenth century. In their sections on geography, the 1827 and 1846 censuses recorded similar mistakes concerning that area, though they recognized that it had not been explored scientifically.

Even though it was said that the El Frijol settlement had been destroyed by the operations Gerónimo Valdés had ordered, this was not so. Rather, as has already been described, it was demolished in the second attack that was made on it. For many years afterward—even in 1848—its site was checked periodically, but there were no more reports of runaways living there again. In fact, the El Frijol settlement had ceased to exist by 1840, but several dozen other, no less important runaway slave settlements were established—and attacked—in the 1840s.

In mid-1841, the governor ordered Eduwiges Domínguez, heading a slavehunting militia of thirty men, to go into the mountains between Santa Catalina and Baracoa and make an attack. This operation was carried out in the rugged area bounded by the Toa, Barbudo, and Quiviján Rivers. According to a report that was made on the slavehunting militia's return and that was included in the governor's official correspondence, the militia attacked the San Pedro, Arroyo del Fango, El Lechero, El Barbú, La Yamagua, and Calunguita *palenques* (ANC, AP, leg. 131, no. 11). No runaways were found in any of the first five settlements, because they had fled when the members of the militia approached, but fourteen runaways were found in the last settlement. Their leader—Eusebio, a Ganga—put up resistance and was killed by a member of the slavehunting militia who was himself wounded in the struggle. The militia captured two males and a female, who turned out to be Eusebio's woman. The documents stated that Eusebio and his woman came from Holguín. In addition to the member of the militia who was wounded in the struggle, two others were injured when they fell into traps containing sharpened stakes. Eight days later, the operation was repeated in the same places, which caused some of the runaways to turn themselves in.

According to a report made by the governor, around six hundred runaway slaves had lived in those mountains before the operations were carried out in 1841. He also stated that, by June 1841, the number of runaways living in settlements had been reduced to four hundred (ANC, AP, leg. 131, no. 11). Those figures seem to have reflected the facts quite closely. When the year ended with the successful operations of Eduwiges Domínguez's slavehunting militia, a list of the number of runaway slaves in each of the territorial divisions in the department was ordered. That list gives the true number of slaves who had run away in the region—which, along with the fact that many runaway slave settlements were scattered through the various mountain ranges, provides solid proof that, in those specific conditions, there could not have been any large runaway slave settlements with more than two hundred members.

Because of the great value of that document—which lists how many slaves had run away before December 31, 1841, and were still runaways—its text is included here (see Appendix 3).[12]

To that list of 176 runaway slaves, which was based on reports from all the territorial divisions in the Eastern Department, the governor of Santiago de Cuba added 30 more runaways, who, according to his calculations, came from the western areas. In this regard, in the note he attached to the list he sent to the captain general, he stated, "There is no doubt, sir, about the exactitude of the report" (ANC, AP, leg. 131, no. 11). In the authoritative opinion of the governor of Santiago de Cuba, 206 runaway slaves were hiding out in the various eastern mountain ranges at that time. It is important to note that, according to the reports made by the local authorities, most of the runaways had fled that same year, though smaller numbers of slaves had run away three, seven, ten, and twenty years earlier.

This information shows how interested the highest-ranking authority in the department was in paying careful attention to this matter. In the same report, he compared the results of his efforts with those of earlier years. In this regard, he said that the operations that had been carried out in 1841 had reduced the number of runaways by half. It should be remembered that his figures were deliberately conservative, for he wanted to demonstrate his control of the situation, but, even so, he had little chance of falsifying the slavehunting militias' reports. Therefore, even though his figures should be accepted with some reservations, it is impossible to think that they contained any gross inaccuracies. In short, the runaways constituted only 0.21 percent of the slaves in the Eastern Department—a fact that was closely linked to the characteristics of the economy and society in that part of the island. The true importance of these historical facts lies not in the number of rebellious slaves but in the number of runaways living in settlements, and there is no reason to exaggerate this aspect of the matter.

This should be kept in mind when making evaluations because, unfortunately, in the necessary work of rescuing the slaves' traditions of struggle and publicizing important events in that struggle, the facts are sometimes twisted. An analysis that sticks to the information set forth here shows that both living in runaway slave settlements—the main form of slave resistance in the eastern region—and running away and living as vagabonds were practices adopted by small groups. However, it should be noted that there were some—few—slaves who ran away and lived in freedom for twenty years, as stated in the official sources, and many others who, as corroborated in the attacks on runaway slave settlements, preferred to die rather than be captured and taken back to the plantations.

I have insisted on the relationship between the levels and importance of slave resistance and two other factors of colonial society: the percentage that slaves constituted of the total population and their concentration in productive units, such as sugar mills, coffee plantations, and mines, where they were exploited. The 1841 report on runaway slaves in the Eastern Department (ANC, AP, leg. 131, no. 11) can be checked by comparing it with some of the data contained in the census that was taken that same year.

The list already cited (see Appendix 3) shows that, in general, the figures on runaways were small. Table 10 gives the figures for the six places that had the highest numbers of runaways. The other areas were

Table 10. Main Origins of Runaway Slaves

PLACE	NUMBER OF RUNAWAYS	PERCENTAGE OF ALL RUNAWAYS
Santiago de Cuba	32	18.08
Hongolosango	24	13.56
Bolaños	22	12.43
Moroto	9	5.08
Bayamo	8	4.52
Morón	8	4.52
Total from these places	103	58.19
Total from the entire territory	176	

Source: Based on data from list of runaways for 1841 (ANC, AP, leg. 131, no. 11).

not considered because they had figures of under eight—and were, comparatively, of little significance. Thus, it can be seen that more than 50 percent of the runaways came from just six places in the department, and it was not by chance that they had high concentrations of slaves and that their economies—except in the case of the city of Santiago de Cuba, where other factors created a different panorama (see Table 11)—were based on sugar mills and coffee plantations.

Even though, by itself, Table 11 falls short of reflecting the situation completely, it does clearly show that all the places where significant figures on runaways were reported had large slave populations. Bayamo and Holguín, where slaves constituted only about 18 percent of the total population, had forty-one and eighteen sugar mills, respectively. The greatest number of runaway slaves was reported in Santiago de Cuba, a city in which slaves constituted about 32 percent of the total population, but factors related to the characteristics of a populous port city with many businesses and a slave market were responsible for this.

The other territorial and governmental divisions, for which fewer than eight runaways were listed in the report, generally had low figures in at least two of the categories included in Table 11.

All this shows that, even though they do not have an absolute value,

Table 11. Slave Population and Production Units for Sugar and Coffee, 1841

PLACE	TOTAL POPULATION	NUMBER OF SLAVES	SLAVES AS PERCENTAGE OF TOTAL POPULATION	NUMBER OF SUGAR MILLS	NUMBER OF COFFEE PLANTATIONS
Santiago de Cuba	24,753	7,933	32.04	0	0
Hongolosongo	3,138	2,583	82.31	11	70
Bolaños	1,118	838	74.95	4	12
Holguín	23,635	4,189	17.72	18	0
Moroto	2,532	1,347	53.19	10	3
Bayamo	27,252	4,933	18.10	41	9
Morón	3,041	1,648	54.19	16	16

Source: Based on data from the 1841 census (Comisión de Estadísticas 1842).

since the relations between them are not always lineal, the three things just listed as being among the factors that caused slave resistance did promote the growth of that resistance. To illustrate the geographic origins of the runaways in 1841, I have included a drawing shows the areas from which the largest numbers of them came, with lines tracing the paths that the groups of runaways took, based on the existence of runaway slave settlements in nearby areas at the time (see fig. 8). I have also included a map that shows the geographic distribution of the units producing sugar and coffee, based on the information given on Pichardo's map ([1875] 1986). Even though there is a time difference between the two sets of information, the correspondence between the areas with the highest numbers of runaways and those with the greatest concentrations of sugar mills and coffee plantations is verified (see fig. 9).

Early in 1842, the lieutenant governor of Guantánamo held a preliminary hearing in a case against several slaves who had attacked the Las Cuevas plantation (ANC, GSC, leg. 617, no. 19,725). This strengthened the decision that had been made the preceding December that a general attack should be made in all the mountain areas in the department. This operation, which was carried out by five mixed columns of military men and civilians in the first few months of the year, was carefully recorded in

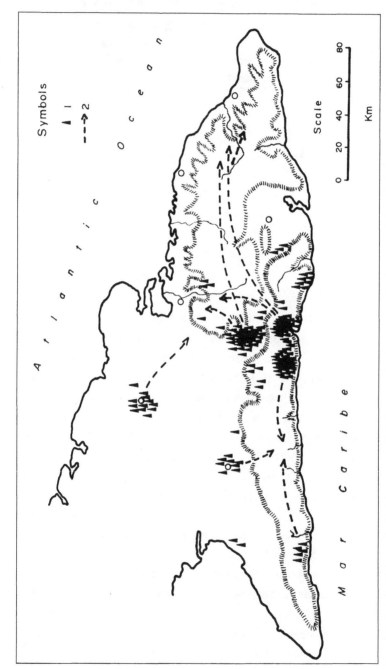

Figure 8. Origins of slaves who had run away from their masters in the eastern region in 1841 and the migratory trends toward existing runaway slave settlements, based on statements by runaways who were captured. Legend: (1) runaway slave; (2) migratory trend.

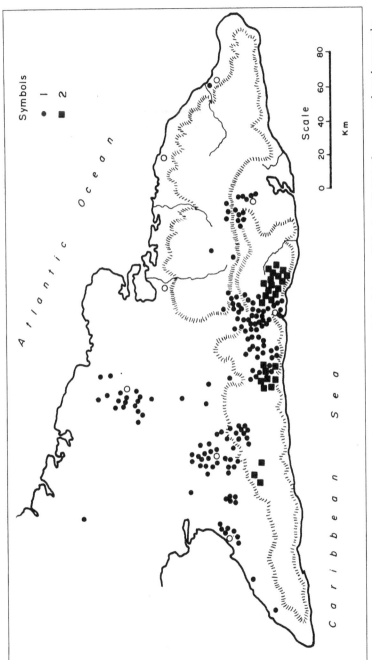

Figure 9. *Concentration of sugar mills and coffee plantations, as given on Pichardo's maps ([1875] 1986). Note the correspondence between the areas where the largest numbers of those production units are concentrated and the places from which the most slaves ran away, even though this information does not refer to the same period as that shown on the map in figure 8. Legend: (1) sugar mill; (2) coffee plantation.*

the colonial documents. The finding of the five diaries of operations has made it possible to reconstruct the facts more completely than in the cases in earlier years and to check some of the constants of the repressive system.

The five columns, each composed of military men and slavehunters, were as follows:

1. *West Column*. Headed by cavalry captain Santiago Guerra. It set out from Santiago de Cuba going westward and carried out operations in the Sierra Maestra between January 12 and March 23.

2. *Manzanillo Column*. Headed by Lieutenant Leandro Melgarez, of the Nápoles Infantry Regiment. It set out from Manzanillo on January 16 and returned on March 16. This slavehunting militia, too, operated in the Sierra Maestra.

3. *East Column*. Headed by infantry brigadier and lieutenant colonel Pedro Becerra. It set out from Santiago de Cuba going northwestward on January 10 and returned on April 4. A slavehunting militia headed by Second Lieutenant Tiburcio del Castillo, of the Nápoles Regiment, operated in conjunction with it.

4. *Baracoa Column*. Headed by Captain Esteban Menocal. It set out from Baracoa going toward the El Frijol Mountains on January 20 and returned on March 20.

5. *Micara Column*. Headed by Captain Pedro Galo. It set out from Tiguabos going toward the El Frijol Mountains on January 20 and extended its operations to Mayarí Arriba, in the Cristal mountain range, returning on March 22.

I studied the operations of these five columns by tabulating the measurable data and summed up the information (so as to avoid repetition) by consolidating the results on a map (see fig. 10).[13]

The first column, called West and headed by Santiago Guerra, which Ensign Mariano Arrieta of the King's Lancers later joined with an auxiliary troop, was assigned the mountain massif between Turquino Peak and the town of El Cobre, west of Santiago de Cuba, as its zone of operations. However, according to the diary of operations, the column concentrated its actions in the mountains between the Bayamito and Sevilla Rivers, an important point in all the operations that had been carried out against runaways living in settlements in that mountain range ever since 1747. The slavehunting militia that set out from Manzanillo, which had been assigned the westernmost part of the Sierra Maestra as its zone of operations, also concentrated its activities in this area, which corroborates that this was the part of the Sierra Maestra that was of the greatest interest to the slavehunters—a matter that was unquestionably related to the fact that it was also the area that the runaway slaves preferred. Not by happenstance, it was the highest, most rugged, roughest part of the mountain range.

According to the "Descriptive Itinerary and Diary of Operations" (ANC, GSC, leg. 41, no. 38) of this column, its members set out from Santiago de Cuba on January 12; went through Palma Soriano; crossed the Cauto River; passed Jiguaní, Bayamo, Baire, and Naranjos; and then climbed into the mountains. It is possible that they went on horseback in the first sections of their route, but, once in the mountains, they advanced on foot. They crossed the range and reached Sevilla, on the southern coast; traversed the heights near the Guamá del Sur and Bayamito Rivers; and then started back. On February 3, while moving along the right branch of the Arriba River, they recorded the presence of an old runaway slave settlement that they called Palenque Viejo de Río Grande, which had been attacked sixteen years earlier—that is, in 1826—about which no earlier references have been found. The slavehunting militia destroyed the banana plants once more, for they had grown back—because, as the document states, they had not been torn out by the roots.

On February 9, they found a temporary settlement used by runaway slaves at the headwaters of the Grande River, and, on March 3, they found the El Cedro runaway slave settlement. According to the description of this settlement contained in the diary of operations, it was in a "picturesque, leafy" valley that had a stream running through it and was surrounded by hills. There, they counted forty-seven plots planted to sugarcane, bananas, and other fruit, all "of an unusual size" (ANC, GSC, leg. 41, no. 38), but the crops had already been destroyed and all the banana plants cut down, which showed that it had been attacked not long before.[14]

From the El Cedro runaway slave settlement, the slavehunting militia set off north along the Guamá River and, after going a little more than

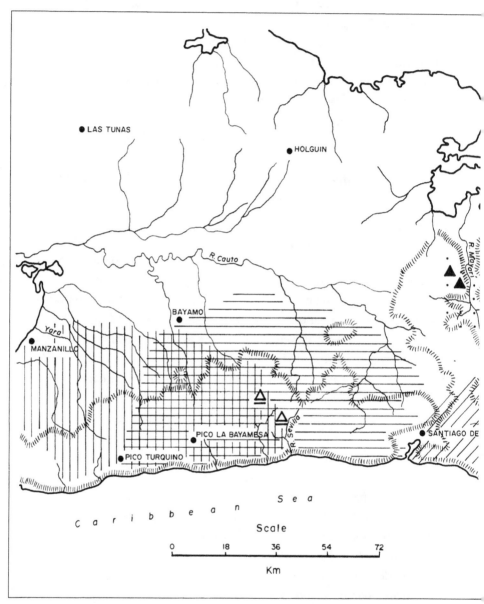

Figure 10. *Zones of operations of the five mixed columns that participated in combined operations in the subregions where runaway slave settlements were located in 1842. Several of the columns covered parts of the same routes. Legend:* (1) Manzanillo Column; (2) West Column; (3) East Column; (4) Baracoa Column; (5) Micara Column

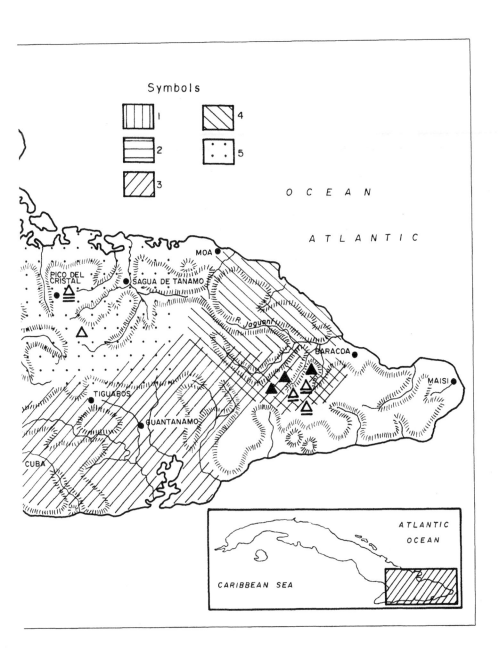

Symbols

1 2 3 4 5

OCEAN
ATLANTIC

MOA
PICO DEL CRISTAL
SAGUA DE TANAMO
R. Jaguani
BARACOA
MAISI
TIGUABOS
GUANTANAMO
CUBA

ATLANTIC
OCEAN

CARIBBEAN SEA

two and a half miles, noted that the Manzanillo Column had attacked a runaway slave settlement known as Palenque de la Cruz, which was surrounded by ditches with pointed stakes and had one hundred plots. It was at the place known as El Copal, nearly eight miles from Boca del Angel.

On March 8, on going by there, the members of the slavehunting militia ran across four runaways—two men and two women—who were armed with machetes and who, it seemed, were heading for the runaway slave settlement. On being discovered, they fled downhill. The slavehunters went after them and managed to catch up with the two women and to wound one of the men, who disappeared in the undergrowth. On narrating these events, Santiago Guerra recorded in the diary of operations the existence of a very well known (but not attacked) runaway slave settlement called El Jagüey, which, according to him, served as a refuge for many runaway slaves from Bayamo and Santiago de Cuba. He also mentioned another settlement, called Pilón. The most interesting information recorded in this diary of operations includes references to the burial practices used in the runaway slave settlements. These are the only references to this important matter that have been found in historical sources in Cuba to date: "Two slavehunters came with a message from Lieutenant Melgarez, informing me that he had not found the wax that I had told him to look for in some huts halfway between La Cruz and the Pilón runaway slave settlement. One of the slavehunters told me that he had found a fresh grave with a plate and a pipe on top of it and that it might be that of the black that the same slavehunter had wounded on the day when Lieutenant Baños caught the blacks" (ANC, GSC, leg. 41, no. 38).

This reveals a custom that was not recorded in earlier studies on *palenques* in Cuba and shows that groups of runaways living in settlements in the mountains in Cuba observed African magical-religious practices. The presence of offerings of this kind on a grave shows that it was that of a runaway slave and opens up interesting prospects for using archaeology to help in the historical reconstruction of settlements founded by such groups.

Another item that was recorded—in this case, by the slavehunting militia that had set out from Manzanillo—corroborates the use of a custom that seems to have been prevalent among the slaves in Cuba during the nineteenth century. On February 13, Leandro Melgarez, the leader of the slavehunting militia, wrote in his diary of operations that, near the head-waters of the Masío River, they had found "a place where there had been a fire, which [he] was convinced of because there was fresh ash—between six and eight days old—and, when it was examined, a paper-wrapped cigarette and the butts of some others that had been smoked were found." He continued, "The guide told me they had not belonged to blacks, be-cause they have no paper and smoke nothing but pipes—except for the criollos, who smoke cigars" (ANC, ME, no. 7,531).

The information about this habit was provided by a person of that same era and therefore is extremely reliable. In his view, pipe smoking was customary among black slaves, especially those who had been brought from Africa. This corresponded to the deeply rooted habit of smoking that many African groups had, which dated from before their introduction as slaves in the Americas. The Africans smoked pipes that they made of wood, clay, and gourds.

Pichardo (1976, 117) corroborates this fact by defining the term *ca-chimba* as the "name that is generally given to an ordinary pipe for smok-ing that is used by blacks from the countryside." In addition to showing how useful the slavehunters' diaries of operations are as historical sources of information about slavery in general and runaway slave settlements in particular, these elements demonstrate the important role that archaeol-ogy and comparative ethnography can play in the historical reconstruc-tion of this kind of settlement.

The final result of the West Column's operations was the capture of eleven runaway slaves. The list of the captured runaways is of particular interest because it helps to establish one of the constants of the runaway slave settlements in the eastern region: contrary to what some people have said and to what some researchers suppose, the runaways living in settlements in the eastern region had not come from the central or west-ern parts of the island (see Appendix 4).

Seven of the runaways who were captured in the operations headed by Santiago Guerra had run away from properties in Santiago de Cuba; two came from Bayamo; and, it seems, two did not say where they had come from. Because they were close by, the heights of the Sierra Maestra of-fered asylum to slaves who ran away from Manzanillo, Bayamo, El Cobre, and Santiago de Cuba. This large mountain range had smaller elevations along its base that were very close to those towns, and runaways used them for climbing quickly to the main range. To seek refuge in the mountain ranges to the north, runaways from those towns had to cross the Cauto River basin and expanses of relatively flat land, which exposed them to danger. Even so, some slaves from Santiago de Cuba preferred to run those risks, for the documents contain some examples of this.

Except for the two unidentified cases, all the runaways who were captured in this operation came from the eastern region. It should be recalled that all the runaways living in the El Portillo settlement who had been captured nearly a century earlier came from Bayamo, and the list that the governor of Santiago de Cuba sent to the captain general in 1842 stated that, although 176 slaves had run away in the Eastern Department, he knew of only around 30 who had come to the mountains from the western part of the island. Thus, all the available information disproves the view that the vast majority of the runaways living in settlements in eastern Cuba had come from the western part of the island.

The list of captured runaways also shows that most of them were from Santiago de Cuba and Bayamo—areas with large concentrations of slaves. The proportion of men to women among the captured runaways is also of interest. In this case, four of the eleven were women—a proportion very similar to that of the runaways who had been captured at El Portillo. However, this should not be taken as an indication of the proportion of men to women in the runaway slave settlements, because when the attacks were made, the women were less likely to escape—which is why the lists of captured runaways always contained the names of many women.

The other column of military men and slavehunters who engaged in operations in the Sierra Maestra was headed by Leandro Melgarez (ANC, ME, no. 7,531) and had set out from Manzanillo. The town of Manzanillo had been officially founded on June 18, 1784, on the site of an old Indian settlement on the coast of the Gulf of Guacanayabo. Its low-lying land, crossed by many rivers and by tributaries of the Cauto, were very fertile and excellent for agriculture. Bayamo lay to the northwest and the Sierra Maestra to the south. Because Manzanillo's economy was mainly based on tobacco growing, there were fewer slaves than in Bayamo and Santiago de Cuba. As has already been seen (see Table 9), the number of slaves and sugar mills had grown in this area, but the same source noted some other aspects of interest. Manzanillo had 476 tobacco plantations, and only 2 percent of its 14,904 inhabitants lived at the sugar mills, 14 percent on the tobacco plantations, 68 percent on cattle ranches and at other workplaces, and the rest in the city. This largely explains why slave resistance was less pronounced in Manzanillo than in other places (Comisión de Estadísticas 1847).

In 1842, the authorities in Santiago de Cuba decided that Manzanillo should contribute a slavehunting militia—more for tactical military reasons than to solve internal problems. The main tactical reason for creating that slavehunting militia—which went eastward into the Sierra Maestra to meet up with the column that had set out westward from Santiago de Cuba—was undoubtedly to catch the runaways between the two forces in the highest part of the Sierra Maestra.

The Manzanillo Column attacked the El Cedro runaway slave settlement and burned its crops on February 5—before the other column arrived there and described it on March 3. As is recorded in Leandro Melgarez's diary of operations, all the runaways living in that settlement scattered when the attack was made, and it was impossible to capture any of them. The members of the column then went on and attacked the Palenque de la Cruz, which was around ten and a half miles north of the El Cedro settlement, at the headwaters of the Sevilla River. The slavehunting militia found the Palenque de la Cruz on Santa Ana Hill, west of a big rock on which the runaways living in the settlement had posted lookouts, as was proved when two rustic beds were found there. Fourteen runaways were in the settlement when the slavehunters arrived. Three of them were killed, and the rest ran away.

The diary of operations states that Ramón Martínez, the head of a slavehunting militia from Baire, and twenty-nine slavehunters had attacked El Cedro in May 1841. The runaway slave settlement was northwest of the Sevilla plantation and had thirty-nine "houses," with individual plots of land, in the foothills of the mountain. Therefore, the two slavehunting militias that were engaging in operations in 1842 made it a point to go by there.

While all this was taking place in the large mountain region west of Santiago de Cuba, infantry brigadier and lieutenant colonel Pedro Becerra set out for Tiguabos (ANC, ME, no. 7,531). Even though all the columns had been told to set out on January 20, the governor had decided to send this slavehunting militia out ten days earlier, so its members could meet in "the little town of Tiguabos, in the middle of the country," and direct all the operations in the northern mountain ranges from there.[15] Within two days of setting out, the members of this column reached Tiguabos, from where they sent messages to the lieutenant governor of Baracoa, the military commander of Sagua, and the military commander of Mayarí—the three other key places in the planned operations. This column was strengthened with the incorporation of several groups from the area: Yatera Arriba contributed many slavehunters and members of the Nápoles Regiment and the detachment from Santa Catalina. The slavehunting militia from Micara, headed by Pedro Galo, had thirty soldiers and twenty slavehunters. Brigadier Pedro Becerra contributed several hunters from the Galicia Regiment and twenty slavehunters. Appendix 5 lists the forces used in those operations.

This meant that a force of 190 men—not counting the slavehunting militia from Sagua, which remained on the alert, and other small groups that joined later, during the march—was mobilized against the runaways who lived in settlements in the mountain ranges in the northern part of the region. On January 20, as had been planned, the column set out from Tiguabos. At Yaterita, Pedro Galo and fifty men split off from the main group and headed for the Mayarí Mountains. Pedro Becerra and his men slept at the Caujeri plantation, whose accommodations consisted only of two houses made of fan-palm fronds. Ten hunters from the Galicia Regiment joined them there. They then went northwest, passing the Belén plantation, the branches of the Los Negros River, the Toa River, the Tribilín Stream, the Alegría plantation, and the Toa plantation. This last, also, had nothing but two rude huts made of fan-palm fronds. The large troop did not operate as a single group but divided into small bands that combed the same area from different starting points and then joined forces again at previously agreed-on places.

The members of this slavehunting militia were supplied with large amounts of jerked beef. Their superiors had ordered them not to take along any "meat on the hoof," because if they did so, the bawling of the cattle would give the runaways warning of where the column was. Their commanders' instructions also stated that there should be no talking or smoking. One thing that was different about this column's operations was that, in their advance, the men did not do what was customary in the department and go from one of the already known runaway slave settlements to another, because, as Pedro Becerra put it, it was "impossible to go to the enemy's usual runaway slave settlements now, because they would not be found there" (ANC, ME, no. 7,531) Therefore, they proceeded to search for tracks, with the idea of following them. Such tracks—and the same source noted that the trackers would know if they were made by blacks because the blacks had no shoes—could show the presence of bands of runaways, means of communication between runaway slave settlements, and tactics the runaways might use to confuse pursuers. In this regard, the skills that the runaway slaves had developed over the course of years of continual attack should not be underestimated. One of the most ingenious defense tactics that the runaways in the eastern region used was that employed by a group of runaways in that same mountain range "who rendered their pursuers' efforts useless by simply following behind the slavehunting militia that was looking for them, maintaining a suitable distance" (ANC, RC/JF, leg. 25, no. 1,364).

The slavehunting militia's tactic of splitting into small groups when exploring the zones of operations allowed it to comb large areas of the mountain system near the Toa River, but it also implied a limitation, because most of the time they advanced along the banks of the rivers, leaving the rivers only to make brief incursions into the nearby mountains when they found tracks. In theory this may have seemed a very good thing to do, but in practice it held back the development of the operations and limited the scope of the results. For example, in order to go from the Caujeri to the Belén plantation, they had to cross the same river fourteen times, and to go from the Alegría to the Caujerí plantation, they crossed the Toa River five times and the Dos Brazos River fourteen times. Therefore, despite the great deployment of forces and the distances covered, they were able to check on only two old runaway slave settlements—the Arroyo del Fango and the El Lechero—that had been attacked in June the previous year.[16]

They found the first of these, the Arroyo del Fango, when they went up a branch of the Quiviján River. It was completely destroyed and the crops scorched. There, they found the body of one of the runaways who had lived in the settlement who, it seemed, had preferred to die rather than fall into the hands of the attackers. After leaving this settlement heading east and crossing the Quiviján River, they found a hut, which they destroyed. Then, after crossing a branch of the same river, they came across two runaways who were crossing it in the other direction but who ran away. They pursued them and shot and killed one of them; the other "disappeared in the thick underbrush" (ANC, GSC, leg. 41, no. 38).

However, as the operations advanced, more and more of the men got fevers. At one time, they had to carry five of them in hammocks, while two others were too sick to carry their own belongings. The operations ended on April 4, with total results of one hut destroyed and one runaway killed. That was a pretty poor showing for the hunters, in view of the enormous resources deployed and compared with the usual results of this kind of operation. In this effort, the method that the slavehunting militia adopted played a negative role, since, in addition to what has already been pointed out, marching along the banks of the big rivers made the troop easy to see from the high mountains and from a distance.

On the date agreed on, Captain Esteban Menocal and his men had set out from Baracoa heading for the mountains to the southwest (ANC, RC/JF, leg. 41, no. 35). They passed the place known as Palmarejo and then went on to the Sitio Viejo plantation and to the Quiviján and Barbudo Rivers. On January 27, advancing along the banks of this last river, they climbed a mountain that was very hard to get to, which was between the two rivers. It took them six hours to do this. On the top of the mountain, they found the Come Palma runaway slave settlement, which had fourteen huts and twenty-six beds.[17] The crops here included bananas, taro, and other root vegetables. Some of the plants bore recent cuts, so the attackers considered that the settlement was being used and had been abandoned when they came close.

Later, they went southeast and, two-thirds of a mile away, after having climbed three great elevations between the Barbudo and Quiviján Rivers, checked on the El Lechero runaway slave settlement, which had been discovered the year before. From there, they headed northwest and, after going around eight miles and climbing four high mountains, arrived at the Palenquito Triste settlement, through which the Bueno Stream ran. Even though the settlement had been destroyed, they managed to find some bananas and taro, which they needed. Then they went on in the same direction along the banks of the Toa River, reaching El Purial and then the Quiviján River. A little more than five miles from the banks of the Quiviján, they checked on the Arroyo del Fango settlement, which was on a very high hill and was surrounded by ditches with stakes. Two huts there had been set on fire recently. They went southeast from this last settlement and, on February 25, after covering ten and a half miles, came across the settlement called El Búfano, about which they noted only that it had been abandoned a short time before.

From there, they went on to the Núñez plantation and, about eight miles away, found a new runaway slave settlement, called Carga Pilón, on the banks of the Quiviján River. They recorded that it was on the top of Azul Peak. This settlement, which was also protected by stakes, had seven huts, and when the attackers arrived there, four runaways who were in the settlement shot at them. That was the last *palenque* that this slavehunting militia attacked that year. Later, the troop went back to the Barbudo River and, from there, headed for Baracoa. A comparison of the results obtained by this slavehunting militia with those of the others shows that this one achieved more. That this group checked on settlements that were already known leads us to think that its members were more familiar with the terrain than the men in the other slavehunting militias were.

For its part, after setting out from Tiguabos, the slavehunting militia headed by Pedro Galo (which was assigned the Mayarí area) went toward Piloto Abajo and, ten days later, discovered the Río Naranjo runaway slave settlement. Here, they found sixteen "houses" and some crops. As in all the other cases, its inhabitants had scattered when they learned the slavehunting militia was nearby. From there, the slavehunting militia went to Micara and the Frío River and, nearly sixteen miles to the south, raided the Palenque del Río Seco, which had eight huts, one of which was burned.[18] The attackers counted thirteen beds in the settlement and came to the conclusion that it had been abandoned a month before.

On February 27, they went back to the Río Naranjo settlement, which had been destroyed, and then visited the old La Zanja settlement.[19] This last had been attacked for the first time in the late 1820s and since 1828 had been used as a meeting place for the slavehunting militias that operated near Cristal Peak. From there, they went on to the Grande River; then

Table 12. Runaway Slave Settlements Attacked, 1841 and 1842

YEAR	SLAVEHUNTING MILITIA HEADED BY	RUNAWAY SLAVE SETTLEMENTS	AREA
1841	Eduviges Domínguez (from Baracoa)	San Pedro, Arroyo del Fango, El Lechero, El Barbú, La Yamagua, and Calunguita	Mountain range between the Toa, Barbudo, and Quiviján Rivers
1842	Santiago Guerra (west from Santiago de Cuba)	El Cedro, Palenque de la Cruz, and Palenque Viejo de Río Grande	Sierra Maestra between the Bayamito and Sevilla Rivers
1842	Esteban Menocal (from Baracoa)	Palenquito Triste, El Búfano, Carga Pilón, and Come Palma	Mountains between the Quiviján, Barbudo, and Toa Rivers
1842	Pedro Galo (from Micara)	Río Naranjo, Palenque del Río Seco, La Zanja, and Maluala	Mayarí Mountains

Source: Based on information from the pertinent diaries of operations.

to a branch of the Miguel River; and then—after a trek that they estimated at twenty-nine miles but that was nothing of the sort—arrived on March 17 at the site of the famous old Maluala settlement, where they found nothing of importance. This leads to the inference that this settlement, which Professor Franco (1973) was the first to describe in historical studies, had been attacked after the incidents he reported. So far, it has been impossible to determine the exact date of that attack, though it must have taken place early in the 1830s, because slavehunting militias who did not know exactly where it was were still going out to attack it in the late 1820s.

Correcting the exaggerated estimates of the distances covered by this slavehunting militia and analyzing other, collateral aspects, such as the place-names recorded in the diary of operations, leads me to conclude that the runaway slave settlement was at the headwaters of two branches of the Levisa River, south of Cristal Peak, which is in accord with the estimates of one of the slavehunting militias that attacked it in 1830.[20]

Table 12 sums up the results of the operations that were carried out in 1841 and 1842. It lists the names of the runaway slave settlements that were attacked or explored and the areas where they were located. Nearly three hundred men—military men and slavehunters—took part in the operations, in which seventeen runaway slave settlements were explored or destroyed: six in 1841 and eleven in 1842. Reference is made to two others, the El Pilón and El Jagüey settlements, but they were not found. In addition, two huts were destroyed in 1842. Eleven of these settlements had never been attacked before. According to the records, thirty-four huts, with a total of fifty-four beds, were destroyed. But, since not all the diaries of operations included figures on how many huts and beds there were, the real figures might easily have been close to fifty huts and a hundred beds.

The map on which all the operations carried out in 1842 and the locations of the *palenques* were entered (in all these cases, their locations were inferred) shows that no slavehunting militias were sent into the mountain area east of Santiago de Cuba that is known as the Gran Piedra range as part of the general plan of attacks for that year. Even though the center of the operations and of the settlements was in the highest part of the Sierra Maestra, between the Turquino and Sevilla Rivers, few new runaway slave settlements were found.

The same situation was observed in the Mayarí Mountains: few runaway slave settlements, most of them already known and attacked in previous years. Most of the settlements that had not been discovered prior to these operations were concentrated in the El Frijol Mountains. The underlying reason for this was that the virgin land in all those mountain subregions (except for the last) was being settled. Root vegetables and grain had been planted, animals were being raised, tobacco farms and coffee and cotton plantations had been established, and lumbering and many other economic activities were being carried out that promoted the settlement—albeit a slow one—of those mountain areas.

The years after the 1840s brought some changes, both in the system of *palenques* and in the repressive system. Basically, the system of runaway slave settlements reached its peak and began to decline.

4

Expansion and Decline

arlier chapters have shown the progressive increase in resistance and rebellion by the masses of slaves in eastern Cuba, as well as the continual tightening of the repressive system created to oppose them. The first important manifestations of the main means of resistance used by the slaves in the eastern region arose in the eighteenth century. The first significant events took place in the first half of that century—not the second half, as has been sometimes supposed—in correspondence with the development of the area's population and economy.

Even though, traditionally, most Cuban authors have placed the beginning of the plantation economy in the 1760s, more recent studies of the development of the Cuban economy have shown that the roots of that interesting process are to be found in the first half of the century. This development was reflected in the ever growing import of African workers, the founding of new settlements and towns, a modest increase in the number of products that could be exported and in trade, and the birth of new economic units (mainly sugar mills and tobacco plantations).

In this regard, though recognizing that the great expansion of sugar production began in 1740 and was accelerated by 1760, noted historian Moreno Fraginals pointed out that "sugar production grew throughout the 18th century" (1986b, 45). This view, which takes into consideration all the factors that had anything to do with that process, improves on the traditional approach, which placed emphasis only on the last few decades of the eighteenth century. It also provides an explanation for the great increase in slave resistance in the eastern region, whose first milestones were two events that occurred in the first half of that century: the protests and creation of a runaway slave settlement by the slaves from the El Cobre mines, starting in 1731, and the existence of the El Portillo settlement, which was attacked in the 1740s and 1750s.

Beginning in the last few years of that century, the abusive, exploiting nature of slavery was accentuated in correspondence with the burgeoning of a new economic stage, mainly defined by sugar production, that had advanced even though not enough slaves were brought in to meet the demand—a problem that was solved when all limitations on the slave trade were lifted in 1789. That stage, which Moreno Fraginals (1986b, 45) called the "sugar boom" and which lasted approximately up to the second decade of the nineteenth century, also affected the eastern region of the island, though to a lesser degree. There, along with the mines and coffee and cotton plantations, conditions were created that were so cruel that they resulted in the development of the system of slave resistance that was to prevail in the region. During that stage, slave resistance experienced a veritable explosion, extending to all the mountainous subregions in the department. The Sierra Maestra—not only in its highest part, near Turquino Peak (west of Santiago de Cuba), but also in the Gran Piedra range (east of Santiago de Cuba) and in the Mayarí, Sagua, Moa, and El Frijol Mountains, to the north—served as a refuge for the slaves who fled from the plantations.

That was the stage in which the first regulations against vagabond runaways and runaways living in settlements—reflecting the levels slave resistance had reached—were issued (1814), and it was also when the first large-scale attack was made on the El Frijol settlement and plans and projects for doing away with runaway slave settlements were drawn up.

The 1820–50 period was a stage of impetuous development of slave plantations, a period in which the possibilities of sugar production to meet the demands of the capitalist market using methods based on slavery were exhausted (Moreno Fraginals 1986c, 1:96), and the system entered into crisis. An analysis of the decline of the slave regime in Cuba and its causes would be beyond the limits of this work, in which the manifestations of that regime in the eastern region of the island were taken as a sample or model of the system. However, some brief comments are required to explain the rapid decline in the system of runaway slave settlements, especially from 1849 on, and the appreciable variations that came about in the repressive system.

The capitalist market's growing demand for sugar, coffee, and other products had had a direct influence on production—and therefore on the pressing need to increase the workforce that was required for that production. But when the import of African slaves was hindered by contradictions among the big powers and by the development of capitalism as a system, the plantation owners on the island sought solutions to meet the needs of the production process and experimented with several of them. To the demands of world capitalist development were added the factors of a class nature that the owners contributed in their search for solutions for the growing difficulties caused by the shortage of manpower, with the process of exploitation based on slave labor quickly exhausting the slaves. Many proposals were made, including the use of free and contracted workers and the intensified renting out of slaves, all of which brought out the crisis of the system.

One of the immediate consequences of the difficulties in supplementing the workforce—and of the considerable resultant rise in the price of slaves when the number of slaves who were brought in decreased—was that the slave owners showed interest in prolonging the slaves' working life and replacing losses by means of reproduction. The same thing seems to have occurred in other colonies in the Americas when sources of slaves ran dry. Concerning this, the historian A. Gebara stated that, in Brazil, "when the slave trade was abolished, the level of violence against the slaves changed appreciably. Slaves were treated better" (1986, 91). Moreno Fraginals (1986c) has studied this process in Cuba.

From then on, measures aimed at facilitating procreation—birth and the growth of slave children—were strengthened. Incentives were offered to slave women who gave birth, and the system of raising their children was consolidated and extended. Slaves were also urged to plant and sell agricultural products in their free time. The slave quarters, in which all the slaves working on a single plantation were forced to live under a prison regime, gave way to small, separate huts. And with the passing of time, even though they were not eliminated, the cruel punishments to which the slaves were subjected became less frequent and were replaced by other, more subtle methods of repression. Moreover, the possibilities of manumission increased.

All this was part of the picture of slavery in Cuba starting in the late 1840s, which was reflected in a decrease in the number of runaway slaves—and also in the number of runaway slave settlements. The Eastern Department was also influenced by other factors. They included the facts (already noted) that the plantations in the eastern region were less developed than those in the rest of the island; the crisis appeared more quickly and was more visible there; and a large part of the region's economy was still based on cattle ranches and tobacco plantations. In addition, there were high levels of racial mixing and evidence of a process of manumission for the offspring so produced.[1] A final factor was the coffee crisis—which caused coffee production on the island as a whole to decline considerably but was particularly acute in the eastern area. A large part of the slaves were linked to that kind of production unit, serious difficulties arose in the technical improvement of the production processes, the "crisis" of 1857 and the depression of 1866 made it much more difficult to obtain credit (Le Riverend 1965, 172), and most of the coffee plantation owners in the region had holdings of less than 270 hectares (Iglesias 1982, 126).

In addition to all this, many of the sugar and coffee plantations were destroyed in Cuba's 1868–78 war of liberation, which was especially violent and hard fought in the eastern areas. As a result, the decline in slavery in the eastern region was expressed very dynamically and was reflected in an appreciable decrease in slave resistance—at least in what had traditionally been its main expression.

The last large-scale attack on runaway slave settlements in the department took place in 1848. From 1849 on, the only such settlements that remained were some small ones in the El Frijol Mountains. Throughout this stage, there had been a process of land settlement, resulting in a displacement of and reduction in the areas containing runaway slave settlements—and, consequently, a decline in military operations against them.

However, prior to 1849, when this form of slave resistance began to decline, its highest levels were in the Eastern Department. It is true that fewer slaves became vagabond runaways in the easternmost part of the island than in other areas, and this had always been the case, but in those years the number of those runaways fell off markedly. Figure 11 shows the insignificant number of vagabond runaway slaves in the Eastern Department and the number of vagabond runaways sent from the depots where runaways were held outside Havana. These numbers show—though not absolutely—how many runaways there were and how many of them were captured, and they bear out one of the theses put forward in this work: that the highest figures on runaway slaves corresponded to the places where the slaves were exploited the most.

Figure 11 presents the figures on how many captured runaways were sent back to Havana between 1847 and 1854,[2] so it also shows the declining trend in the number of slaves who ran away. During that period, 927 runaway slaves were sent to the central depot of runaways in Havana from other parts of the island, but here I included only the places that sent the largest number of runaways. Cárdenas sent 375; Matanzas, 229; Sagua la Grande, 47; the Eastern Department (Baracoa, Gibara, Manzanillo, and Santiago de Cuba), 38; Cienfuegos, 33; Trinidad, 27; and Remedios, 22, for a total of 771.

It is no accident that Cárdenas and Matanzas were in first and second place. At that time, they were the areas with the largest concentrations of slaves and the highest sugar production on the island. The eastern region was responsible for only 4 percent of the runaways who were sent to the Havana depot.

White settlement seemed to have results in certain mountain areas, such as in the Gran Piedra range, where runaway slave settlements had practically disappeared. In the Sierra Maestra and Mayarí Mountains,

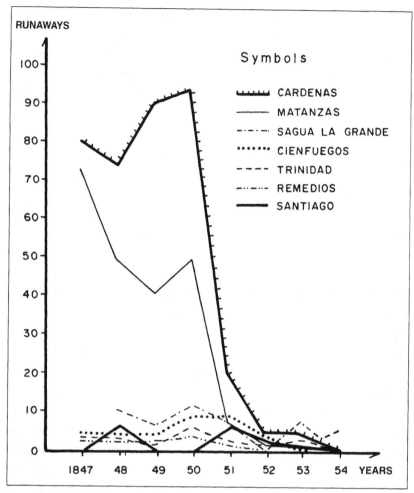

Figure 11. *Decrease in the number of vagabond runways captured outside Havana in the period 1847–1854.*

where the number of runaway slave settlements had decreased considerably, the plantation owners and eastern authorities continued to mull over the project of white settlement, and the occupation and use of that land were slow. But the El Frijol Mountains were an exception to this, which is why, on July 1, 1844, Antonio María de Escobedo, acting on behalf of the Board of White Citizens, undertook a study concerning the already old idea of having whites settle in those mountains (ANC, RC/JF, leg. 192, no. 8,559). The study noted that there were uninhabited and uncultivated areas in Manzanillo, Bahía de Nipe, Mayarí, Sagua, and (mainly) Guantánamo and Baracoa and suggested that families of white immigrants be urged to settle there. The document also acknowledged that the main difficulty, in the cases of the mountains in the Baracoa and Guantánamo areas, was the presence of runaway slave settlements and proposed that the following measures be taken:

1. slavehunters should go after the runaways living in settlements;
2. runaways who had been captured should be used for going after the runaways still living in those settlements, so as to reduce their number; and
3. the land in those places should be turned over to families of white immigrants.

In general, this proposal, which was discussed in the Royal Consulate of Havana at the end of that year, maintained the same measures and principles as the plan that Eusebio Escudero, then governor of Santiago de Cuba, had drawn up in 1816.

This new project had only one new element: the statement that the third measure could not be applied until the first two had been carried out in full. This demonstrated greater understanding of the matter and showed that the system of runaway slave settlements was complex and permanent. The project called for the destruction of the runaway slave settlements: "It will take some time to destroy them in the extensive and mountainous countryside, and very active measures by the government will be required. The runaways living in settlements defend themselves by fleeing to nearly inaccessible mountainous terrain. They are accustomed to the noxious humidity of the forests and to maintaining themselves on animals and fruits that are useless to the slavehunting militias that pursue them."

Early the next year (ANC, RC/JF, leg. 192, no. 8,559), a slave conspiracy—in which, it seemed, only a few slaves were involved—was discovered in Santiago de Cuba. Four of those implicated were executed when it was considered that their participation in the plan had been proved (Bacardí Moreau 1925, II, 368). As was nearly always the case with this kind of conspiratorial activity aimed at promoting rebellion, one member of the group gave it away, informing on the others. The four leaders were shot in the back, and the others were whipped and imprisoned.

An isolated report in January 1846 about the fate of a group of captured runaways who had lived in a settlement revealed one of the links of the repressive system. According to that source (Bacardí Moreau 1925, 11, 383), seven of the runaways who had lived in a settlement were put up for public auction. The purpose of the sale was to raise 2,077 pesos to pay the costs of maintaining them in the royal jail of Santiago de Cuba, where, it seems, they had spent some time without being claimed by their owners. The solution for the case of these seven runaways was no different from what had been done a hundred years earlier in the case of the runaways from the El Portillo settlement who were not claimed by their owners.

During 1846, incidents and reports related to runaway slave settlements in the mountains in the region continued to be significant. Official correspondence sent from Baracoa denounced the presence of a "very big" temporary settlement of runaway slaves on the heights opposite the Come Palma settlement, whose members fled when caught off guard while taking the honeycombs out of wild bees' hives (ANC, RC/JF, leg. 144, no. 7,110). This incident, though not of key importance, contains information that corroborates how the runaways living in settlements organized their economic activities and the use of temporary settlements as occasional shelter when they were engaged in such jobs as hunting, trapping, and collecting food. The fact that many runaways were taking the honeycombs out of wild bees' hives (the honey would be used as food, light, and medicine) and that they used a temporary settlement for shelter enables us to infer the link that existed between some temporary settlements and the permanent runaway slave settlements, since this was done in many other cases, as well. The same correspondence also denounced the presence of "many runaway slave settlements" in the woods in that jurisdiction. The Baracoa authorities particularly expressed concern over a runaway slave settlement that was very close to the road that was being built from Santiago de Cuba to Baracoa.

That runaway slave settlement was attacked in September of that year, as José Pérez Malo, a captain of engineers, reported later on. While near the work on the road to Baracoa, he saw signs of the settlement, so he decided to make a reconnaissance and found its exact site. After identifying it, he asked the authorities for permission to attack it.[3] On September 28, a force composed of one commanding officer, two sergeants, two corporals, and twenty men, who were joined by an equal number of volunteers working on the road project—who were surely attracted by the possibility of sacking the settlement—set out toward it. They split into four groups and headed for the Verde range. One of the groups came across the settlement, which was on a foothill of one of the rugged mountains that was a little more than two and a half miles from the end of the trail cut through the woods for the construction of the road to Baracoa.

The members of the group found nine large huts, two medium-sized ones, and a group of small huts in the runaway slave settlement and estimated that around thirty runaway slaves lived there. They found some land planted to bananas, with three hundred plants; twenty plots planted to corn, most of which was dry; and an equal amount of land planted to "second-harvest rice," but it was not ripe yet.[4] They also recorded that there were areas planted to taro of "an extraordinary abundance," some yams and sweet potatoes, peanuts, green tobacco, and some fruit. After listing what they had found, the slavehunters set fire to the huts and took the crops for the road builders (ANC, GSC, leg. 618, no. 19,763).

In the middle of 1844, the town hall of Baracoa petitioned the queen, by means of the governor and captain general of the island, to extend the 50 percent tax reduction on products exported from that port to ten years, to protect its development and promote trade. One of the arguments the Baracoa authorities used to back up their request was the presence of runaway slave settlements in their territory. As the authorities explained, two things held back Baracoa's economy: the first was the old and well-known problem of the town's lack of communication with the rest of the island other than by sea, and the second was the presence of runaway slave settlements in its mountains, which held back the settlement of new land. The queen of Spain agreed to the petition and, in a royal order dated April 26, 1847, stated, "Since the continued existence of runaway slave settlements constitutes an obstacle to the development of the territory of Baracoa, Your Excellency should endeavor to eliminate them, offering rewards to those who dedicate themselves to this service" (ANC, GSC, leg. 1,292, no. 50,369).

Unquestionably, the presence of runaway slave settlements in those mountain ranges held back the settlement of those uncultivated areas by whites, but that was not the only factor. As will be remembered, the exploitation of land in the Gran Piedra range, mainly through the creation of coffee plantations, practically wiped out the runaway slave settlements in those territories. In addition, a comparison of the geographic characteristics of those areas in which runaway slave settlements were giving ground to white settlement shows that the geographic factor had much weight in the slow advance of white settlement in the mountains. Those steep mountain ranges hindered the logical and necessary movement of people and products from the plantations that were founded there.

Last Large-Scale Attacks on the Eastern *Palenques*

Early in 1848, the Santiago de Cuba authorities decided to mount a general attack on the runaway slave settlements with operations very similar to those of 1842. Five slavehunting militias were created. Three of them were to operate in the mountain ranges to the north and the other two in the Sierra Maestra, since those were the areas that contained runaway slave settlements at the time. The slavehunting militias were as follows:

1. *Tiguabos slavehunting militia*. Headed by Lieutenant Miguel Pérez, with thirty-five slavehunters. It was to operate on the heights northwest of their starting point—that is, in the El Frijol, Jaguaní, Quiviján, and Santa Catalina areas, going as far as Mayarí.

2. *Baracoa slavehunting militia*. Headed by Segundo Suárez, with a second in command and forty slavehunters. This militia was to operate in the mountains near the Quiviján, Barbudo, Toa, and Jaguaní Rivers.

3. *Sagua slavehunting militia*. Headed by Benigno Cura, with twenty-five slavehunters. It was to extend its operations from the Mayarí Mountains to Sagua and Baracoa, especially in the El Frijol Mountains.

4. *El Cobre slavehunting militia.* Headed by Eduardo Busquet, with twenty-five slavehunters. It would head west along the coast, going as far as the spurs of Turquino Peak.

5. *Bayamo slavehunting militia.* Headed by Antonio Lora, with twenty-five slavehunters. It would set out toward the southern coast and cross the Sierra Maestra to join the El Cobre slavehunting militia and comb the mountains near the Sevilla, Guamá, and Bayamito Rivers.

The operations were carried out simultaneously throughout that extensive region, starting in late January 1848. A total of 156 men took direct part in this attack. Following routes previously agreed on, they combed their respective territories for sixty days.

Of all the slavehunting militias that operated in that period, the one headed by Lieutenant Miguel Pérez, of the Tiguabos slavehunting militia, was the most effective in terms of the slavers' interests. In a period of fifty-nine days, the men in this slavehunting militia covered more than 210 miles. They left Tiguabos on January 28, headed east and then north, and entered the mountains at what is now the Guaso Plateau. After concluding their operations in the El Frijol Mountains, between the Toa and Jaguaní Rivers, they went up the Toa toward the Santa Catalina plantation; crossed the Sagua River and then the Miguel River; and, on descending along the banks of the Cabonico River going toward the north coast, went to the El Quemado plantation. They then headed west again. They crossed the Sagua River and then retraced their steps, once again entered their favorite area, and finally set out on their return journey.

During the first stage of their return, when they were in the area between the Jaguaní and Toa Rivers, in the section known as the Mal Nombre Mountains, they found a temporary runaway slave settlement, which they razed. A little more than five miles away, they destroyed a runaway slave settlement that they did not identify, which had abundant provisions. It was at the head of the Peñas Prietas Stream, on the way to Mal Nombre. Later, they went north, toward the Jaguaní River, to inspect a runaway slave settlement called El Hato, which another slavehunting militia had attacked earlier. There, they observed that, following that earlier attack, the runaways had used the place for planting tobacco.

From there, they went to the already known and abandoned runaway slave settlement called El Justo, where they found abundant root vegetables, which they destroyed.

They then went back to the Mal Nombre River. After going by the La Yagruma runaway slave settlement, which was already known, they happened on a settlement they had never heard about. Therefore, they surrounded it, preparing to attack. They had arrived unexpectedly and caught its inhabitants off guard. Two of them put up resistance and were killed in the fray after having wounded one of the slavehunters with a pike. The others fell back.

After occupying the settlement, the slavehunters wrote in their diary of operations that there were fifty-nine "houses" and thirty-five "huts." These last were very low, rudimentary structures and were used as storehouses. The attacking party seized 200 sacks of rice and 625 pounds of jerked meat and noted that there were 7 pigpens, containing 14 pigs, and "a church with a sham altar on which there was a piece of wood with which they had tried to portray Christ, as the sign on it said" (ANC, GSC, leg. 625, no. 19,879).

In another document, which was written later on, the Santiago de Cuba authorities reported on the destruction of that important runaway slave settlement, noting that it was laid out formally, with public squares and blocks, and that every adult male inhabitant had a woman—which had inspired the inhabitants to give the settlement its name: Todos Tenemos (We All Have).

These last aspects, considered together, are very important in the analysis of the historical phenomenon of runaway slave settlements. As may be seen, the runaway slaves did not always try to re-create their African villages or hold fast to the roots of their ancient cultures, as has been generally believed, to defend themselves against the dominant culture. Some of the examples included in this work show that this phenomenon was certainly present in some runaway slave settlements, but when this occurred, it was a response imposed by the need for survival. The survival of African habits and customs in a runaway slave settlement was dependent on many factors, such as the preponderance of certain ethnic components in the group and the degree to which the dominant culture had been assimilated. There were differences among the various African groups, and some of them caused bloody conflicts in the slave quarters between men who were united by slavery under the same severe regimen of exploitation and extermination. It is very possible that such differences were not manifested in the runaway slave settlements, where all members were ruled by the same law: that of survival against an enemy that was stronger than they and that harassed them continually.

In Cuba, no single ethnic group predominated in any of the runaway slave settlements—except, perhaps, for the Palenque de los Vivís, near Sigua, which was explored in 1815. In all other cases, the range of ethnic groups seems to have been quite varied, as the lists of captured runaways show. The runaway slave settlements contained Congos, criollos, Gangás, Carabalís, Vivís, and others. The important cultural element that made it possible for them to join together was the language they had learned from their oppressors: Spanish.

In a runaway slave settlement, everything had to be subordinated to resistance if the group was to remain free. All expressions of material and spiritual culture served the vital needs of the settlement. The runaways living in the settlement used trenches containing sharpened stakes—a defense tactic used in many African villages—pikes, bows and arrows, amulets, and other magical-religious practices that were expressions of their old cultures, but they also used machetes, pistols, and blunderbusses, which had nothing to do with their African heritage. In their kitchens, they used both trivets—iron pots from England and the United States that were suspended over the flames—and ceramic pots that they had made themselves. These last did not have any African decorations and were purely utilitarian.

The runaways living in the El Frijol settlement used the body of one of their number who was killed in the first attack on that settlement, in 1815, for magical-religious practices, but the runaways living in the Todos Tenemos settlement built a village with a church in the center and, within it, an altar with a wooden figure of Jesus Christ.[5] Obviously, the habits and beliefs of most of the runaways living in the Todos Tenemos settlement had been completely transformed.

The aspects mentioned here do not complete the analysis of this complex subject. Rather, they point out the need for a scientific discussion that will gain ground as the existing unknowns are cleared up—but on the basis of solid documentation and sufficiently representative samples, not old suppositions or hypothetical studies that lack scientific backing.

Even though some other authors have mentioned the Todos Tenemos settlement, since the documents of the period contain references to it, it was never studied in depth before. It had an extension of "around sixty-seven hectares of land" that was planted to bananas, taro, sweet potatoes, yucca, yams, sugarcane, tobacco, corn, ginger, greens, and fruit trees. It also had stores of rice and smoked meat. With regard to the rice, it should be noted that the conditions of the terrain and humidity—both here and at the runaway slave settlement in the Verde range, where rice had been planted—made it possible to grow this crop and tomatoes without irrigation. The fifty-nine "houses" had auxiliary structures—low thatched-roof huts and pigpens.

All these details show the group's tendency to live in family units. In this regard, it should be noted that the slavehunters seized two small children during the attack. The presence of fruit trees contributes an important element for measuring how permanent the settlement was, both in terms of how long it had been in existence and as an expression of the confidence its inhabitants had that it would continue to exist in the future. It would hardly be likely that runaway slaves would plant trees if they did not intend to pick their fruit years later. Moreover, the planting of greens—by runaway slaves who were being hunted down—shows the cooking refinement and taste of the group that had settled there. For all these reasons, the Todos Tenemos settlement was the most developed of all such settlements studied here—even surpassing the El Frijol settlement, which has traditionally been considered the most developed one.

After the attack, the leader of the Todos Tenemos settlement, known as Bota, along with the women and children, sought refuge in another settlement that had been prepared for this purpose. For this reason, the latter was called the Guardamujeres (Protect Women) *palenque*. The slavehunters tried to attack it as part of the same operations but were unsuccessful because the settlement was completely surrounded by ditches containing sharpened stakes. Several slavehunters were injured in the attempt. Almost certainly, later operations were mounted to destroy it, but, so far, no documentary information has been found that states what finally happened to this group.

Following the attack on the Todos Tenemos settlement, Miguel Pérez left twenty men—who were joined by nine more later on—at the site and, with the remaining fifteen men, headed for the Toa River and Pulgas Stream, following the runaways' tracks. During those operations, they came across a lookout and then a temporary settlement that had just been abandoned. They then went south and found another temporary settlement—also just abandoned—that had five dwelling places in which they estimated around twenty runaway slaves lived. After this, they returned along the Toa River and went on to the Cruzadas, Alegría, and Palenque plantations and to the Sagua and Mayarí Mountains.

The authorities who planned the attack had ordered Miguel Pérez to be on a branch of the Grande River at the place at the foot of Cristal Peak that was known to be a "holy place of runaway blacks" (ANC, GSC, leg. 625, no. 19,877) on February 28, and he obeyed those instructions. Then, on March 10, nearly a month after having attacked the Todos Tenemos settlement and after their long trek to Mayarí, the members of the slavehunting militia returned to that settlement. This time, they surprised a large group of runaway slaves there. The runaways scattered when the attackers arrived, but after an intense pursuit, the slavehunters managed to capture five of them.

It may be that statements extracted from these captured runaways gave the slavehunting militia information about a new runaway slave settlement that was identified in the diary of operations as the Chinibunque settlement. They reached it after a day's travel but found that it had just been abandoned. This settlement had twelve "houses" and crops, all of which the slavehunters destroyed. Later, they attacked the Calunga runaway slave settlement, which was on a mountain at the headwaters of the Calunga Stream.[6] This settlement had twenty-six "houses" and was northwest of the Todos Tenemos settlement—a day's trek, due to the ruggedness of the terrain. From there, the members of the slavehunting militia went on to a temporary runaway slave settlement, which they considered to have been abandoned shortly before and where they found a large store of provisions.[7] Here, they counted twelve small and "big houses." For some time, they continued to pursue Bota, the leader of the runaways who had lived in the Todos Tenemos settlement. The runaways who had been captured said that he and all the women from the settlement would be in a refuge, but the slavehunters could not find it (ANC, GSC, leg. 625, no. 19,877).

In the course of its operations, this slavehunting militia destroyed four runaway slave settlements and explored three that had been discovered and attacked in the past; killed two runaways who put up resistance; captured two small children in the second attack; and destroyed 109 houses or huts, 97 of which were dwellings in permanent *palenques* and 12 in temporary settlements. The operation cost a total of 367 pesos and 30 centavos. A map (see fig. 12) shows the route taken by this slavehunting militia, the sites of the Todos Tenemos and Calunga settlements (verified by fieldwork), and the (inferred) locations of the other permanent and temporary runaway slave settlements that Miguel Pérez and his thirty-five slavehunters attacked in 1848.

Another of the five slavehunting militias that took part in the attacks made against the eastern *palenques* that year was commanded by Segundo Suárez. Its members set out from Baracoa and covered nearly as much ground as those in Miguel Pérez's militia. A comparison of the routes of these two slavehunting militias shows that the one from Baracoa operated in combination with the one that set out from Tiguabos, for the two diaries of operations make reference to the same landmarks. In line with calculations based on the information from the diary of operations of Miguel Pérez's militia, its members covered almost two hundred miles and concentrated their interest in the mountain area between the Jaguaní and Toa Rivers. The militia from Baracoa, commanded by Segundo Suárez, focused its operations a little farther to the east—in the mountains between the Barbudo and Quiviján Rivers (see fig. 13).

After leaving the town of Baracoa on January 28, the members of Segundo Suárez's militia headed west, through the area north of the Jaguaní River. Near the Naranjo Stream, they explored the Buen Consejo runaway slave settlement, which had been discovered and abandoned years earlier. Very close to it, toward the headwaters of the Jaguaní River, they found the Santa Cruz *palenque*, which had also been discovered and destroyed in past years. Then, after a long trek, they reached Cristal Peak, in the Mayarí area, and, following the orders they had been given, joined Miguel Pérez's militia on the banks of the Grande River and visited the old

La Zanja settlement. They then descended the mountains going north, toward the El Quemado plantation, near Cabonico.

Still later, they began their return journey, passing through the town of Sagua and the Casanova and Moa plantations. Going up the Moa River, they reached the headwaters of the Jaguaní River. From there, they went down its right bank to carry out the bulk of their operations in the area bounded by the Toa, Barbudo, and Quiviján Rivers. During this second stage of their trek, they attacked two abandoned temporary runaway slave settlements, one in the woods near the Barbudo River, close to where it ran into the Toa, and the other in the woods near the Jaguaní. They captured two runaways—who, even though armed with pikes and machetes, did not put up any resistance when caught off guard. One of the two came from the El Lechero settlement, which slavehunters had first attacked in 1841 and which had been destroyed. The members of the slavehunting militia also visited the old runaway slave settlement called El Hato.[8]

Even though the members of the militia from Baracoa covered great distances, their operations had far fewer results than those of the militia from Tiguabos, for they captured only two runaways who had lived in settlements; explored five old runaway slave settlements; and attacked two temporary settlements, one of which, they estimated, housed around forty runaways. This militia's operations cost a total of 608 pesos and 4 reals.

For its part, the militia of twenty-five slavehunters commanded by Benigno Cura set out from the town of Sagua on the date agreed on. Calculations show that the members of this slavehunting militia must have covered around 185 miles. When they left the town, they headed northwest, toward the place known as Casanova. Then they crossed the Moa and Arroyón Rivers; passed the headwaters of the Jaguaní River; and went west, crossing the Castro, Sagua, Miguel, and Cabonico Rivers. They skirted Cristal Peak and went down the Levisa River to the north. Then they went by Quemado; climbed the mountain range; and returned to Sagua, so ending the first stage of the expedition. During that journey, they passed the old runaway settlements of El Bobal, at the headwaters of the Jaguaní River, and El Ojucal.[9] Then, following the tracks of several

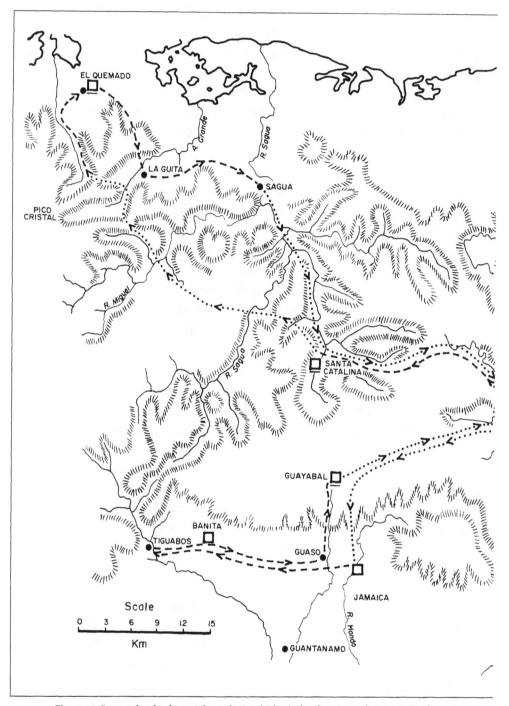

Figure 12. *Route taken by the members of Miguel Pérez's slavehunting militia in 1848. They set out from Tiguabos and, after going to the Banita, Guayabal, and Palenque plantations, checked the El Hato, El Justo, and La Yagruma runaway slave settlements. Then they discovered and attacked the Todos Tenemos* palenque, *a temporary runaway slave settlement,*

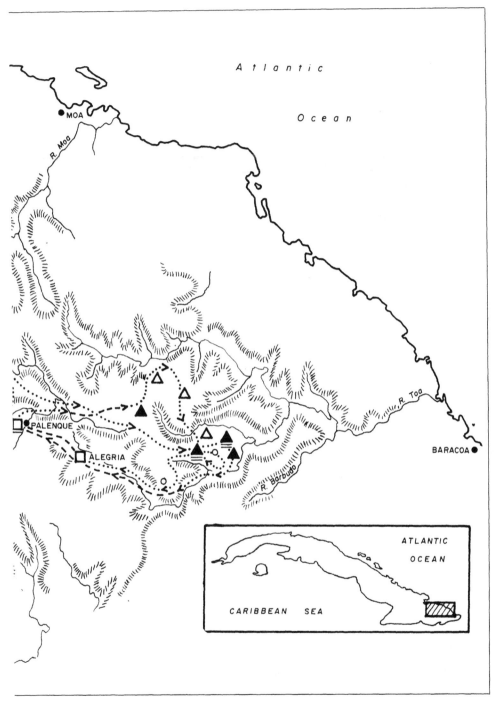

the Chinibunque and Calunga palenques, and one more temporary settlement. They then
went west, as far as the Cabonico River and the El Quemado plantation, before returning to
Sagua, the Santa Catalina plantation, the Todos Tenemos settlement, Jamaica, and Tiguabos.

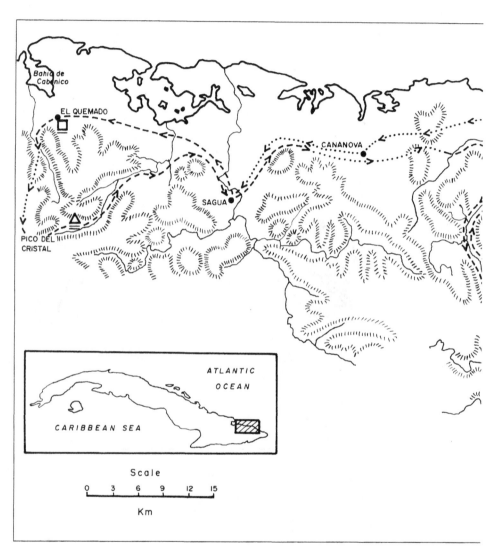

Figure 13. *Route taken by the members of Segundo Suárez's slavehunting militia in 1848. They set out from Baracoa and headed toward the El Frijol Mountains. Between the Naranjo and Jaguaní Rivers, they checked on the Buen Consejo and Santa Cruz runaway slave settlements, which had already been discovered and attacked. Then, after a long trek along the Moa River, they went to the Cananova and Sagua plantations and visited the old La Zanja palenque at the foot of Cristal Peak. Following this, they returned toward the El Frijol Mountains, where they attacked two temporary runaway slave settlements and then checked on the El Lechero palenque and another one that they mistakenly thought was the El Hato settlement.*

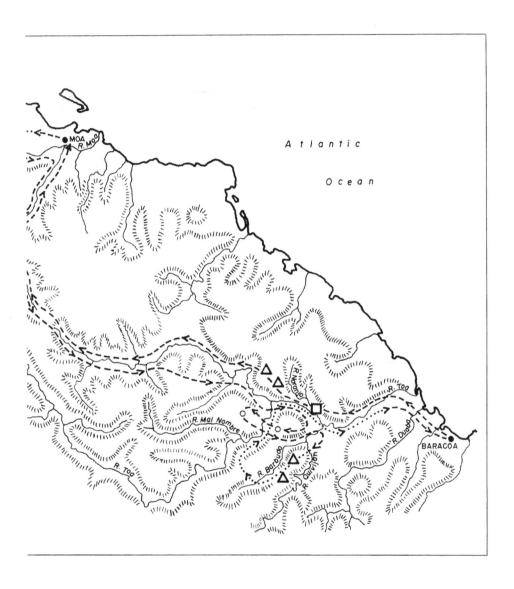

A t l a n t i c

O c e a n

MOA
R. Moa

R. Naranjo

R. Toa

R. Mal Nombre

R. Barbudo

R. Duaba

R. Quiviján

BARACOA

R. Toa

blacks, they came to a hut that they decided belonged to a band of seven vagabond runaways who had spent the night there. They continued to follow the same tracks and found the Palenque Viejo and then the Palenquito, which they attacked.

The second stage of their operations began when they left the town of Sagua heading for Casanova again. This time, however, they climbed the steep El Frijol Mountains instead of going toward Moa. Once more passing by the headwaters of the Jaguaní River, they happened upon the Sao de Veras runaway slave settlement in the Mal Nombre Range and checked on the Quemayal *palenque*, a temporary settlement, and the El Hato settlement—which was between two branches of the Jaguaní River—all of which had already been destroyed.[10] After this, they headed south to the Todos Tenemos settlement, which the members of the militia from Tiguabos had told them about not long before (see fig. 14).

In the course of their operations, the members of the militia from Sagua destroyed two temporary runaway slave settlements; checked on seven permanent settlements that had already been discovered and abandoned; and attacked a small settlement identified as Palenquito, where they captured four runaways—three men and a woman—who had lived there. Those runaways were captured after the death of the captain of the group, who, as recorded in the diary of operations, "died because of his stubborn resistance" (ANC, GSC, leg. 625, no. 19,879). As in the case of the slavehunting militia from Baracoa, these results fell short of those obtained by the militia from Tiguabos. Total cost of this militia's operations: 368 pesos.

While these three slavehunting militias were operating in the mountain ranges in the northern part of the department, the twenty-five slavehunters in the militia headed by Eduardo Busquet were carrying out operations from the town of El Cobre, west of Santiago de Cuba.

At the Sevilla plantation—at Tabacal, on the southern coast, a little less than forty miles from Santiago de Cuba—this group joined the slavehunting militia under Antonio Lora, which had set out from Bayamo.[11] Thus, even though the two militias started out from different points and separated after the operations were over, they followed the same route on the map of operations (see fig. 15).

The orders to explore the mountains between the Sevilla and Uvero

Rivers had been precise: the militias were to destroy the runaway slave settlement that had been discovered at La Plata, in the Sierra, around ten days before the large-scale attack began. The settlement had been found when a group of seventeen slavehunters, acting on the orders of the political and military governor of Bayamo, had carried out combing operations in those mountains and found a hut that they recognized as a "lookout post" for a large *palenque* in the territory of Santiago de Cuba. Because they believed that the runaways living in the settlement greatly outnumbered the men in their group, the slavehunters decided not to attack at that time, but they sent a report to the governor of Santiago de Cuba when they ended their operations on February 10.

Therefore, when a general attack was planned in the department, the slavehunting militias from Bayamo and El Cobre were ordered to join forces to destroy the runaway slave settlement at La Plata. The members of the militia from El Cobre set out along what was called the "southern road" on February 20 and reconnoitered the rugged terrain. The members of the other militia left Bayamo five days later; went through Jiguaní; entered the Sierra Maestra along the Mogote Arriba River; and headed toward the southern slope along the Sevilla River, where they joined the militia from El Cobre on February 29. From there, they headed west, toward the Bayamita plantation.[12] The members of the militia from Bayamo split up for a while and searched the banks of the Guamá and Uvero Rivers, going up to their headwaters, but without results.

The members of the various slavehunting militias joined forces again at the Bayamita plantation and then went up the Bayamita River as far as Cueva Grande, where they found a hut in which the runaways had smoked meat and dried honeycombs not long before. They followed some tracks from that hut and, always heading upriver, came across another hut that was similar to the first one. From there, they saw smoke coming from the highest hill, so they were convinced that the first two huts served as lookout posts for the runaway slave settlement that was on the highest part of the mountain—now known as Bayamesa Peak. They spent the night at the foot of that elevation and, at dawn, split into two groups to attack the settlement from two flanks. When the slavehunters drew close to the settlement, some of the runaways' dogs barked.[13] A runaway armed with a rifle came to investigate and then ran back to the settlement, from

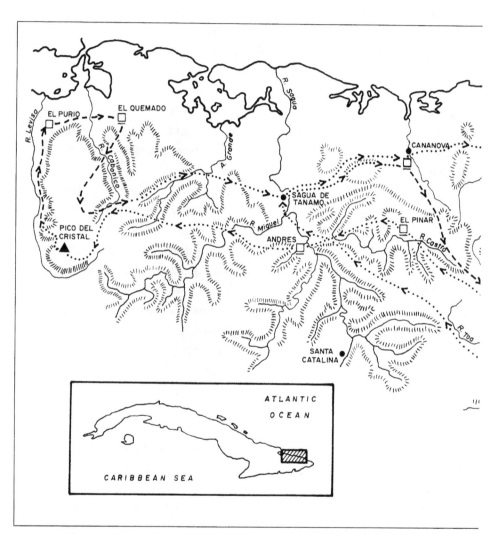

Figure 14. *Route taken by the members of Benigno Cura's slavehunting militia in 1848. They set out from Sagua de Tánamo, went to the Cananova plantation, crossed the Moa River, climbed El Arroyón, and passed the headwaters of the Jaguaní River. In that area, they checked the El Bobal, Ocujal, and Palenque Viejo runaway slave settlements, all of which had already been discovered and attacked. During their trek, which went as far as the Mayarí Mountains, they attacked the Palenquito settlement. On their way back to the El Frijol Mountains, they checked on the Sao de Veras and Quemayal palenques, a temporary runaway slave settlement (attacked), and the El Hato and Todos Tenemos settlements and then returned to Sagua de Tánamo.*

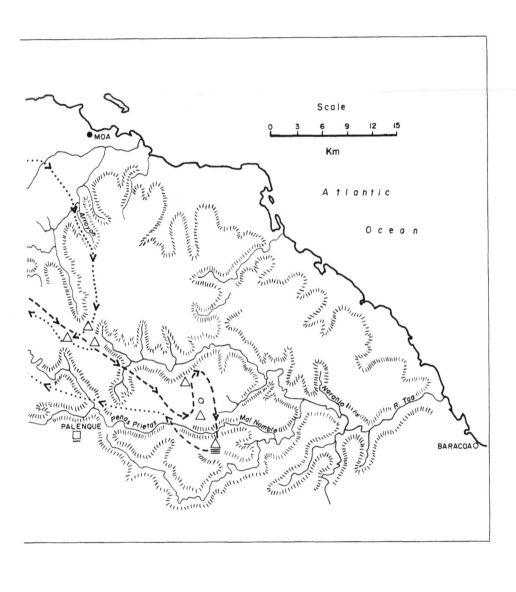

Scale

0   3   6   9   12   15

Km

MOA

Atlantic

Ocean

Arroyón

PALENQUE

Peñas Prietas

Mal Nombre

Naranjo

R. Toa

BARACOA

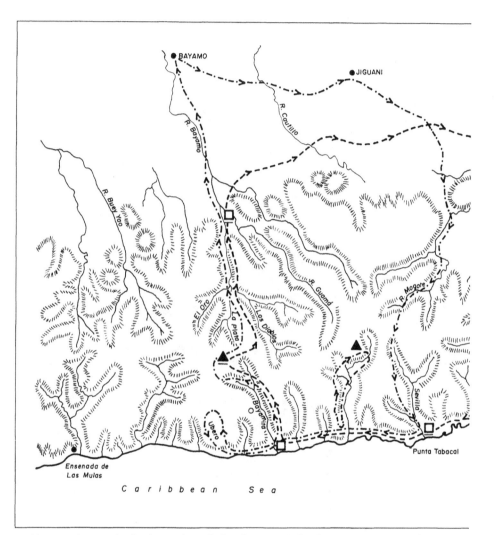

Figure 15. *Routes taken by the members of Eduardo Busquet's slavehunting militia (from El Cobre) and Antonio Lora's slavehunting militia (from Bayamo) in 1848. The two militias joined forces at the Sevilla plantation and went west along the banks of the Guamá and Bayamito Rivers. During their operations, they attacked two temporary runaway slave settlements, a permanent* palenque *on top of Bayamesa Peak, and another on a branch of the Guamá River.*

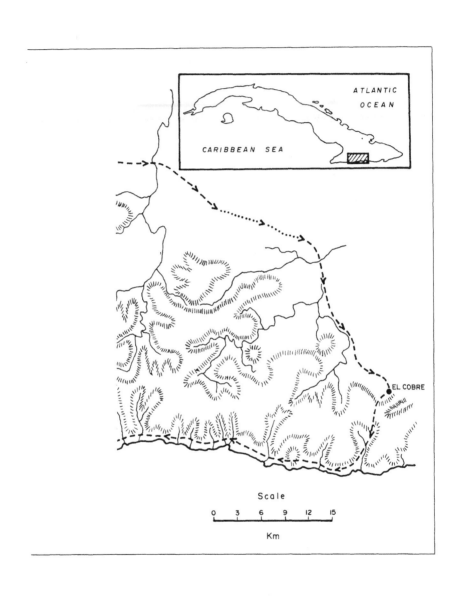

ATLANTIC
OCEAN

CARIBBEAN SEA

EL COBRE

Scale

0   3   6   9   12   15

Km

which the runaways shot and threw pikes. It seems, however, that, when the runaways in the settlement became aware of the enemy's superior numbers, they decided to scatter through the woods.

Atanasio and Jesús María, two runaways who had been living in the settlement, were killed in the first skirmish, and four others—two men and two women—were captured without being wounded. From statements extracted from the captured runaways and from their exploration of the place, the members of the slavehunting militia reported that the settlement consisted of twelve runaways, all of whom except for the leader of the settlement had been the property of José Antonio Medina, the honorary quartermaster general of the province, who lived in Santiago de Cuba.[14] After the attack, the two columns split into small bands that combed the area and discovered "eleven plots" planted to root vegetables of various kinds, but all the huts had been burned, because the head of the settlement had set fire to them before withdrawing.

This report contains several aspects that should be analyzed: the small number of inhabitants (including some women) in the *palenque* and the fact that they seem to have designed the settlement on Bayamesa Peak with very scattered housing units, since, as reported in the diary of operations, it was only after the attack—which must have been made at the highest point, which gave access to the inhabited area—that the slavehunters discovered the eleven plots, which meant that every male runaway living in the settlement had a small plot next to or near his hut, where he grew root vegetables. Of all the runaway slave settlements studied, only three—Bayamesa, El Cedro, and Palenque de la Cruz—had this form of cultivation in small plots, called *conucos* or *estancias* in the documents.

These three settlements were the only ones to have this specific kind of distribution and exploitation of the land, which supposes a difference not only in form but also in organization. In the other cases, reference was always made to large areas of cultivated land, which supposes collective work and, therefore, collective distribution. In these three, however, individual cultivation of the land—and, consequently, individual distribution—seem to have prevailed. The fact that the three examples were in the same geographic area raises some questions of interest: Was there some experience in the runaway slave settlement in the Sierra Maestra that was repeated by several groups at different times? Was that experience related to the places from which the runaways living in the settlements came? So far, no conclusive answers to these questions have been found.

By 1842, several references had already been made to the existence of runaway slave settlements in those mountains that had small plots or strips of cultivated land separated by hedges of underbrush that hid them. This may well have been in response to their defense tactics. The groups living in the Sierra Maestra became quite developed, with huts for lookouts; guard dogs; well-separated huts, which made it possible for them to burn them before withdrawing; and, always, settlements with small numbers of inhabitants. All these aspects are closely related to or integrated in defense tactics, so the plots may have been part of their system of protection. In any case, the small plots separated by hedges of underbrush were harder to find than a large cultivated area would have been.

From statements extracted from the captured runaways, the slavehunters learned that there was another runaway slave settlement between the two branches of the Guamá del Sur River. After sending the captured runaways to Santiago de Cuba, they ended their activities with an extensive combing operation in the Pulgatorio Hills, on La Plata Peak, and in the Jigüe area, where they lost the track of the runaways who had fled from the settlement they had attacked. From there, each slavehunting militia headed back to its starting point. The members of the militia from El Cobre had covered nearly 110 miles, as had the members of the militia from Bayamo, even though they had different routes in some sections. The operations of the two slavehunting militias cost 380 pesos and resulted in the destruction of one runaway slave settlement and two lookout huts, the deaths of two runaways who had lived in the settlement, and the capture of four runaways—two men and two women.

At the conclusion of the operations of the five slavehunting militias that searched the most isolated areas of the Eastern Department in 1848, the governor of Santiago de Cuba compiled a statistical summary that was sent to the captain general. This summary was used in checking some of the calculations and data taken from the diaries of operations (see Table 13).[15]

A comparison of this information shows that the least expensive and, at

Table 13. Results of Operations Carried Out by Slavehunter Militias, 1848

STARTING POINT	COMMANDER'S NAME	WAGE (IN PESOS)	NUMBER OF SLAVEHUNTERS	MILITIA'S COST (IN PESOS)	NUMBER OF RUNAWAYS CAPTURED	NUMBER OF RUNAWAYS KILLED
Tiguabos	Miguel Pérez	60	25	367.2	7	2
Baracoa	Segundo Suárez	80	40	608.4	2	0
Sagua	Benigno Cura	60	25	306	3	1
El Cobre	Eduardo Busquet	40	25	190	3	0
Bayamo	Antonio Lora		25		4	2
Total			140	1,533.6	19	5

Source: Data based on the summary report for that year (ANC, GSC, leg. 625, no. 19,877).

the same time, the most effective operation in terms of the slave owners' interests was the one carried out by the slavehunting militia that Miguel Pérez, of Tiguabos, headed. Table 13 does not include the number of runaway slave settlements that were destroyed but, along with the preceding paragraphs, reaffirms what has been presented.

Payment for captured runaways, which was a powerful incentive for the bands of slavehunters who operated in the western and central parts of the island, was not the main factor in the Eastern Department. Even supposing that all the runaways who were captured in those operations were immediately returned to their owners, the payments for them would not have covered the expenses of the operations, since the regulations in effect in the eastern part of the island stated that only eight pesos could be collected for each runaway who was returned.

The destruction of the runaway slave settlements in the eastern part of the island was not a profitable business for the authorities or for the Commission of Eastern Plantation Owners, but even so, they spared no efforts to destroy them. This was mainly a political decision, though there were underlying economic reasons, as well, because, as a form of slave resistance, those settlements were a constant incentive for slaves to run away. The example of runaway slaves had to be eradicated in order to end the threat that there would not be enough manpower left to maintain production. Additional reasons included fear of revenge and attacks, the possibility that the runaways would join forces with foreign enemies, and even personal motivations.

The documents summing up the results of the operations that were carried out that year mentioned other resources employed by the repressive system—resources that had not been recorded earlier and that were used to hunt down and destroy the runaways living in settlements. Eight observation and support bands of slavehunters were formed and stationed at places that gave access to or egress from the various regions while the operations were being carried out, to cut off possible flight or movement from one area to another by the runaways who had been living in the settlements.

Only the number of captains of these bands and the places where they were posted were recorded—neither their cost nor how many members they had was noted. Because of the little importance given them in the documents, especially regarding cost, they probably consisted of small groups of cowhands led by local authorities. Those eight observation and support bands were stationed as follows: one band at San Andrés, two at Sabanilla, four at Bolaños, and one at the Seco River (ANC, GSC, leg. 625, no. 19,879).

Another communication that the eastern authorities sent to the Development Board of Havana, dated June 2 of the same year, reported on the plan of attacks and their results. This report, checked against the data taken from the diaries of operations, makes it possible to corroborate several matters of interest. The five slavehunting militias that took part in the operations had 140 members and cost 1,533 pesos and 6 reals, which the Commission of Eastern Plantation Owners had advanced on the understanding that it would be repaid by the Royal Treasury. Among the most outstanding results evaluated in the official report, the destruction of the Todos Tenemos settlement occupied a prominent place, because many runaways had lived there.

At the time the report was written, the twenty-seven runaways who had been captured had already been turned over to their respective owners. This is very important because the information corresponded to early June, so the captured runaways had been returned to the system within two months—which proves that all of them belonged to owners in the

Eastern Department, because the procedure established by the Royal Consulate could not be applied so rapidly in the case of runaways returned to other departments. As of that date, therefore, none of the reports supported the idea that the runaways living in settlements in the mountains in the eastern part of the island had come from the west.

I have analyzed the operations that were carried out in 1848 in great detail, not only because it was possible to find all the diaries of operations or summaries of activities of the slavehunting militias but also—especially—because that year marked the high point in the development of the system of active resistance, whose main form in the eastern region of Cuba was the creation of runaway slave settlements.

At the same time, the specialized repressive system—which had been constantly honed in the course of a century of attacks on this specific form of slave protest—achieved its most polished form that year. From then on, a process of decline could be observed in both systems.

That year saw the largest number of attacks on runaway slave settlements and the most alarming incidents. During that same year, other forms of rebellion—such as uprisings and rebellions—appeared that were symptomatic of slavery's having reached a turning point. The members of the colonial government in Havana became very worried by this kind of problem, as shown by the document that the captain general issued on August 26, 1848, in which he ordered that each of the local authorities on the island make a detailed report setting forth the number and characteristics of the runaway slave settlements existing in his territory. The data in all the reports that were sent to the captain general were gathered and analyzed at the end of that year, making it possible to sum up the picture that was officially presented in each of the regions. The reports for the Eastern Department stated that there were no runaway slave settlements in the jurisdictions of Santiago de Cuba, Bayamo, Holguín, Manzanillo, Las Tunas, and Guantánamo but that there were three such settlements in Caujerí, in the Baracoa jurisdiction: Todos Tenemos (with two hundred runaways), El Hato (with sixty), and Lavapies (with ten) (ANC, RC/JF, leg. 145, no. 7,166).

Thus, those reports stated that there were only three runaway slave settlements, with 270 runaways, in the department at that time. However, this information, which was provided by the heads of the slavehunting militias, contradicts other data from different sources. For example, the diaries of operations of Eduardo Busquet and Antonio Lora, which had been written just two months earlier, stated that several groups of runaway slaves were living on Bayamesa Peak and at the headwaters of the Guamá del Sur River. Therefore, the report that was sent to the captain general should be approached cautiously—it may well be that the local or departmental authorities wanted to play down the matter to show that they had the problem under control. Moreover, the figure of two hundred runaways living in the Todos Tenemos settlement, which had already been attacked and destroyed, was also contradictory; the report on the first attack on that settlement had stated that around one hundred runaways lived there.

The figure of two hundred runaways may have referred to the estimated total of runaway slaves living in those mountains, which would include not only the ones who managed to escape from the slavehunters at the Todos Tenemos settlement but also an equal number who were in the mountains of the Mal Nombre Basin, the area where the Todos Tenemos settlement was located. It is interesting that the report listed a new runaway slave settlement—the Lavapies—which was not mentioned in any of the diaries of operations that dated from that period and corresponded to the area where it was said to be located.

In any case, the report consolidated the situation of the runaway slave settlements in the eastern part of the island in the last few months of 1848 and recorded the trend concerning the regional aspect of the matter, since the operations that were launched at the beginning of the following year were concentrated in the El Frijol Mountains. Miguel Pérez (head of the slavehunting militia from Tiguabos) and Damián Pérez were ordered to attack the runaways in those mountains. Eight support bands were formed for the rest of the territory in the department. They were stationed at Sabanilla, Corralillo, Bolaños, San Andrés, Baracoa, El Cobre, Bayamo, and the Seco River and cost the authorities nothing. This new tactic, first reported in 1849, was symptomatic of the decline that was occurring in runaway slave settlements as the main form of slave resistance in the region.

Miguel and Damián Pérez's diaries of operations on the activities they carried out from Tiguabos have yet to be discovered, but the summary

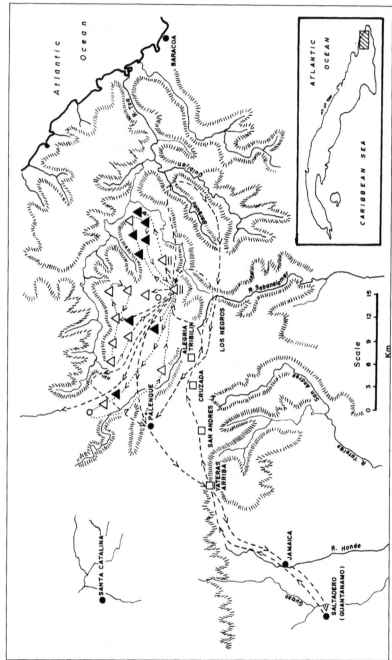

Figure 16. *Routes taken by the members of Miguel Pérez's and Damián Pérez's slavehunting militias in 1849. They used the old Todos Tenemos runaway slave settlement as a base. Note how these operations differed from earlier ones, with their routes extending out from their base camp somewhat like the spokes of a wheel, indicating intensive operations in a single area. The slavehunting militias' attacks were among the most productive for the slave owners' interests.*

that was made in Santiago de Cuba on April 28, 1849, based on those diaries of operations has been found and contains so much information that we can analyze those operations just as we did earlier ones. The map of the routes taken by those two slavehunting militias shows that they carried out an intensive raid in a single geographic area, which shows that the authorities' main fears unquestionably concerned the groups of runaways living in settlements in the El Frijol Mountains (see fig. 16).

The activities that were launched in February 1849 against the runaways living in settlements showed symptoms of the decline of the repressive system, since operations were simplified considerably. From that year on, there were no more simultaneous movements of large columns of military men and slavehunters, and after 1849, all the operations were handled by Miguel and Damián Pérez, each with a militia of twenty-five slavehunters combing the same main area.

The activities were concentrated not only from the general point of view of the region but also within the mountain range itself. The long treks that the oppressive forces had had to make in the past were eliminated, and their operations became more rapid and intensive. With these changes, the attacks achieved greater results. As was common practice and experience dictated, the two slavehunting militias set out from the town of Saltadero at the same time and headed straight for the former site of the Todos Tenemos settlement, going through Jamaica, Yatera Arriba, and the San Andrés, Cruzada, and Alegría plantations. They crossed the Tribilín Stream and, at the Toa River, split into two groups. One went up the Toa River, and the other climbed toward Galán Peak. Later, they joined forces at the site of the Todos Tenemos settlement, which they found deserted but stocked with root vegetables. At one of the settlement's northern entrances, they also found traces that runaways had been there not long before.

The slavehunters in the group that had gone up the Toa River captured a runaway who, acting on orders given by the head of the Calunga runaway slave settlement, was exploring near the Todos Tenemos settlement to see if the militias of slavehunters were nearby. After taking him prisoner, the members of that militia decided to go to the Calunga settlement. When they got there, they found it inhabited, but all the runaways—

except Gregorio Rector, the captain, who confronted the attackers with a firearm and was killed in the fighting—fell back quickly.

The Calunga *palenque* had been attacked once before, in 1848. At the time of the second attack, the slavehunters saw that, judging from the size of the plants, its inhabitants must have begun to work the land again around six months earlier. They estimated that about eighty hectares of land were under cultivation and that fifty-four "dwellings without any furniture" had been built. The absence of furniture shows that the reconstruction was very recent. The large number of dwellings—nearly double the number found at the time of the first attack—can be explained if the runaways who had lived in the Todos Tenemos settlement and escaped when it was attacked had joined the ones at the Calunga settlement.

During earlier operations, the members of this slavehunting militia had found a temporary shelter near Mal Nombre Stream where, according to the tracks they found, several runaways had spent the previous night. They came across two runaways who were armed with pikes and machetes and captured one of them alive; the other was killed in the clash. Then they went on to attack the La Yagruma settlement on February 15, capturing three runaways and a "little black woman" and killing one of the group who put up resistance. During all these operations, the members of the slavehunting militia used the former Todos Tenemos *palenque* as their camp. They also attacked the El Hato settlement, where they captured one runaway, and destroyed another new runaway slave settlement (which had two houses) and its crops.

Almost in the middle of the El Frijol Mountains, they went to the Quema Sal and Vuelta Pariente settlements, where they caught a runaway who had come from the Calunga settlement. Near the Jaguaní River, they inspected the Ochavo and San José settlements, where they captured two runaways; the others got away. They also destroyed the Ajengiblar settlement, in the Mal Nombre Basin. While pursuing a runaway who had been at the Todos Tenemos *palenque*, they discovered the Guardamujeres settlement a little more than two and a half miles to the west, but they could not attack it "because of the stakes that surrounded it."[16]

In March, they attacked the Leva Buena runaway slave settlement, whose inhabitants had just abandoned it, leaving many good clothes in two trunks. Among other things of value, the trunks contained hand-kerchiefs, lengths of muslin, and percale.

After this, they went on to the Come Berraco and Enciende Vela settlements. On March 12, they attacked the La Palma settlement, which had five "houses" and some dogs, which warned the runaways, who scattered before the slavehunting militia arrived. They also burned down the Convite settlement, which had six "houses" and was surrounded by trenches containing stakes. Its occupants had been warned by the runaways who lived in the La Palma settlement, so they managed to scatter before the attack.

Thus, the members of the slavehunting militia headed by Miguel Pérez went about the destruction of the settlements in those mountain ranges with an unprecedented intensity. In the final days of the operations, they attacked the Palenque del Saltadero del Toa, which had two "houses," and the Cupey settlement, which had seventeen; went to the El Viento settlement (but found it already destroyed); and attacked a temporary runaway slave settlement that had twenty-two beds. They planned to make another attack on the Guardamujeres settlement at the end of their operations but lost their way while heading east, wound up somewhere else, and finally gave up that attempt.

The operations ended on March 31 with the militias' return to the town of Saltadero. The summary dated April 28, 1849, reported that, in those activities, the slavehunters captured a total of nineteen runaways and killed five, and the support bands, which were posted at the points of access to and egress from the mountain ranges, captured a total of sixty-three runaways. The departmental authorities described these results as "brilliant." Total cost of the operations was 2,128 pesos. No earlier operation had been as effective.

An analysis of the summary of those diaries of operations shows that those results also included the destruction of four permanent runaway slave settlements and nine temporary ones (note the growth in the number of temporary settlements over the numbers reported in earlier operations, which reflected the increase in armed bands of runaway slaves) and the inspection of eight permanent settlements that had already been discovered.

Except for the Calunga settlement, where fifty-four new dwellings were found, the number of huts and beds in the runaway slave settlements was really very small, which indicated a basic change in those settlements. Since they were subjected to continual attack, the runaways responded by forming smaller groups, which made it easier to hide their settlements and to flee when attackers appeared. Nearly all the runaway slave settlements that were discovered from then on bore out this trend, which may have been what enabled some groups to live in isolation for many years. Many of their members joined the insurrectional troops that waged the war of national liberation that began on October 10, 1868. Moreover, their settlements were used as refuges and hospitals for those wounded in the war.

A summary made by the political and military government makes it possible to compare the final results of the operations carried out that year with those of the preceding one. Appendix 6 contains a copy of the report. As may be seen, few runaways were killed, and the numbers were nearly the same for the two years. The figure of runaways captured alive, however, rose from twenty-seven to sixty-three. The slavehunting militias headed by Miguel and Damián Pérez captured a total of thirty-three runaways, including those who were killed. The observation band from Baracoa also captured a large number (thirty-three) of runaways, mainly because of the operations that Miguel and Damián Pérez carried out in the nearby mountains, since their attacks led many runaways who had lived in settlements to move to other places, where they were caught.

It should be emphasized that the repressive system in the Eastern Department continued to operate very differently than the systems used in other regions of the island, especially with the changes that were introduced in the way runaway slaves were hunted down in the El Frijol Mountains—with the posting of small observation and support bands at various points of access to and egress from the area of operations. In 1848, bands of this kind captured eleven runaways alive and killed three who had lived in settlements and were fleeing from the mountains near the Seco River and in the Sagua, El Cobre, and Bayamo areas. In 1849, however, the small slavehunting militias posted there failed to capture any runaways who had lived in settlements, but the band from Baracoa caught a large number of them. Thus, the authorities' tactic of concentrating operations in the El Frijol Mountains was productive.

Some small groups of runaways must have continued to live in settlements in the other mountain ranges, but they were so isolated and small in number that their pitiless old enemies did not bother about them.

Last of the Runaways Living in Settlements

During the 1850s, in line with the developing crisis of slave plantations, the system of rural runaway slave settlements showed even clearer variations that reflected the decline in this form of slave resistance. Later, those settlements were modified again, in response to the war of national liberation. Moreover, the gradual triumph of capitalist relations of production contributed to the abolition of slavery.

These factors had a decisive influence on slave resistance and on the repressive system that had been created to oppose it—because the characteristics and forms of the repressive system were directly dependent on the nature and forms of the slave resistance. In Cuba, the researchers who have studied the phenomenon of runaway slave settlements—who have always done so in a very general way—have not established the necessary differences between this form of resistance and the other forms that the slaves' struggles took; nor have they provided any convincing explanations for the considerable decline that was registered in this form of resistance from the 1850s up to the disappearance of slavery per se. The methodological assumptions that underlay the treatment of the subject precluded any understanding of the changes that had occurred in the phenomenon studied and the explanation of its virtual disappearance from then on as a key problem for the colonial power structures.

In a lineal way when ending their descriptions or historical analyses of the process of slave resistance—especially the specific form of runaway slave settlements—nearly all the works that have been published in this regard have closed by repeating the conclusion that Franco (1973) reached, based on a document that Carlos Manuel de Céspedes, head of the insurrectional forces, wrote in 1868. That document, in which he declared the runaway slaves living in settlements to be free and gave them the right to join the ranks of the revolution as fighters, offers some of the last historical testimony about the existence of those small, clandestine hamlets.

This formula enabled the outstanding Cuban historian to link runaway slave settlements, the main form of slave resistance in the eastern part of the island, with the movement of national liberation, which was initiated in the same region. In its ideological bases, or principles, the revolution that was initiated on October 10, 1868, called for the abolition of slavery, so the two historical happenings were indivisibly linked. This aspect, which Franco brought out, contributed to the historical analysis of this subject and made it necessary to explore the variations that could already be seen in the system of slave resistance.

Thus, on the eve of the war of 1868, runaway slave settlements unquestionably existed—but, as proved in previous pages, this resource used by the slaves showed clear signs of decline. Few facts or reports of incidents concerning runaway slave settlements at that time have come down to us, and the few that have survived are of little importance. No attacks were made against runaway slave settlements in the Eastern Department in the final decades of slavery in Cuba. Some of those settlements still existed, but the colonial authorities and slave owners no longer considered them a serious problem. What happened then?

In mid-1850, the governor of Santiago de Cuba still complained that groups of runaways were living in settlements in the mountains between Sagua, Baracoa, and Guantánamo, the area in which the main operations had been concentrated in the late 1840s (see fig. 17).[17] In those letters, he made it clear that that was the only subregion in which the problem persisted.

That same year, Miguel Pérez, then a second lieutenant in the militia, was ordered to take thirty slavehunters from Tiguabos and comb the El Frijol Mountains along with another slavehunting militia that was to set out from Baracoa and join him in the area of operations. This was to be the last time that the old, elaborate method of using more than one slavehunting militia at the same time was employed.

Between 1747, when the first combined attack using several forces was made on the El Portillo settlement, and mid-1850, the repressive system had adapted to the characteristics and levels of slave resistance. After that, it was not considered necessary to form large slavehunting militias for carrying out simultaneous combined operations—almost certainly because the number of reports of runaway slave settlements had decreased and they no longer occupied such an important place in the concerns of the colonial government.

From then on, the ruling sectors' attention was directed to other, more pressing problems than the existence of runaway slave settlements. An analysis of the diaries that were kept on the operations Miguel Pérez carried out that year reveals the real nature and levels of the problem and the changes that had taken place in the tactics used to hunt down the runaways living in settlements. The members of the slavehunting militia headed by that well-known slavehunter set out from the town of Tiguabos, but in a different way than on previous occasions. The review of troops was held outside the town—not in it, as had been traditional. This probably was done to avoid upsetting the population; the slavehunters had been asked not to go into towns unaffected by the problem, so as not to create an unnecessary state of alarm that would be harmful to the inhabitants.

Miguel Pérez and the members of his slavehunting militia left Tiguabos on March 31 and, after the slavehunters had been reviewed outside the town, set out northwest along the Guaso trail. They went through the plantations and past the landmarks of earlier marches, heading for the old Todos Tenemos settlement, where they had camped in 1848 and 1849, after their first attack on it. This kind of operation created conditions in the area that were propitious for white families to move into some of the former runaway slave settlements, which seems to have given rise to the towns of La Zanja and La Cueva, the only two geographic points studied here that correspond to the sites of runaway slave settlements.

After following tracks that led out from the Todos Tenemos settlement for about eight miles, the members of the militia found a new runaway slave settlement and attacked it, destroying forty-two dwellings and around thirteen and a half hectares of cultivated land. The runaways living in the settlement had abandoned it as soon as they became aware of the militia's approach, and since the slavehunters had not captured anyone whom they could force to tell them the name of the settlement, they

Figure 17. *Panoramic view of the Mal Nombre range in the El Frijol Mountains: (A) top of Galán Peak, where the Vereda de San Juan runaway slave settlement was attacked in 1850; (B) area where the Guardamujeres palenque was located; (C) top of Guardamujeres Peak;*

recorded it in their diary of operations as No Se Sabe (Unknown), a name that was also used to refer to it in other reports. After this, the attackers went on to the Jaguaní River. On the way, they went to the Sotamundo runaway slave settlement, which had already been discovered, and the famous old El Frijol settlement, without finding anything of interest in the latter. Thirty-four years had passed since the first attack on that settlement, yet they still kept an eye on it!

After going back south, they went by the No Se Sabe settlement again; went on to the Galana mountain range; and, on its highest peak, discovered the Vereda de San Juan runaway slave settlement, which had only two entrances, one to the north and the other to the south. The settlement was surrounded by cliffs, which enabled the runaways living there to defend it by bombarding invaders with rocks from piles they had made earlier. This is the only one of the eastern *palenques* studied here where this defense tactic was used, though it was quite common in other

(D) Todos Tenemos Basin; (E) top of Lazos Peak; and (F) Mal Nombre Basin. Place-names preserved in the oral tradition are one of the main resources for locating the sites of the former runaway slave settlements. (Photo taken during the expedition made in 1987)

regions, such as Vuelta Abajo—its use being determined mainly by the characteristics of the terrain, for it required places with very steep slopes and an abundance of rocks on the peaks. The Vuelta Abajo ranges, which consisted of large pincushionlike hills, were ideal for employing this defense tactic. In all of the Mal Nombre mountain range, which forms part of the El Frijol Mountains, where such important runaway slave settlements as Todos Tenemos, Calunga, Guardamujeres, and Ajengiblar were located, only Galán Peak—nearly thirty-two hundred feet high, where the Vereda de San Juan settlement was located—had the conditions for this type of defense: a height surrounded by cliffs with an abundance of rocks on top.

Chronologically, the Vareda de San Juan settlement was the third runaway slave settlement whose inhabitants put up all-out resistance against attacks by slavehunters. The first was the El Frijol settlement, at the time of the first attack against it, in 1815, and the second was the Bayamito settlement, also when it was first attacked, in 1831. The main defense tactic employed against attacks on the runaway slave settlements in eastern Cuba was retreat—almost never total confrontation of the attackers, though it should be emphasized that, in many cases, the head of the runaways living in the settlement and two or three other members of the group fought off the aggressors while the others scattered (and whenever runaways were killed in the settlements, it was while doing this). The descriptions of many of the attacks recorded here bear this out.

In the case of the attack on the Vereda de San Juan settlement, when the fighting was at its height and the slavehunters managed to get through the obstacles, the runaways scattered among their dwellings, and the attackers were able to capture only one of them.

Later, the slavehunters split into two groups and checked the Calunga, El Viento, Cupey, and La Palma settlements. On April 14, they joined up with the militia from Baracoa at a small, abandoned runaway slave settlement between two branches of the Mal Nombre River. After this, they made a long trek westward, going past the Guayabal and Palenque plantations and checking on the Bobalito settlement and Palenque Viejo, which had been abandoned long before.

On April 19, while heading for the Las Yaguas River, the slavehunters came upon an armed band of ten runaway slaves and managed to capture six of them (ANC, GSC, leg. 261, no. 19,820). This incident, though accidental, reflected one of the changes that were occurring in the system of runaway slave settlements in the eastern part of the island. Armed bands of runaway slaves who kept on the move and only occasionally sought refuge in a temporary runaway slave settlement had been common in the central and western parts of Cuba, whereas conditions in the eastern part of the island had favored the development of permanent settlements. By 1850, however, because of intensive harassment by the slavehunters under Miguel Pérez, who knew the eastern mountains extremely well, the system of runaway slave settlements had been reduced to the El Frijol Mountains. This not only led the runaways living in those settlements to form smaller groups (except for those in the Calunga and No Se Sabe settlements) but also resulted in an increase in the number of armed bands of runaway slaves, since it was more difficult for slavehunters to destroy those groups.

As reported in the last diaries of operations that have been found and studied, there were many tracks of armed groups of runaway slaves, and the slavehunting militias followed them—nearly always without catching the runaways, though the tracks often led the pursuers to temporary or permanent runaway slave settlements.

In response to greater harassment by the repressive system (in the sense of their being pinpointed), the runaway slaves in the region adopted more dynamic tactics, adapting to circumstances. Therefore, references to armed bands of runaways—which had been few and far between up until then—began to appear quite frequently in documents about slave resistance. Therefore, it was not surprising that, two days after the incident already noted, Miguel Pérez's slavehunting militia came across another armed band of runaways. Caught off guard, the runaways tried to escape, but the slavehunters managed to capture two of them and killed two others.

After eight more days of operations in those hills, the members of the slavehunting militia withdrew toward the southwest, heading for the Banita plantation. Eleven of them had been wounded (ANC, GSC, leg. 625, no. 19,877). They had spent two months carrying out the operations, during which time they had checked the old Todos Tenemos, Sotamundo, El Frijol, Calunga, Cupey, El Viento, La Palma, Palenque Viejo, and Bobalito settlements and attacked two new ones: the No Se Sabe and Vereda de San Juan. The attack on this last settlement marked the turning point in the system of *palenques* in the region. Located on Galán Peak—the highest, steepest, most rugged mountain in the region, with extremely difficult conditions for raising crops and living in groups, as was confirmed by fieldwork carried out in 1987—it was one of the last great efforts by a large group of runaway slaves to survive by employing the main traditional means of resistance.

The old runaway slave settlements and the new ones that had just been attacked were quite different, as were the methods employed in attacking them. This time, the operations were directed by the experienced hunter Miguel Pérez, who was quite successful in the operations he had carried out two years before. This was very symptomatic of a process in decline.

Even though no diaries of operations for later operations have been found, many other data and cross references show that the system of repression was maintained, but at less intensity. Operations were carried out when outbreaks of resistance occurred. In this regard, the last entry in Miguel Pérez's diary of operations for 1850 is eloquent. On his return with a large group of sick and wounded men—they had fallen into trenches that contained sharpened stakes—he said that he hoped for "their recovery so they [could] go out once again to complete the job or to continue for more time if so needed" (ANC, GSC, leg. 625, no. 19,877).

Among the results of its operations, the band of slavehunters that had set out from Baracoa and joined the members of Miguel Pérez's slavehunting militia recorded checking on the Come Palma, El Lechero, and Arroyo del Fango runaway slave settlements; capturing a woman runaway; and pursuing an armed band of five runaways, whose tracks they followed for several days until they caught up with them. Only one of the runaways managed to survive the ensuing clash. One of the final comments in that diary of operations stated that the members of the slavehunting militia withdrew "without incident except for having found all of the old runaway slave settlements abandoned," persuaded that "the runaway blacks had sought refuge on the Imías and Palenque plantations, because it [was] not customary to pursue them there" (ANC, GSC, leg. 625, no. 19,877).

Those two plantations were south of the Toa River, and the runaways living in settlements had traditionally tended to seek refuge on the northern side of that river—that is, between the Toa and Jaguaní Rivers. The assumption that the head of the slavehunting militia from Baracoa made was probably mistaken, because the Imías and Palenque plantations were relatively easy to get to from Tiguabos and Saltadero, and many cowhands went there.

The visits to runaway slave settlements that had already been destroyed were made in compliance with orders from above—which, in turn, were based on experience. The diary of operations cited earlier said in this regard, "Following the practice established in this department, according to records of earlier attacks, . . . if the blacks who live in runaway slave settlements scatter, as they customarily do, and then gather again after the slavehunting militias have withdrawn, a second attack on them—because unexpected—causes greater terror" (ANC, GSC, leg. 623, no. 19,847).

This was one of the tactics that the militias of slavehunters used, and it had enabled them to catch large groups of runaways off guard in former years—as at the Todos Tenemos and Calunga settlements, where the second attacks decimated the runaways and proved very effective for their pursuers. But in the operations that were carried out in 1850, both by the slavehunting militia from Tiguabos and by the one from Baracoa, the results fell far short of those obtained in former years (see fig. 18).

In messages sent to the governor of Santiago de Cuba early in 1852, several plantation owners from Monte Líbano, Yateras, Ramón, and Las Yaguas expressed concern over the existence of runaway slave settlements in the mountains in the Guantánamo and Baracoa areas—and particularly in the El Frijol Mountains, from which some armed bands of runaways descended and "forcibly seized" peaceful slaves. The writers claimed, "They have started to form runaway slave settlements again because they have been left in peace for some years" (ANC, GSC, leg. 623, no. 19,847). Those messages, which were sent in April, and another one that was dated October 14 were considered grounds for launching a new operation against the runaways—which was carried out by two slavehunting militias from Tiguabos and Baracoa that operated in much the same way as in 1850.

According to the only information that has been found about that operation, which was carried out in late 1852, the Todos Tenemos, El Bruto, and La Yagruma runaway slave settlements were attacked.[18] Fifteen of the runaways living there were captured: four at the first settlement and eleven in the other two. Seven slavehunters were wounded on stakes. Five years after those activities against the three settlements, another combing operation was launched to find runaway slaves who had hidden in the El Frijol Mountains. That operation, too, was made in response to a denunciation—in this case, one that the lieutenant governor of Guantánamo presented to the departmental authorities on May 22, 1857, stating that a group of runaways living in a settlement had stolen food and animals from a property in the Yateras area. The document continued, "The number of runaways has grown too large because many years have passed since the runaway slave settlements in the mountains of that jurisdiction have been attacked, so it is considered advisable to make a large-scale attack on them" (ANC, RC/JF, leg. 146, no. 7,229).

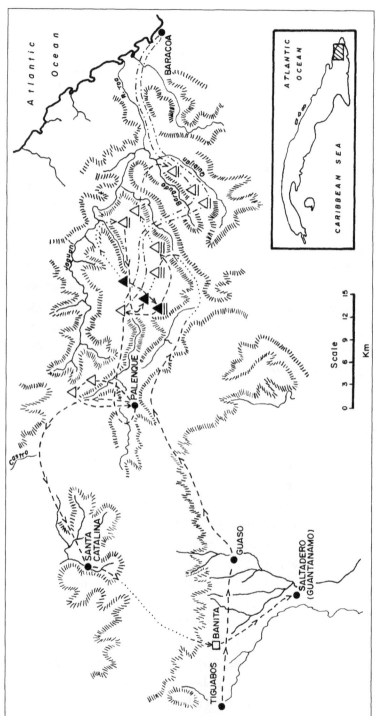

Figure 18. Routes taken by the members of Miguel Pérez's slavehunting militia and a slavehunting militia from Baracoa in 1850. It was an intensive operation, limited to the El Frijol Mountains, in which the slavehunters managed to attack only two new runaway slave settlements: the No Se Sabe and the Vereda de San Juan. The others—Todos Tenemos, Sotamundo, El Frijol, Calunga, Cupey, El Viento, La Palma, Palenque Viejo, and Bobalito—had been discovered and attacked in the past. Once more, the slavehunters used the site of the old Todos Tenemos palenque as their base camp.

Two aspects should be considered here. First, it seems that no attacks had been made since 1852, and, second, the incident that triggered the complaint by the Guantánamo official was very different from the violent attacks that had occurred in earlier decades. It is also noteworthy that the runaways' action was undertaken to obtain food—a matter usually associated with the activities of an armed band of runaways and never before with those of runaways living in settlements, who grew their own food.

Even though what had happened in Yateras was far from serious, the authorities acted quickly. Three militias of twenty slavehunters each were formed in Sagua, Baracoa, and Saltadero, and they engaged in operations for a month (Bacardí Moreau 1925, III, 364). The documents that have been found to date make no further references to this incident, so it is impossible to assess the results of the operations.

The only other report that has been found about incidents related to runaway slave settlements after 1850 concerns an attack that was made on the Bayamito runaway slave settlement—which had been discovered in 1831 near El Cobre, in the Sierra Maestra—in 1864. Six runaways who had been living at the settlement were captured.

An important political and military event occurred in 1868 that marked a turning point in the concerns and repressive activities of the ruling classes and sectors—the outbreak of Cuba's first war of national liberation, which posed much more of a threat to the colonial and slave owners' interests than did the various forms of slave resistance, including sporadic uprisings. The crisis of the slave system on the island was caused by historical, technological, political, and demographic factors.

A detailed study of the complex crisis of slavery and its abolition is beyond the scope of this book, but some of its most important aspects warrant discussion, because this crisis was the historical framework in which the runaway slave settlements in the eastern part of the island disappeared.

By the 1860s, the period in which the last references to attacks on these runaway slave settlements were made in colonial documents, slavery had already been abolished in most countries.

The abolition process was long and tortuous and filled with contradictions. For example, the Revolutionary National Convention in France had proclaimed the emancipation of all slaves in the French slaveholding possessions in the Americas in 1784, but with the overthrow of the French Revolution and the restoration of the Bourbon monarchy in 1815, slavery was revived. It was not done away with permanently until thirty-three years later, in 1848.

Great Britain declared the abolition of slavery in its colonies in 1838, and the struggles for independence in territories under the Spanish flag were indissolubly linked to the emancipation movement right from the beginning. The Central American countries (Nicaragua, Guatemala, Honduras, El Salvador, and Costa Rica) that gained their independence in 1823 outlawed slavery in 1824. The link between the declaration of independence and the abolition of slavery was a constant throughout the first half of the nineteenth century in nearly all of Spanish-speaking America.

In the latter half of the century, few countries still allowed slavery, and those few soon joined the new order. Ecuador declared the abolition of slavery in 1851; Colombia did the same in 1852; Venezuela and Peru, in 1854; the Dutch colonies and the United States, in 1863; and Puerto Rico, ten years later. Thus, in all of the Americas, only two bastions of slavery remained: Brazil and Cuba.

Attacks were made on the recalcitrant slave owners in Cuba, who clung to slavery for practical reasons linked to their economic interests—they had no desire to see their wealth threatened.[19]

Bringing slaves into Cuba became not only expensive but also very risky. Spain and Great Britain had signed a treaty on September 27, 1817, that outlawed the slave trade. It became applicable in Cuba in 1820, but this in no way meant that fewer Africans were brought into Cuba as slaves. The slave traders, plantation owners, and colonial authorities were all in cahoots and inveterately thumbed their nose at this treaty and later agreements and laws that reaffirmed that policy, such as the treaty of June 28, 1835 (even though mixed tribunals were created under it) and the Penal Law of 1845. A reduction in the number of slaves that were imported was noted in the years immediately following 1845, but this was mainly due to the slave owners' fear caused by the great slave rebellions that had swept the plantations in the Matanzas region in 1843 and 1844.

One of the most effective treaties was the one that was signed on September 29, 1866, and ratified on May 17, 1867, which imposed heavy penalties on those who violated it. As a result, starting in 1867, the decrease in the number of slaves brought into Cuba, which had begun in 1860, was accelerated.[20]

After the 1840s, the economic projections of the large slave owners in Cuba were strongly influenced by the need to replace their slaves with a free workforce. However, even though the vast majority of them considered the end of the slave trade to be necessary and trade restrictions interfered to an ever greater extent with illegal slave-trading operations, slaves continued to be brought in.

The world demand for sugar increased, however, and, improved technologies, better transportation, and a more efficient workforce were required if more sugar was to be produced. Many attempts were made to replace slave labor with free gradually, but that process was too slow for the interests at stake.[21] Therefore, slaves continued to be brought in, though in ever more adverse conditions, at ever greater cost, and not in numbers large enough to make up for the annual losses on the plantations.

The price of slaves soared. Whereas in the 1840s a healthy young male slave could be purchased for 350 pesos, the price rose to more than 1,000 pesos in the late 1850s.[22] This had direct repercussions on two important processes of a social and demographic nature. Between 1840 and 1860, the white population increased from 41 to 56 percent of the total and the free black population from 15 to 16 percent, whereas between 1841 and 1860, the slave population dropped from 43 to 28 percent of the total (Knight 1970).

Between 1861 and 1877, the slave population dropped from 27 to 14 percent of the total, while the free black population rose from 17 to 19 percent (Friedlaender 1978, 58). The drop in the percentage of slaves was the result both of natural causes and of an increase in the number of slaves who were given their freedom. According to the 1862 census, 9,462 slaves had been freed during the past four years. This was three times as many as had been freed in a similar period in earlier decades (Centro de Estadística 1862).

The import of emigrants from Spain and the Canary Islands and of indentured workers from China and Yucatán was stepped up. In the late 1850s, around 6,000 emigrants from Spain and the Canary Islands entered Cuba each year. According to demographer J. Pérez de la Riva,

Chinese laborers were hired to meet 50 percent of the need for sugar workers between 1853 and 1857. Thousands of contracts for Chinese laborers were purchased each year, with the highest figures corresponding to 1866, when 12,391 were contracted, and 1867, when the figure reached 14,263. It is estimated that 150,000 Chinese had immigrated to Cuba by 1874 (1975, 472).

The shortage of slaves also resulted in some changes in the repressive nature of their regimen of servitude. In those years, special emphasis was placed on importing slave women, to promote the birth of slaves on the plantations. The authorities offered incentives to plantation owners of more than fifty slaves who obtained the highest percentages of births and the lowest mortality rates among their slaves. Slave women who became pregnant were rewarded; those who had just given birth were freed from heavy work; and, in general, the feeding and care of slaves were improved (ANC, GSC, leg. 949, no. 33,549) because the owners needed to prolong their working lives so as to avoid the expense of replacing them.

The movement for independence was taking shape in the midst of the crisis of slavery, and public protests against colonial despotism began to be heard in the 1850s. Anticolonialist groups and movements monopolized the attention of the colonial authorities, and a royal decree dated May 28, 1852, empowered the captains general of the island to govern in besieged conditions.

When the war of independence broke out in the eastern part of the island on October 10, 1868, the plantation owners and intellectuals who headed it freed their own slaves and also considered all other slaves who joined their forces to be free. However, because they wanted the big slave owners in the western region to join in and support the anticolonial struggle, their official documents stated that they sought "the gradual abolition of slavery, with compensation for the owners" (Pichardo Viñals 1965).

On December 27, 1868, two and a half months after the outbreak of the war, the leaders of the republic in arms issued a decree about the many runaway slaves who lived in settlements in the mountains in the region. It fell short of abolishing slavery but did state, "Of course, the slaves in the runaway slave settlements who present themselves to the Cuban authorities will be declared free, with the right to live among us or to continue in the settlements in the mountains" (Pichardo Viñals 1965).

This failure to free all slaves reflected the contradictions that existed within the leadership of the insurrectional movement, and slavery was not abolished in all the occupied territories until December 25, 1870.

Meanwhile, in July 1870, the Spanish government had decreed the Law of Free Birth (Moret law), under which all children born of slave mothers on or after September 17, 1868, and all slaves over sixty years old were declared to be free. The official figures state that 50,405 newborns and around 20,000 slaves over sixty years old had been emancipated under that law by the end of 1876 (Friedlaender 1978, 525).[23]

The Ten Years' War ended with the signing of the Zanjón Pact in February 1878. Among other things, it stated that the Chinese and blacks who had been indentured workers and slaves and were in the ranks of the insurrectional forces at that time were freed, as were the slaves who had served under the Spanish flag during the war. However, slavery was not entirely abolished in Cuba until October 7, 1886.

No large-scale operations had been mounted against the runaways living in settlements in the eastern region for many years. During the war, their freedom was recognized, and this was ratified by the agreements that were signed with the Spanish Crown when the war ended. The runaway slave settlements were abandoned. None of the settlements mentioned in this monograph became towns inhabited by the freed runaways or their descendants. The runaways who had lived there did not stay in those inaccessible, isolated places. After they were freed, they could offer their services to an economy that was based on free rather than slave labor.

It should be kept in mind that, by the end of the war, the economy of the eastern region had been practically destroyed, many places were uninhabited, and there was a great exodus to other territories. Only 65 of the 238 sugar mills that had been functioning in the eastern region in 1861 were still there in 1877, and only 107 of the 426 coffee plantations that had been there in 1862 still existed in 1877 (Friedlaender 1978).

What the masses of slaves did during that period—how many of them joined the insurrectional forces, how many remained in servitude, and how many stayed in the mountains—and their later incorporation in Cuban society once slavery had been definitively abolished have yet to be studied in depth.

Cuban historian Francisco Pérez Guzmán is working on the slaves' incorporation in the independence struggle, and U.S. historian Rebecca Scott is studying the former slaves' integration in Cuban society, but all that is another story.

Runaway Slave Settlements
as a System of Resistance

This chapter is not a summary but simply touches on—or, in some cases, enlarges on—some of the topics discussed in earlier chapters. Far from closing this subject, these notes should serve as a starting point for future work. Therefore, the chapter presents some partial conclusions and suggests methodological criteria and ideas that will facilitate the work of reconstructing history and forming opinions on the basis of new information.

Two new resources contributed to the reconstruction presented in this book: fieldwork and the diaries of operations of the slavehunting militias that, for years, attacked the runaway slave settlements in the region studied. In fieldwork, both archaeological and ethnographic aspects were helpful, but in this phase of the work, obtaining on-the-spot knowledge of the geographic conditions that favored the founding of runaway slave settlements as a form of active slave resistance was most important, since, in order to understand and explain this phenomenon, it was necessary to make direct contact with the environment in which the incidents and actions took place. Doing this enabled me to assess each group's possibilities of survival, the inaccessibility of the settlements, and their communications.

In order to avoid the risk of giving either undue or insufficient importance to incidents and actions, historians must have direct contact with the topography, flora, and sources of water. Moreover, fieldwork facilitates a view of the whole and helps to determine which aspects are constants and which are specific to the social phenomenon under study. Concerning this important aspect or resource of research, Moreno Fraginals has correctly stated that "a specialist in the social sciences must have a physical relationship with the environment he studies. If he lacks this relationship or experience, he may have erudition (sometimes excellent, useful erudition), but he will never have a grasp of living anthropology, sociology, and history. The territory or environment is not just climatic or geographic data; man and society establish very specific relations with their environment. These relations give the dimension not only of the environment but also of the men who move in, transform, and control it" (1986a, 294).

Thus, this study is based not only on the slavehunters' diaries of operations and other documents from that era but also on several expeditions I made to some of the areas where events related to *palenques* took place. In accord with Moreno Fraginals, I wanted to delve more deeply into the human element that transformed and sought to control that environment and that gave rise to the hidden runaway slave settlements that were attacked so savagely.

In geography, the term "settlement" has two meanings: the process of occupation of a territory by a group of human beings and the place thus occupied (Sociedad Geográfica y Centro Científico del Extremo Oriente de la Academia de Ciencias 1984, 11). In various documents issued in this regard, the Secretariat of the World Conference on Habitat has stated that the concept is applicable to any kind of human community, no matter what its size or place, and that it includes all the material, social, organizational, spiritual, and cultural aspects that support it (Comité Cubano de Asentamientos Humanos 1977, 2). From this viewpoint, runaway slave settlements are indeed settlements, the means by which the runaways created a system of active resistance, both to the exploitation to which they had been subjected as slaves and to the attacks that were made against them as runaways living in the mountains.

The geographic conditions of the large eastern mountains and the absence of any nearby population centers favored the development of this specific form of resistance, which attained notable characteristics in the region studied. As already stated, the places in which runaway slaves chose to settle had to meet the most basic prerequisites for living under attack: *distance* (as far as possible from colonial population centers and from means of communication), *inaccessibility* (that is, they had to be in places that were difficult to reach by passersby, farmers, and cowhands and that had few probabilities of being stumbled upon), and *natural concealment* (a place whose topography and vegetation offered it protection). These three conditions, which often overlapped, corresponded to three different—though related—spatial levels.

This aspect, which can be seen at the insular level, explains why, even though there were runaway slave settlements in all parts of Cuba, they became most important in the eastern region, since it was the part of the island that offered the best conditions in terms of distance, inaccessibility, and natural concealment.

This geographic element was not independent of the other factors studied—such as the presence of large groups of slaves who were subjected to intensive exploitation. This last was really the starting point, the basis for everything that happened later on, but once that level of development had been reached, the system operated on the basis of another factor, which was the existence of areas with the characteristics just listed. In regions where the geographic conditions were not favorable to the formation and isolation of groups of runaway slaves, slave rebellion took other forms. This is why, when colonial communications and settlement penetrated the large forests, the runaway slaves living in settlements were forced to move them or to adopt more dynamic forms of resistance, such as joining armed bands of runaways.

During the years of the greatest development of slave plantations in the eastern region of the island, there were four areas or subregions in which many important *palenques* were concentrated, but those subregions did not maintain the same degree of importance all the time. The authorities paid a great deal of attention to some of them at certain moments only to ignore them at others. The reduction in the number of runaway slave settlements and their displacement to the El Frijol Mountains reflected the fact that it was the area in which the population density was lowest during the colonial period.

Among the subregions to which reference is made, that of the Sierra Maestra, in the southern part of the eastern region, was very important. Significantly, all the runaway slave settlements there were on the southern slopes, between Turquino Peak and the Sevilla River—which, not by coincidence, was the highest, most rugged, least populated area in the mountain range. Eight of the nine runaway slave settlements studied here were in that subregion.

The second major area that contained important runaway slave settlements was the Gran Piedra range, east of Santiago de Cuba. During the first decade of the nineteenth century, the runaways living in settlements and the armed bands of runaways there attacked some plantations violently on occasion; however, it was also the first subregion in which the *palenques* suffered a serious decline, starting in the second decade of that same century, when the land was settled by Franco-Haitian immigrants, who created coffee plantations. Six runaway slave settlements were located in this subregion. Another factor in the rapid decline of runaway slave settlements in this area was its propinquity to Santiago de Cuba, which made it very vulnerable to attack.

The two other subregions were in the mountain ranges in the northern part of the region. (This division in subregions is used only for the purposes of studying these phenomena; it does not correspond exactly to geographic criteria.) The first subregion in the northern section was called the Mayarí Mountains subregion. All the fifteen runaway slave settlements that were found here had similar characteristics and became famous in the 1820s and 1830s.

The second of these northern subregions was called the El Frijol Mountains subregion, because most of the runaway slave settlements in the mountain ranges near Sagua, Moa, and Baracoa were located in that area. Most of those settlements were in the El Frijol and Mal Nombre Mountains, which are between the Jaguaní and Toa Rivers before they

Table 14. Number of Runaway Slave Settlements in Each Subregion, by Period

| | 18TH CENTURY | 19TH CENTURY | | | | | |
| | 1740–1799 | 1800–1819 | 1820–1829 | 1830–1839 | 1840–1849 | IN AND AFTER 1850 | TOTAL |
SUBREGION							
1. Sierra Maestra	1	1		1	6		9
2. Gran Piedra range		6					6
3. Mayarí Mountains	1	1	5	5	3		15
4. El Frijol Mountains	1	1			45	5	52
Total	3	9	5	6	54	5	82

merge. This fourth subregion was the area in which the runaway slave settlements persisted longer than elsewhere.

The first important operations against runaways living in settlements—not only in the eastern region but in all of Cuba—were carried out in the highest part of the Sierra Maestra (the first subregion, in line with the order given here to the large settlement areas). The attacks on the El Portillo runaway slave settlement in 1747 and from 1750 through the 1760s were the first measures of this kind that the repressive system in the eastern part of the island took. However, this subregion had few runaway slave settlements in subsequent decades, and earlier, even though it had some settlements that were very important from the viewpoint of defense tactics and forms of working the land, it seems not to have had large settlements with many inhabitants. In the 1820s and 1830s, the Mayarí Mountains subregion was more important than this one.

Table 14 presents figures on the number of new runaway slave settlements discovered in each subregion by period, showing the changes that occurred in each of those areas.[1] Percentagewise, 63 percent of the runaway slave settlements were in the El Frijol Mountains subregion; the Mayarí Mountains subregion had the second largest number of settlements, with 18 percent. The Sierra Maestra subregion contained 11 percent, and the Gran Piedra range subregion 7 percent of the total.

Most of the runaway slave settlements existed in the first half of the nineteenth century, especially between 1820 and 1850. The largest-scale operations against those settlements were carried out in the 1840s, when many denunciations were made of the existence of runaway slave settlements—which were then attacked. Subregion 4, that of the El Frijol Mountains, had the most *palenques*. This continued to be true until the last expressions of this form of slave resistance disappeared.

The continual shifting of runaway slave settlements toward more isolated areas, to some extent in response to the colonization of new land, was a constant and reflected the basic principles of safety that made it possible for settlements of this kind to exist. The conditions considered valid throughout the island and on a regional basis (distance, inaccessibility, and natural concealment) were also manifested on the local scale— that is, in the case of each settlement. This is why the size of the place inhabited or occupied, the length of time the runaways stayed there, its enlargement, its repopulation after attack, the kinds of crops and size of plots planted to them, and the defense system were all determined by safety conditions.

A morphological analysis of these settlements shows a wide variety of forms and distribution of the elements composing them. All were based on the same principles of safety for the group. Forms and resources were not repeated; they were combined with the environment, and thus variety prevailed. The runaway slave settlements made the most of their environmental conditions, which included the more or less intensive attacks to which they were subjected.

Thus, temporary runaway slave settlements had from one to twenty dwellings, which were mainly used as transit quarters. Permanent runaway slave settlements had from two to sixty dwellings, which ranged from small, low ones covered with weeds to large ones with inner divisions. The rooms were anything from less than three feet long, with dirt floors, to more than twenty-six feet in length. Some dwellings had one door; others, two. The settlements were located on the peaks of mountains, surrounded by cliffs; on foothills; or in valleys. Some had large cultivated areas that were worked collectively; the crops of others were planted in streambeds or in small plots that were separated by hedges of underbrush and were worked by individuals. Some runaway slave settlements had streams running through them; others were on the banks of large rivers; and still others, in rare cases, were not close to any sources of water.

In some cases, these clandestine settlements had better dwellings and rooms than some of the towns or famous plantations of the era. For example, in 1842, the Alegría plantation, which was located at the place that still bears its name, north of the Toa River, had two primitive dwellings made of fan-palm fronds; that same year, the town of Saltadero de Santa Catalina had only fifty dwellings; the Toa plantation consisted of two dwellings made of fan-palm fronds in which a militia of slavehunters who were passing through were not able to spend the night; and the El Jobo plantation had only ten huts made of fan-palm fronds (ANC, AP, leg. 41, no. 38). In 1848, when the Calunga runaway slave settlement was attacked for the first time, it had twenty-six "houses," and the Todos Tenemos *palenque* had fifty-nine dwellings and some auxiliary buildings. Both were better than all of those colonial rural settlements, and the Calunga and Todos Tenemos settlements also had very diversified crops.

As for the tactics and means of defense employed at the runaway slave settlements, it was supposed in the past that all of them had ditches or trenches covered over with grass, with sharpened stakes point-upward embedded at the bottom, but not all *palenques* used the same means of protection. For example, the Todos Tenemos, Calunga, and Bayamesa settlements, which were among the most important ones, did not use that kind of defense. The high level of development they achieved within the system of runaway slave settlements indicates a prolonged stay at the site selected—which in turn corresponded to the selection of places that had considerable natural protection. The number of dwellings and inhabitants and the diversification of their crops showed the (always relative) stability attained in them and justified the absence or early abandonment of trenches with stakes as a means of defense.

It was also supposed that, when an enemy attacked—and the enemy was always superior in terms of arms and often in numbers, as well—the runaways living in the settlement responded with a massive defense. This belief was based on the mistaken hypothesis that the runaways living there wanted to preserve their hamlet and on an idealization of the facts. Earlier chapters showed that the runaways in only three of the runaway settlements studied here put up all-out resistance to attack. Nearly always, the runaways abandoned their settlement when enemies approached. For them, the most important thing was to get away from the attack alive so they could regroup later on, either in the same place or in another that had been selected earlier. The tactic of falling back—which the runaways living in settlements used in most cases when they were caught off guard—was often supported by two or three of them, along with the captain of the settlement, who fought against the enemy while the others scattered through the woods to avoid capture.

This very generalized defense tactic also brings out the principles and nature of this kind of settlement: the runaways living in them did not develop a sense of territorial permanence that was stronger than the need for survival. It was a setback when slavehunters discovered the settlement, destroyed their crops, and burned down their huts, but the runaways were able to recover quickly and easily. If they were captured, however, that was the end. To consider that all the runaways living in settlements were fierce warriors who would fight to the death when a settlement was attacked is a forced interpretation that does not correspond to reality. They developed means of struggle in accord with the conditions of the terrain they occupied and the material resources and possibilities they had as a social group. The most distinctive aspect of this form of slave resistance was the fact that everything was determined by the survival needs of the group of humans who were being hunted down. This united, sustained, and strengthened them.

In short, slave uprisings, which were a much higher form of struggle, occurred in Cuba at fleeting moments of very heated, violent emotions. They took place in very brief, unconnected periods of time and were put down quickly and violently. The establishment of runaway slave settlements, however, offered the rebels greater possibilities and had broader, more permanent temporal and spatial connections.

Whereas the traditional repressive bodies of the colonial government were used to put down uprisings, the authorities created special administrative apparatus and amassed specialized human and material resources for attacking and destroying the runaway slave settlements in the eastern region of the island. Unlike the norms for repressing riots and uprisings, which were established in ordinary legal decrees and codes, the norms for opposing runaway slave settlements (the regulations of 1814 and 1832) had a specific nature. The war on the eastern *palenques* in Cuba was prolonged and ongoing, and its components were polished and adapted to the changes that came about in this specific form of resistance.

Specific Characteristics of the Eastern Settlements

In line with the characteristics prevailing in each of the subregions studied, the runaway slave settlements in those subregions had some interesting specific characteristics. During the investigation—especially as the sites where the settlements had been built were located—I was able to confirm the presence of some elements that were repeated and others that were not commonly shared.

All the runaway slave settlements in the Sierra Maestra were between Turquino Peak and the Sevilla River—an area covering about a quarter of the length of that hundred-mile-long mountain range—and on the southern slopes, which were the steepest, least populated parts of that section. This occupation of the most isolated, roughest, least populated areas was repeated in all the other subregions, but it was not the only shared characteristic. three of the four subregions had a network of communications and relations that linked several permanent and temporary runaway slave settlements (see fig. 19). Several sources contained information about the communications and close links that existed among several runaway slave settlements in the same subregion. The many references made to them in the slavehunters' diaries of operations made it possible to confirm this and to show that some runaway slave settlements were dependent on others.

The form of cultivation that existed in some of the runaway slave settlements in subregion 1, the Sierra Maestra—which was described in the diaries of operations—was one of the most interesting aspects of the settlements there. According to those descriptions, some of them had small plots next to the dwellings in the settlement, which indicated that they were worked individually. This contrasted with the form of cultivation

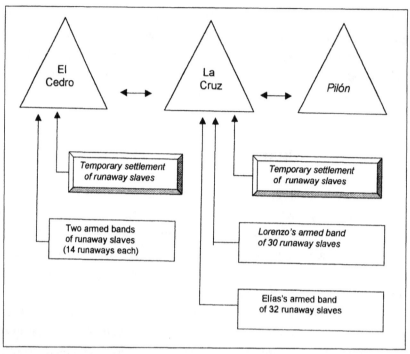

Figure 19. *Communications routes among the runaway slave settlements in the Sierra Maestra subregion.*

that prevailed in the other subregions, which had large cultivated areas that required collective work—and thus it may be inferred that distribution followed the same principle.

Some of the same characteristics noted earlier obtained in the permanent and temporary slave settlements in what was called subregion 3, the Mayarí Mountains. Thus, the settlements in that subregion were concentrated in the mountains and small mountain valleys in the highest parts of the range, close to the headwaters of the main rivers that ran through those mountains. Those settlements were at their peak in the 1820s, and they declined sharply in the following decade when trees were felled on large tracts of land and tobacco plantations were created. It has been proved that the runaway slave settlements in this subregion had communications links (see fig. 20) and some very interesting relations of dependency and that the runaways living in those settlements considered themselves to be one big "family."

Generally speaking, the runaway slave settlements in this subregion

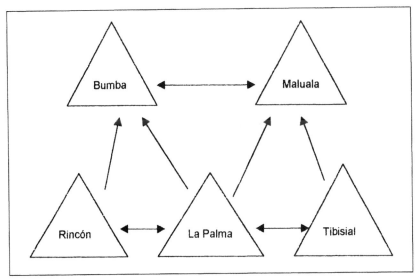

Figure 20. *Links among the runaway slave settlements in the Mayarí Mountains subregion.*

did not develop agriculture very much, and few runaways lived in each of them. This last aspect may be due to the fact that, unlike the mountains in subregions 1 and 4, this mountain range was not very difficult to climb, and more white families lived here than in the others.

Subregion 4, the El Frijol Mountains, was the most important of these subregions in terms of this form of slave resistance. When the number of runaway slave settlements declined in the other mountain ranges and subregions, it increased in this area, which became the last and strongest bulwark of this form of slave resistance. The colonial authorities had had their eye on this subregion ever since the mid-eighteenth century, and since the first few decades of the nineteenth century, it had contained important runaway slave settlements—such as the famous El Frijol settlement. In the 1840s, it became the center of the system of *palenques*, which attained levels that alarmed the authorities and caused them to concentrate their interest on those mountains.

The first diaries of operations that were analyzed described permanent and temporary runaway slave settlements on the periphery of this subregion—that is, at the headwaters of the Jaguaní and Toa Rivers, at Cuchillas de Moa, and between the Barbudo and Quiviján Rivers—but, as

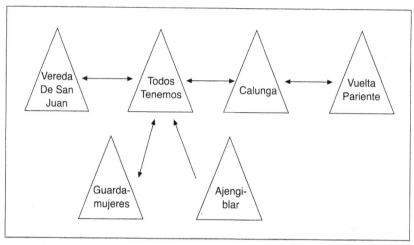

Figure 21. *Links among the runaway slave settlements in the El Frijol Mountains subregion.* Legend: *(〈=〉) reciprocal relations; (—) one-way relations; (—〉) occasional contacts in the direction indicated by the arrow.*

operations against the *palenques* that had been found there were stepped up, the settlements practically disappeared from those peaks and were concentrated in the area between the Jaguaní and Toa Rivers. The El Frijol Mountains and the Mal Nombre range are located in this wide strip of very high mountains, which contains many places that still bear the names of runaway slave settlements: Todos Tenemos Stream, Guarda-mujeres Stream, Guardamujeres Mountain, Ajengiblar Stream, Calunga Stream, and Calunga Mountain.

As for the presence of internal relations and relations of dependency among some of the runaway slave settlements in this area (see fig. 21), it was possible to confirm that there had been very strong links among the Vereda de San Juan, Todos Tenemos, and Calunga settlements and com-munication between the Todos Tenemos and Ajengiblar settlements and between the Calunga and Vuelta Pariente settlements. The Guardamu-jeres *palenque* was a backup settlement for the inhabitants of the Todos Tenemos settlement, to which they withdrew when they were attacked.

One of the main characteristics that distinguished the runaway slave settlements in this subregion was their size, for they included the largest ones, with the greatest number of inhabitants and most extensive and diversified agriculture. Figure 21 shows that the Todos Tenemos settlement (the largest of all), with fifty-nine dwellings and animal husbandry, was the center of the group. Messengers were sent out from it, and visitors from the Calunga and Ajengiblar settlements were welcomed there.

The slavehunting militia that attacked the Calunga runaway slave settlement in 1848 went straight to it from the Todos Tenemos settlement, following the tracks of runaways. There are also many references to runaways who lived in one settlement but were captured in another.

The Vereda de San Juan settlement was built on the highest point of Galán Peak, nearly 3,200 feet above sea level, a place from which all the surrounding mountains could be seen; the Todos Tenemos and Guardamujeres settlements were on foothills of the mountains on the northern bank of the Todos Tenemos Stream, which had its beginnings at the base of Galán Peak. The Calunga settlement was on a mountain 1,811 feet high near the Toa River end of the same basin.

Forms of Settlement

Survival—which was promoted by both the conditions in the place selected and the experience of the runaways who sought refuge there—was the basis on which the form and main characteristics of each runaway slave settlement were determined. Therefore, it is not only simplistic but also difficult to use a single adjective to describe the multiple forms that the runaway slave settlements took. Fieldwork made a satisfactory contribution to the reconstruction of some of the designs of this specific kind of hamlet. The authorities and slavehunters, who were more interested in destroying those settlements than in learning about them, recorded little about their forms.

In this regard, I know of only two manuscripts that specifically contained drawings of this kind of settlement. One is the sketch showing the site and location of the huts in the Maniel de Neiba runaway slave settlement, in the Bauruco Mountains in Hispaniola (now the Dominican Republic) (see fig. 22), which was drawn on November 16, 1785, and reproduced in a book by Esteban Deive (1985, 80). The other is the drawing of an unidentified runaway slave settlement (see fig. 23) that Franco found in the National Archives of Cuba (ANC, CCG, leg. 30-A, no. 60). An

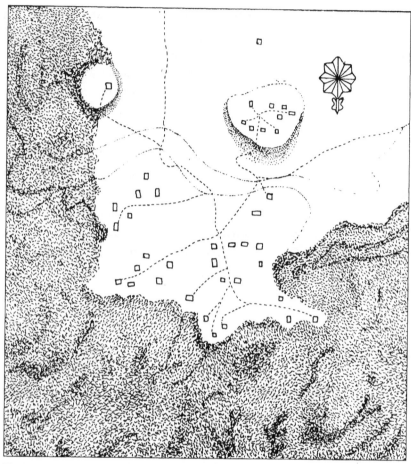

Figure 22. *Drawing made on November 16, 1785, of a runaway slave settlement in the Bauruco Mountains, Hispaniola. (Esteban Dieve 1985)*

interpretation of the plants (fig. 24) and location of the dwellings was made on this second drawing (the original manuscript) to compare all the information and show the possible presence of both common and unexpected elements.

The runaway slave settlement in the Bauruco Mountains had four nuclei or concentrations of dwellings, which were situated on the highest, most exposed parts of that mountain range. The drawing shows the paths that connected the groups of dwellings and the presence of some rooms that were somewhat apart from the main nuclei—that is, that were not completely integrated into those groups. The dwellings were grouped

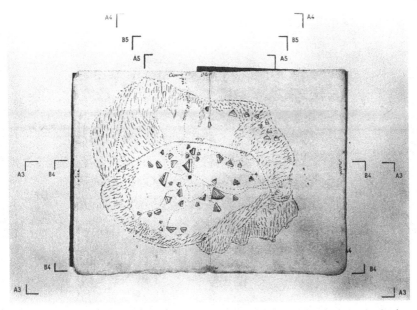

Figure 23. *Drawing of an unidentified runaway slave settlement in the eastern region of Cuba.* (*ANC, CCG, leg. 30-A, no. 60*)

around what may be considered a small square or clear space. Thus, that first drawing, which was made by those who attacked that settlement of thirty-nine dwellings, shows that the main characteristic was the concentration of all the dwellings in a relatively small area, within which some dwellings were related to others, forming small squares, though not all were built in the same way. The grouping contained some discordant elements, but they did not break the spatial framework of the settlement, except for the sentinels' huts, which were clearly differentiated on the drawing.

The second of the original drawings was interpreted and reworked on bases similar to those of the other drawing. This made it possible to add a new element to the analysis (which could not be done in the first case)— that of differentiating among the diverse sizes of the huts in a runaway slave settlement. Nearly all the documents related to that aspect attest to this diversity, and it could also be checked during fieldwork, when the sites of the Calunga and Todos Tenemos settlements were found in the Mal Nombre mountain range, in the El Frijol Mountains. This second

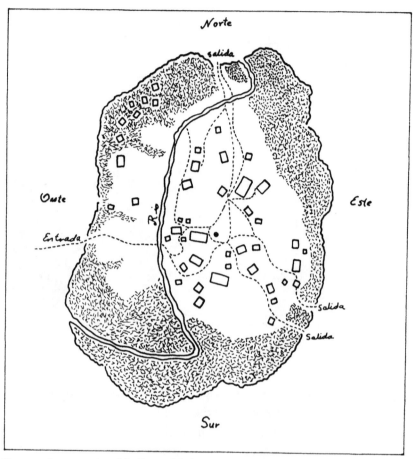

Figure 24. *Interpretation of the floors of the huts and internal communications of the runaway slave settlement depicted in figure 23, showing the grouping of the dwellings and their different sizes.*

original drawing corroborates that the concentration of houses in a small area prevailed in this kind of settlement, and another element that was present in the earlier drawing was also repeated: the existence of small internal groupings of some dwellings and the slight dispersion of some others, without breaking the framework determined by the area that served them as protection.

In this case, most of the huts were concentrated on the eastern bank of the river that ran through it. As in the other drawing, this more concentrated area was on the steeper side. It was well surrounded by underbrush and had an entrance and three exits. Even though all the dwellings were in groups, some inner dispersion can be seen. Thus, in correspondence with the two original drawings that were studied, it can be said that there was some irregularity concerning the location of some dwellings with respect to others, within the limits dictated by the need for security.

For the reconstruction of this kind of settlement, I had not only the two drawings just mentioned but also the descriptions given in some of the diaries of operations kept by slavehunters, though these descriptions were less precise than the drawings. The commander of the slavehunting militia that attacked the Palenque de la Cruz in 1841 said that it was northwest of the Sevilla plantation and consisted of thirty-nine "houses" built around a clear area. He added that there were plots of land with abundant crops behind the houses, in the foothills, which provided additional information for making more detailed observations concerning the forms of those settlements. The description of the Bumba runaway slave settlement, in the Mayarí Mountains, stated that it was built on the highest point of a mountain and consisted of seventeen huts that were widely separated from one another, since the attackers found them one after another after the attack. The Bayamesa runaway slave settlement was somewhat similar. It had only eleven huts—each one with some plots of land—scattered on the mountainside, which made it possible for the runaways living in that settlement to burn them before the slavehunters broke into the area. These are some of the variants contributed by documents dating from the era concerning the form of the runaway slave settlements.

As already stated, I also used fieldwork for reconstructing this kind of settlement and managed to find several of the areas occupied by runaway slave settlements, including the exact location of two of the settlements studied here. In 1985, I made an expedition to the Cuchillas del Toa area and, drawing on the oral tradition and using material evidence of this kind of settlement, found the place where the Calunga runaway slave settlement had been. Each of its dwellings had been built on a human-made slope, so it was possible to make a topographical drawing of the area and draw part of the settlement. In this case, the floors of fourteen of its twenty-six dwellings were located (see fig. 25). The finding of remains of rudimentary cooking stoves consisting of three stones on the lower

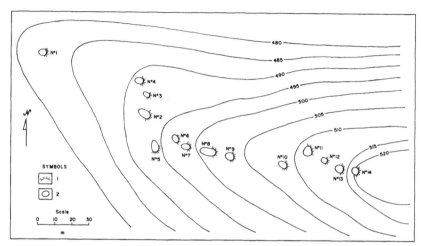

Figure 25. *Topographical drawing of part of the Calunga runaway slave settlement, showing where fourteen dwellings were located. Legend: (1) manmade slope; (2) leveled area. (Drawn by J. J. Guarch Rodríguez under the author's direction during the expedition made in 1985)*

parts of some of the slopes and the different dimensions of the slopes proved that there were rooms of different sizes and that the runaways cooked outside their dwellings, as was also done in Indian settlements and even in some African villages.

The floors of the dwellings in the Calunga settlement that were found described a path that went down from the highest part of the mountain (slightly more than 1,710 feet above sea level) to 1,575 feet above sea level, from which point the terrain drops abruptly to the Calunga Stream (see fig. 26). The floors showed lineal continuity, determined by what may be called the foundation of the elevation—that is, the least sloping area. From the highest part, where the floor of dwelling 14 was located, to the lowest, where the floor of dwelling 1 was found, everything was covered with enormous old trees that give the place wonderful protection, as it is impossible to see it from other heights, yet all the surrounding mountains can be seen from its peak.

Another of the drawings, which was made as part of this study and used the same procedures, was of the Todos Tenemos runaway slave settlement (see fig. 27). In this case, the description of the attack made by the slavehunting militia that carried out the operation in 1848 also served as a basis for fieldwork. The route the slavehunters had taken made it

Figure 26. *The Calunga Stream was named for the runaway slave settlement that was built near its headwaters. (Photo taken during the expedition made in 1985)*

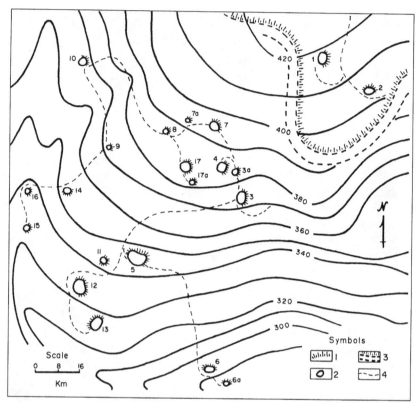

Figure 27. *Topographical drawing of part of the Todos Tenemos runaway slave settlement, showing where seventeen dwellings and four auxiliary buildings were located. Legend: (1) manmade slope; (2) leveled area (3) path to the coffee plantation; (4) possible inner paths. (Drawn by R. Riquenes, M. Leyva, F. Valdés, and V. Marín under the author's direction)*

possible to deduce where the settlement had been. This was then corroborated by the oral tradition of the farmers of the Toa; by the finding of material evidence; and, above all, by the discovery of the floors of the dwellings, which had also been built on human-made slopes. The leveling of the floors of the rooms and their hardening through use created conditions that made it possible to differentiate clearly between the areas that the huts had occupied and the rest of the terrain.

According to the diary of operations, this runaway slave settlement had fifty-nine "houses," many of which had auxiliary buildings with dirt floors close to them, which served as barns or corrals for animals. Seventeen floors were found, three of which had another, smaller space that had also been leveled close to them—the site of an auxiliary building. The drawing that was made—in this case, by members of the August 1987 expedition—shows the presence of some of the elements noted in earlier examples, but this one was differentiated by the presence of the small areas of land that had been leveled close to the dwellings, an aspect to which no references have been found in any of the other cases studied.

The drawings made at the time, the descriptions contained in the slave-hunters' diaries of operations, and the reconstruction of those drawings by locating the settlements all showed the diversity of forms that a runaway slave settlement might adopt. However, they also showed a similarity: the concentration of dwellings in a relatively small area, in a place that was difficult of access. This is the main distinguishing characteristic of this kind of human settlement, though the inner designs had variations that included scattered dwellings; clusters of dwellings that were joined harmoniously, forming small inner squares, with separations between the clusters; several huts in a line that seems to have corresponded to an inner path; and several of these combinations.

In Cuba, human settlements in isolated rural areas have exhibited great dispersion, with enormous distances between the dwellings. Basically, this reflects socioeconomic reasons—that is, it is related to landholding and to the working of the land. Therefore, the drawings of settlements that have characteristics similar to those noted earlier have considerable weight in identifying the runaway slave settlements, along with place-names, the oral tradition, descriptions by slavehunters, and the presence of objects associated with inhabitants of this kind. An extensive analysis of this last aspect is not necessary for the purposes of this historical reconstruction. It is sufficient to point out that archaeological evidence has been used as an element proving that the areas studied were occupied by humans in the historical periods of interest. The utensils and fragments of utensils that were found in those places have already been the subject of a special study (La Rosa Corzo 1990).

Types of Dwellings in Runaway Slave Settlements

Dwellings were one of the important elements of the material culture of the runaway slave settlements, for they expressed the level of social development attained by the group outside society and, to some extent, showed how sedentary it was, to what extent its members had adopted another culture, their ability to use certain techniques and knowledge, and some of the interests of the various groups. Stated simply, most of the dwellings in the runaway slave settlements were rustic huts made of fan-palm fronds, but there were also some specific characteristics that showed the wealth and variety of these components in the system and reflected the social reality of the runaways who lived in each settlement.

Documents from the colonial period contain very little information about the dwellings in runaway slave settlements because the repressive system was not particularly interested in details of this kind. Yet it is still possible to reconstruct some of the main types and forms of dwellings. There were four main types:

1. Low, thatched-roof huts with dirt floors
2. Small huts on piles
3. Huts with walls of royal palm fibers and roofs made of palm fronds
4. Houses

The contents of the various slavehunters' diaries of operations with which I worked showed that the third type of dwelling (in some cases, in combination with the first) prevailed in the eastern region, although, as was stated in earlier chapters, there were also quite a few examples of the fourth type. Since none of the documents studied reported the presence of windows in this kind of dwelling, it may be thought that, in this regard, they followed the style of Indian dwellings, dwellings dating from the earliest times of colonization, and some African hamlets, none of which were reported to have had windows. The forms and measurements that were described in some cases have led me to believe that they were rectangular. The inventory made by the members of the slavehunting militia that attacked the El Frijol settlement states that they destroyed "twenty-two huts forty-four feet long with wide, palm-frond roofs and walls of royal palm fibers" and also "thirteen walled huts that ranged from a little under fourteen feet to twenty-two feet across" (AHSC, GP, leg. 554, no. 2). These examples were repeated in many other accounts and descriptions. The notation that they had walls leads to the inference that,

Figure 28. *Site of one of the dwellings in the Todos Tenemos runaway slave settlement, found in the course of fieldwork during the expedition made in 1989.*

in the runaway slave settlements—as in the rural areas today—there were also many open-sided huts that consisted of four wooden columns, the beams they supported, and a rustic roof of palm fronds.

Tradition, building possibilities, and one of the drawings that was found indicate that most of the roofs had two slopes—at least, none of the descriptions contradicts this. It should be emphasized that the floors of the dwellings in the Calunga and Todos Tenemos settlements showed the presence of "houses" or huts of different sizes. Some of the floors measured thirteen feet one and a half inches by six feet seven inches, nineteen feet eight inches by thirteen feet one and a half inches, seventeen feet eight inches by seven feet four and a half inches, and twenty-six feet three inches by thirteen feet nine inches. In the case of the Todos Tenemos settlement, in which some of the dwellings had had small, low huts with dirt floors next to them, I found some smaller floors measuring seven feet ten inches by five feet eleven inches, five feet one inch by four feet three inches, and seven feet three inches by six feet seven inches, among others, always very close to the larger floors (see fig. 28).

Dwellings of the first type—that is, the low, thatched-roof huts with dirt floors—seem to have been more commonly used and more convenient in places where the conditions did not facilitate the development of a long-lasting, safe settlement. The report of an attack that was made on a group of runaways living in a settlement in the Cajío Swamp (south of Havana) in 1838 recorded the existence of around twenty "low huts with dirt floors and royal palm walls, with bits of fresh bones from cows they had stolen scattered around" (ANC, GSC, leg. 616, no. 19,700).

No references were found to small huts on piles in the region studied, but there were many reports of them in the low-lying, swampy regions along the northern coast of the Vuelta Abajo region and in Puerto Príncipe. It is said that, in the combing operations that the slavehunter Francisco Estévez carried out in the mangrove swamps of Bahía Honda, he found a temporary runaway slave settlement "that was built on piles over the mangrove swamps and cattails and consisted of seventeen blacks, at a spot that is so impassable that dogs cannot get there" (Villaverde 1982). On February 7, 1848, a runaway slave settlement was discovered at the entrance to the Curajaya plantation in the low-lying area in the southern part of Puerto Príncipe. Concerning this discovery, the slavehunter Pedro Antonio Parrado reported that he had caught the runaways "in a fan-palm hut thirty-three feet long by twenty-two feet wide, that was supported on six forked piles on each side and five in the middle" (ANC, RC/JF, leg. 148, no. 7,151).

Finally, it is important that some of the diaries of operations recorded the existence of "houses" in temporary and permanent runaway slave settlements. Even though none of the cases in which the term "house" was used includes an explanation of the elements that differentiated them from the huts, it was possible to confirm that the runaway slave settlements in which that term was applied were the more developed ones, which had existed for quite a long time. It is not advisable to engage in conjecture when there is little evidence, but one thing can be stated: when the Bayamito runaway slave settlement—one of the cases in which the term "house" was applied—was attacked in 1831, forty-five "houses," each with "a living room and bedroom," were found, and its inhabitants returned the attackers' fire for nearly two hours. It should also be emphasized that, in writing about this, the governor of Santiago de Cuba described "the establishment of formal houses and farming" as "scandalous" (ANC, RC/JF, leg. 150, no. 7,462). The dwellings in the Calunga and Todos Tenemos runaway slave settlements were also described as "houses."

When, in these examples, the term "houses" is used and especially when it is said that they had bedrooms, this reflects the impression that the solid appearance of those dwellings must have made on the slavehunters, even though—as was surely the case—they were made of royal palm fibers and fan-palm fronds. The slavehunters must have been led to believe that these towns were more settled, more finished. In the huts of that era, the only space was the bedroom, and all activities took place there. When mention was made of a house with a bedroom, this surely meant that it had an inner division, so there was an interior aspect of the dwelling—which, in that case, was very important. The separation of some of the functions or activities that took place in the hut or "house" gave rise to a higher form of dwelling. The runaway slaves who built their homes in that way showed a higher level of development as a social group outside society, a level determined by their motivations and interests, all of which may have led them to separate the bedroom from the rest of the activities that were carried out inside. This kind of dwelling was more than a mere hut in which to sleep or take shelter from the elements: it was a place in which to live and have a family life. This may be the reason why the slavehunters did not use the term "hut"—which appeared so frequently in their diaries of operations—to refer to these dwellings.

To sum up, even though other kinds of dwellings may still be found to have existed in runaway slave settlements, these were the four types that were found in this study.

The runaways living in settlements did not create any new kinds of housing, for all the types that have been identified corresponded to the more traditional, popular forms of rural dwellings in Cuba, even though the dwellings of some groups in Africa were not very different from the ones used here. I have not referred here to the dwellings in caves or rocky shelters, because they were most often used by armed bands of runaway slaves and are the subject of another study. Table 15 shows the number of dwellings, beds, and inhabitants in the runaway slave settlements in eastern Cuba, grouped by the subregions studied.[2]

Table 15. Number of Dwellings, Beds, and Inhabitants in Runaway Slave Settlements in Eastern Region (by Subregions)

RUNAWAY SLAVE SETTLEMENT	HUTS	BEDS	INHABITANTS	OBSERVATIONS
Subregion 1. Sierra Maestra				
Bayamito	45		160	Houses with living room and master bedroom
Palenque de la Cruz	39			One hundred plots of land
El Portillo			21	Abundant crops
El Cedro				Forty-seven plots of land and fruit trees
Bayamesa			12	Eleven plots of land
Subregion 2. Gran Piedra Range				
La Cueva	50			Abundant crops
Candelaria	35			
San Andrés	More than 8		25	Inhabitants attacked three coffee plantations
Subregion 3. Mayarí Mountains				
Bumba	17	30	30	
Río Naranjo	16			Some crops
Río Levisa	9	24		Root vegetables and sugarcane planted
Palenque del Río Seco	8	13		
Río Miguel	7	14		
Río Yaguasí	5			
Palenquito	1			Few crops

Table 15. *Continued*

RUNAWAY SLAVE SETTLEMENT	HUTS	BEDS	INHABITANTS	OBSERVATIONS
Subregion 4. El Frijol Mountains				
Todos Tenemos	59		100	Animal husbandry, fruit trees, tobacco, coffee plants, etc.
Calunga (1st attack)	26			Abundant crops, fruit trees, coffee plants, tobacco, and ginger
(2nd attack)	54			Recently planted crops
No Se Sabe	42			About thirteen and a half hectares of cultivated land
El Frijol	35	120 (hammocks)	100	Abundant crops
Cupey	17			Abundant crops
El Viento	17			Abundant crops
Come Palma	14	26		Abundant crops
Chinibunque	12			Abundant crops
Sierra Verde	11			Abundant crops
Carga Pilón	7			Abundant crops
Convite	6			Abundant crops
La Palma	5			Abundant crops
El Búfano	2			Few crops
Palenque del Saltadero del Toa	2			Few crops
Palenque de Dos Casas	2			Few crops

Adaptability of the Repressive System

In view of the strength and permanence of runaway slave settlements (see fig. 29) as a form of slave resistance, the repressive system that was created to find and destroy them (see fig. 30) acquired special regional characteristics that have already been analyzed, but one aspect of that system requires commentary. This was the repressive system's adaptability to the specific historical conditions created by the evolution of the methods used by the runaway slaves.

The bases—which have already been described—of the system of repression in the eastern region can be summed up as follows:

1. The existence of special regulations for the region
2. The preponderance of mixed slavehunting militias rather than bands of slavehunters
3. The scheduling of simultaneous operations in different areas
4. The posting of observation bands at points of access to and egress from the subregions in which attacks were being made on runaway slaves
5. The pre-planning of routes, which defined the areas of operations
6. The routing of slavehunting militias through runaway slave settlements that had already been discovered, to prevent their being used again

The behavior of the repressive system shows that the ruling sectors' response had an insular nature, but the structure, resources, strategies, and tactics were adapted to the conditions that prevailed in each region. This was the broadest level of the system's adaptability—flexibility in adjusting to regional characteristics—but it was also exhibited on other planes.

This runs contrary to what has, on occasion, been thought in the past: that the repressive tactics and apparatus were of a rigidity that prevented their adapting to the conditions and forms of slave resistance. In this regard, in the introduction to his book, R. Prince (1981, 17) stated, "Throughout the hemisphere, the runaways developed extraordinary skill in guerrilla warfare. To the amazement of their European enemies, whose rigid, conventional tactics were learned on the open battlefields of Eu-

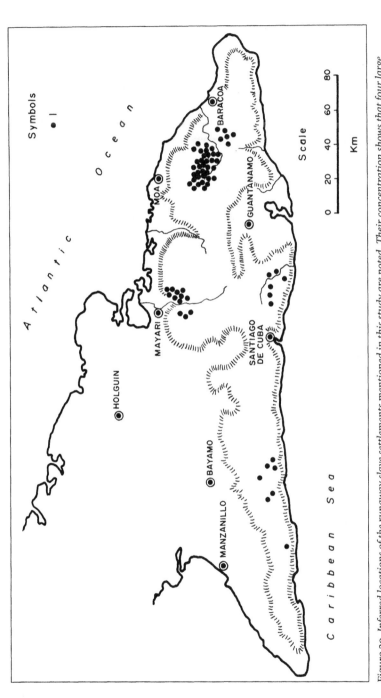

Figure 29. Inferred locations of the runaway slave settlements mentioned in this study are noted. Their concentration shows that four large subregions contained most of the settlements. Legend: (1) runaway slave settlement.

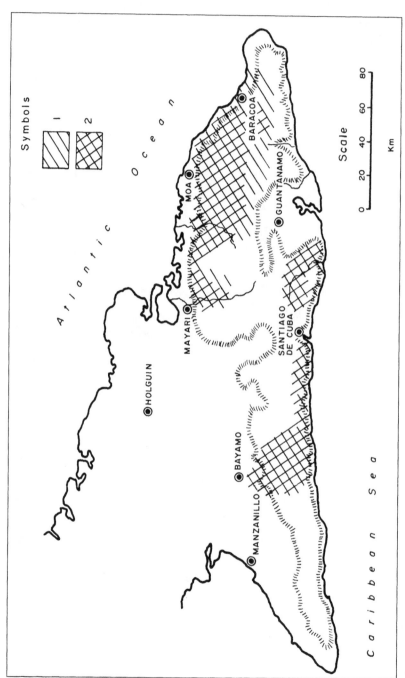

Figure 30. *Areas in which most of the operations by slavehunters and mixed columns were concentrated, according to the diaries of operations studied. Legend: (1) sporadic operations; (2) intensive operations.*

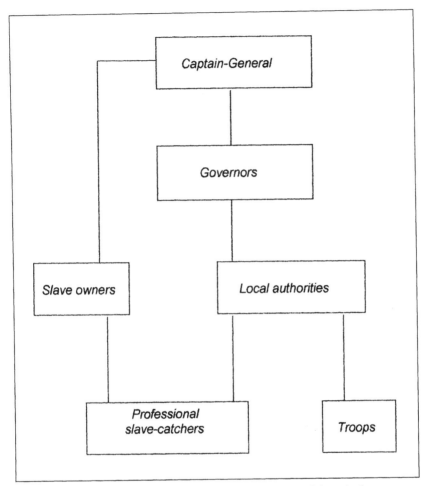

Figure 31. *Structure of the colonial repressive apparatus that opposed the active forms of slave resistance prior to 1796.*

rope, these highly adaptable and mobile wars made the most of the local terrain, with fighters attacking and withdrawing with great rapidity and frequently laying ambushes to catch their adversaries in cross fire."

His comments on the tactics and mobility of the runaway slaves were entirely correct, but what he said about the tactics of their pursuers was not—at least in the case of Cuba, where, as has been shown in preceding chapters, the repressive apparatus showed a great capacity for adaptation, both to regional conditions and to the historical evolution of events. In this regard, two main stages can be distinguished, in which the sys-

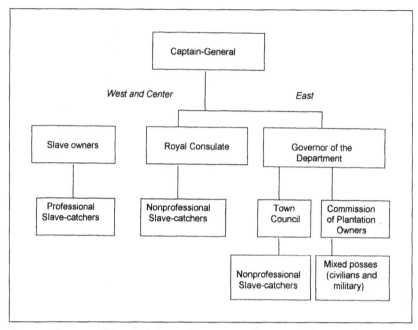

Figure 32. *Structure of the colonial repressive apparatus that opposed the active forms of slave resistance from 1796 on.*

tem's structures changed considerably. Figure 31 shows the structure of the colonial repressive apparatus prior to 1796, the year in which regulations were established for hunting down and exterminating vagabond runaways and runaways living in settlements in Cuba. This structure corresponded to the low levels of that form of slave resistance. Starting in the last decade of the eighteenth century, however, there was a notable development in the various forms of slave resistance, which led to an adjustment in the repressive structure. Figure 32 shows the form that the repressive apparatus adopted in 1796.

The colonial governmental apparatus used the traditional military resources in the case of slave uprisings. Before 1796, slave owners employed professional slavehunters against runaway slaves, but from 1796 on, when the Royal Consulate assumed the function of crushing all forms of active slave resistance, such slavehunters were not used as frequently.

Appendixes

1. Diaries of Operations for Activities Carried Out against
Runaway Slaves Living in Settlements in the Eastern Region

SLAVEHUNTING MILITIA	DATE	COLLECTION
Felipe Quintero (Gran Piedra mountain range)	February 20–March 30, 1815	Asuntos Políticos, leg. 109, no. 34.
Ignacio Leyte Vidal (Mayarí)	April 20–May 19, 1828	Gobierno General, leg. 584, no. 28,861.
Santiago Guerra (west of Santiago de Cuba)	January 14–April 4, 1842	Asuntos Políticos, leg. 41, no. 38.
Leandro Melgarez (Manzanillo)	January 16–March 16, 1842	Miscelánea de Expediente no. 7,531.
Esteban Menocal (Baracoa)	January 20–March 20, 1842	Asuntos Políticos, leg. 41, no. 38.
Pedro Becerra (east of Santiago de Cuba)	January 10–April 4, 1842	Asuntos Políticos, leg. 41, no. 38.
Pedro Galo (Mayarí)	January 20–March 22, 1848	Asuntos Políticos, leg. 41, no. 38.
Miguel Pérez (Tiguabos)	January 28–March 28, 1848	Gobierno Superior Civil, leg. 625, no. 19,877.
Segundo Suárez (Baracoa)	January 28–April 6, 1848	Gobierno Superior Civil, leg. 625, no. 19,877.
Benigno Cura (Sagua)	January 28–March 30, 1848	Gobierno Superior Civil, leg. 625, no. 19,877.
Eduardo Busquet (Bayamo)	February 20–March 27, 1848	Gobierno Superior Civil, leg. 625, no. 19,877.
Miguel Pérez (Tiguabos)	February 5–March 31, 1849	Gobierno Superior Civil, leg. 621, no. 1,820.
Miguel Pérez (Tiguabos)	May 31–July 29, 1850	Gobierno Superior Civil, leg. 621, no. 1,820.

1. *continued*

SLAVEHUNTING MILITIA	DATE	COLLECTION
Slavehunting militia from Baracoa (which joined the preceding one)	May 31– July 6, 1850	Gobierno Superior Civil, leg. 641, no. 1,820.

Source: ANC.

2. Captains of Eastern Runaway Slave Settlements

CAPTAIN	RUNAWAY SLAVE SETTLEMENT	YEAR	OBSERVATIONS
Cayetano Solórsano	La Cueva	1815	Directed attacks on several plantations.
El Francés (The Frenchman—alias)	San Andrés	1815	Had twenty-five runaways under his orders.
Eusebio Gangá	Calunguita	1841	Had fourteen runaways under his orders. When the settlement was attacked, he fought to the death. One of the captured runaways who had lived in the settlement was his woman.
Lorenzo	Not identified (in the Sierra Maestra)	1842	Turned himself in after prolonged persecution.
Bota	Todos Tenemos	1848	Sought refuge in the Guardamujeres runaway slave settlement when the Todos Tenemos settlement was attacked.
Gregorio Rector	Calunga	1849	Killed while fighting in the second attack on the settlement. Had firearms.

3. "List Showing the Blacks Who Have Fled in This Province, According to the Reports Received from Its Lieutenants, Governors, and Captains of Slavehunting Militias"

HOLDING	NUMBER OF RUNAWAYS	TERRITORIAL DIVISION	NUMBER OF BLACKS
Holguín	11	Niminima	6
Manzanillo	1	Dajao	2
Baracoa	0	Corralillo	1
Cobre	0	Zacatecas	1
Jiguaní	0	Guanímar	0
Moa	0	Ti Arriba	0
Bayamo	8	Homgolosongo	24
Territorial Companies		Sevilla	0
Manantuaba	2	Guaninicum	2
Sagua	0	Dos Bocas	5
Sabanilla	1	Brazo del Cauto	2
Tiguabos	0	Andalucía	6
Mayarí	0	Demajagua	1
Maroto	9	Yarayabo	0
Palma Soriano	3	Paz de los Naranjos	2
Contramaestre	0	Armonía de Limones	1
San Andrés	2	Morón	8
Bolaños	22	Damajayabo	3
Mayarí Arriba	2	Candelaria	1
El Ramón	5	Lagun	0
Piloto Arriba	0	Guantánamo	2
Guaninicum de Leonard	3	Güira	0
Cauto Abajo	1	Río Frío	0
Caimanes	5	Fled from the city	32
La Amistad	2	Total	176

Santiago de Cuba, January 29, 1842

Source: ANC, AP, leg. 131, no. 11.

4. Slaves Captured by the West Column

NAME	SEX	OWNER	RESIDENCE
Modesto	M	Gertrudis Echevarría	Santiago de Cuba
Pascual	M	Gertrudis Echevarría	Santiago de Cuba
Sabá	M	Gertrudis Echevarría	Santiago de Cuba
Jadeo	M	Mario Portuondo	Santiago de Cuba
Basilio	M	Vicente Portuondo	Santiago de Cuba
Domingo	M	Unknown	Santiago de Cuba
Basilio	M	Unknown	Santiago de Cuba
María de la Cruz	F	Nicolás Lazo	Unknown
María Manuela	F	José Antonio Eduardo	Unknown
Teresa Tamayo	F	Esteban Tamayo	Bayamo
Manuela	F	Francisco Arias	Bayamo

Source: ANC, GSC, leg. 617, no. 19,725.

5. Forces Employed in Operations in the Northern Mountain Ranges of the Eastern Department

PLACE	COMMANDER	FORCES
1st column, from Sabana la Mar (east of Santiago de Cuba)	Pedro Becerra, of the Nápoles Regiment	Thirty hunters from the Galicia Regiment and twenty slavehunters.
Slavehunting militia from Santa Catalina (joined with Column E)	Tiburcio del Castillo	Twenty men from the detachment from Santa Catalina and twenty slavehunters.
2nd column, from Baracoa	Esteban Menocal	Thirty soldiers and twenty slavehunters.
3rd column, from Micara	Lieutenant Pedro Galo, of the Nápoles Regiment	Thirty soldiers and twenty slavehunters.

6. Results Obtained by Slavehunting Militias Ordered to Destroy the Runaway Slave Settlements in the Sierra Maestra, 1848 and 1849

STARTING POINT	NAME OF COMMANDER	MONTHLY WAGE (IN PESOS)	NUMBER OF SLAVE-HUNTERS	TOTAL COST IN A MONTH AND 27 DAYS (IN PESOS)	RESULTS IN 1849		RESULTS IN 1848	
					CAPTURED	KILLED	CAPTURED	KILLED
Tiguabos	Miguel Pérez	80	25	2,128	19	5	7	2
Saltadero	Damián Pérez	40	25			1	2	
Sabanilla	Observation band	None			4			
Corralillo	Observation band	None			3		4	
Bolaños	Observation band	None			1		1	
San Andrés	Observation band	None			5		2	
Baracoa	Observation band	None			31		1	
Sagua	Observation band	None				3		
El Cobre	Observation band	None				3		
Bayamo	Observation band	None				4	2	
Río Seco	Observation band	None		Total		1	5	
					6	27		

SLAVEHUNTING MILITIA	RUNAWAYS CAPTURED	RUNAWAYS KILLED	TOTAL
Slavehunting militia of 1848	27	5	32
Slavehunting militia of 1849	63	6	69
Total for the two years	90	11	101

Glossary

acoso: pursuit, continual attack, hunting down, repression

administrador: manager

alcalde de la Santa Hermandad: head of the —— branch of the Holy Brotherhood

alcalde mayor: town magistrate

aldea: hamlet

amo: master

amotinamiento: refusal to work

apalencamiento: runaway slave settlement (usually) or the establishment of runaway slave settlements

ayuntamiento: town hall

barracón: slave quarters

batey: sugar mill community

batida: attack, raid

caballería: 13.4 hectares (1 hectare = 2.47 acres)

cabildo: municipal council

capitanía de partido: seat

caserío: group of huts

"casta": ethnic group

cimarrón simple: vagabond runaway slave (not in any settlement, steals from plantations; machete only; was the least dangerous)

comandante de armas: military commandant (of a territorial division)

comandante de partida: commandant of a slavehunting militia

comarca: district

Comisión de Hacendados orientales: Commission of Plantation Owners (or) Commission of Eastern Plantation Owners

conuco: plot of land (small, next to the slave's hut, to be worked on holidays)

corral: enclosure

cuadrilla: band

cuadrilla de cimarrones: armed bands of runaway slaves (used temporary settlements of runaway slaves the most; had firearms; were very dangerous)

cuadrilla de observación y auxilio: observation and support band

Cuchillas del Toa: mountain—the Cuchillas del Toa area

curata: Indian settlement administered by a Spanish priest *departamento oriental*: the Eastern Department

devinir: future

dotación: the slaves on a single plantation

dueño: slave owner

economía de consumo: consumption economy

estancia: plot in a runaway slave settlement (planted to vegetables, separated from one another, each one with a hut)

factor: agent

fondo: collection

garrote: cudgel

hacendado: plantation owner

hacienda: plantation, estate

hato: hut; territorial division

historiografía: historical studies (usually), historiography

hoja de ruta: planned route

indio feroz: rebellious Indian

indulto: branding as proof that their owners had paid the tax required to legitimize their entry

Junta de Fomento: Development Board

Junta de Hacendados: Board of Plantation Owners

Junta de Población Blanca: Board of White Citizens

Junta de Policía: Police Board

jurisdicción oriental: the Eastern Jurisdiction

justicia: authority (person)

legua: league (2.63 miles)

Leyes de Indias: Laws of the Indies

lo particular: the specific

lo singular: the unique

mayoral: overseer

montero: cowhand

Ordenanzas de Cáceres: Cáceres Ordinances

padrón: census

palenque: runaway slave settlement (with crops and a self-sufficient economy)

partida mixta: mixed slavehunting militia (civilians and military)

partido: territorial division

patricio: aristocrat

perseguir: hunt down or (occasionally) pursue

pieza de indias: Indies piece

poblado: town

púa: stake

rancheador: slavehunter

ranchería: temporary settlement of runaway slaves
rancho: temporary settlement of runaway slaves, (sometimes) hut
Real Consulado: Royal Consulate
reales: reals
Real Hacienda: Royal Treasury
redondel: circular area, circular clearing
Río Seco: an area, not a river
Santa Hermandad: Holy Brotherhood
tenencia de gobierno: term of office
título: section (e.g., book 7, section 5)
trabuco: blunderbuss
unidad productiva: production unit
vara: 0.84 meter, or 2.75 feet
vara en tierra: low hut with a dirt floor

Notes

Introduction

1. In Cuba, each band of slavehunters usually had six members, and the head of it was called a captain. Each slavehunting militia, however, always had more than twenty-five men, and the head of it (who was nearly always a military man by profession) was called a commandant.

2. In the literature in English, the term "resistance" was used in *American Negro Slave Revolts*, by H. Aptheker, published in 1969, and the dichotomy between passive and active slave resistance appeared in *The Sociology of Slavery*, by O. Patterson, published that same year. M. Moreno Fraginals introduced those terms in historical studies in Cuba in his work *El ingenio* (The sugar mill) (1986c), but without the required background, and others who studied slave protests in Cuba did not include it in their research. I am entirely responsible for the adjustments that are made between this terminology and the terms in the documents from the era and also for the adaptations made to the facts, events, and incidents.

3. The concept of armed bands of runaway slaves that is used in the colonial documentation clearly described the nonsedentary, bold character of those groups, which were never confused with the runaway slaves living in settlements. However, this difference escaped others studying this topic in Cuba, except for the work of Vento (1976), who described this form of slave resistance when he recorded the existence of a famous armed band of runaway slaves headed by José Dolores. It should be noted that correct guidelines were employed in some of the historical studies on slave rebellions in the Americas to describe and examine the various forms that the slaves' struggles took.

In a study he made (1977) that was based on a large number of documents and that used the terms employed in them, F. P. Bowser distinguished between uprisings and flight and, within this last category, between *cimarrones*, or vagabond runaway slaves, and what he called *bandas cimarronas*, or armed bands of runaway slaves. His analysis of the known armed bands of runaway slaves included their settlements in isolated areas. R. Conrad (1978) established notable differences, considering the runaways who lived in settlements to be a kind of runaway, separating some of the nonviolent forms of struggle, and considering uprisings to be synonymous with rebellion. For his part, D. Geggus (1983) made some important comments about the terms "slave resistance" and "culture of resistance," about the process of searching for what is African, and about creolization and offered a typology of slave rebellions.

F. Guerra Cedeño (1984) analyzed insurrections separately from flight and identified this last as *cimarronaje*, or the flight of vagabond runaway slaves. He also saw two kinds of settlements as a result of flight: *cimarronera*, or that of vagabond runaways, and *cumbe*—which included both the temporary settlements established for mainly tactical purposes and the *palenques*, or permanent runaway slave settlements. In a short but important article, A. Gebara (1986) noted that there was little systematization in the use of correct terms for identifying the various forms taken by the slaves' struggle. He called attention to the inadequate resources for explaining specific social realities in different contexts and eras. This author contributed valuable opinions for scientific discussion and considered the flight of slaves to be a common form of resistance. All these treatments of the subject and the use of different terms, which were solutions for each author, corroborate the depth that historical studies have achieved in recent decades, even if not all of them are compatible with one another. The seriousness of all these approaches constitutes a theoretical base that both enables and obliges us to advance with more rigor in these studies.

4. This work had antecedents in two earlier articles (Pérez de la Riva 1945, 1946).

5. *Batey* is a term is of Indian origin, referring to the central area where the original form of baseball was played. In the colonial period, it referred to the square on each plantation, especially at sugar mills. Regarding plots of land: during the period of slavery in Cuba, some plantation owners gave their slaves small plots of land next to their huts. The slaves worked those plots on holidays.

6. *Barracones* were large depots in which slaves who had just been brought in were held until they were put up for sale. With the development of slave plantations and after the slave uprisings of 1825, it became common to erect large buildings of rubblework with inner divisions in which all the slaves on a single plantation lived under a prisonlike regime, and they were also called *barracones*.

7. The town is in Yateras Municipality, Guantánamo Province, shown at coordinates 694 and 191 on page 5277-III of the 1:50,000 scale map of the Republic of Cuba made by the Cuban Institute of Geodesy and Cartography (ICGC).

8. A few pages later, the document cited stated that there were only 120, not 500, hammocks. This is a key figure for calculating how many people lived there (AHSC, GP, leg. 554, no. 2).

9. Prior to 1796, the judges ordinary and the heads of the local branches of the Holy Brotherhood were in charge of hunting down runaway slaves. Joseph Rivera stated that, in the mid-eighteenth century, the provincial authorities "patrolled the countryside and hunted down runaway slaves and other criminals" (Portuondo Zúñiga 1986).

Chapter 1

1. The ecclesiastical visits by Bishops Sarmiento (in 1554) and Castillo (in 1570) and Cabezas de Altamirano's account (in 1608) are a true reflection of that demographic process (AGI, Santo Domingo, leg. 150; Pichardo Viñals 1965).

2. The figures were reached by tabulating the data in the original document (AGI, Santo Domingo, leg. 116) and differ slightly from the calculations made by I. Macías (1978).

3. The captured runaways who had lived in that settlement said that it was between the Mota and Masío Rivers, near the sea—that is, around nine miles from El Portillo. Therefore, the runaway slave settlement should not be called Cabo Cruz, since Alonso de Arcos y Moreno, governor of Santiago de Cuba, was mistaken when he said it was forty leagues (105 miles) from that city.

4. It seems that the Holy Brotherhood had its origins as an institution during the reign of Alfonso VII of Spain, but it was established by the Catholic kings in 1473, under the Laws of Burgos, and was transferred to the Spanish colonies in the Americas later on. It had ordinary jurisdiction, and its purpose was to repress crime in the rural areas. It had a head and members of bands that, in Cuba, hunted down runaway slaves. This institution appeared in Cuba when Gonzalo de Guzmán became governor of Santiago de Cuba (in 1525).

5. One of the receipts for payment of the members of the slavehunting militia that attacked this *palenque* states that 111 men took part in the operations.

6. The runaway slave settlements in Cuba disappeared during the process of abolishing slavery (1868–86), and—unlike the situation in Jamaica and Dutch Guiana (now Suriname)—none of the descendants of those runaway slaves stayed in their hamlets, so there is no oral tradition to help us in reconstructing a large part of the daily life and history of those hamlets founded by runaway slaves. Consult the works of R. Price (1975a, 1975b) and B. Kopytof (1976a, 1976b) in this regard.

7. Slave traders and members of the colonial administration branded enslaved Africans, using a metal seal that was applied red-hot to visible parts of the body. Carlos III prohibited the practice in 1784, but some slave traders and slave owners continued to employ it in Cuba up to the mid-nineteenth century, as I have shown in an earlier work (La Rosa Corzo 1988b).

8. The Crown allowed the owners of slaves who had been brought in illegally to pay a tax to have them registered. The slaves were then branded with the corresponding mark by a representative of the Royal Ministry of Finance.

9. In this case, the owner had to pay 165 reals for his capture, 43 for his keep, and 12 for the jailer's fee (jail expenses), plus 269 maravedis for the court clerk's services.

10. In María Antonia's case, the fact that she had lived in a runaway slave settlement was not considered a defect.

11. On July 14, 1600, the Town Council of Havana issued fifteen ordinances for the subjugation of runaway slaves—which some authors have considered the first regulation on runaway slaves in Cuba, but, in fact, there was no such regulation. The ordinances in question were aimed at solving the problem of financing the operations against runaway slaves.

12. This aspect has been fully discussed in another monograph on vagabond runaway slaves (La Rosa Corzo, 1988a).

Chapter 2

1. Most of them are in the Real Consulado y Junta de Fomento (Royal Consulate and Development Board) Collection, but some are in the Asuntos Políticos (Political Affairs), Gobierno Superior Civil (Higher Civil Government), and Gobierno General (General Government) Collections and in the National Archives of Cuba.

2. Much speculation on this subject is widespread in Cuba. It has been supposed that anybody was paid for turning in ears torn off vagabond runaway slaves and runaways living in settlements, but this was not really so. The captains of authorized bands of slavehunters presented the ears as proof of the runaways killed in skirmishes, and, along with the runaways captured alive, they were used to show how many runaways had been living in the settlement. The Royal Consulate paid nothing for the ears—it paid only for captured runaways who were still alive.

3. The classifications used in the census have been respected. The terms "free blacks and mulattoes (Spanish)" and "free blacks and mulattoes (French)" refer to individuals who had belonged (as slaves) to owners of those nationalities.

4. According to testimony gathered by R. Rousset (1918, 294), during a tour that Colonel Juan Pico de la Cruz made of the area in 1819, he witnessed the impetuous development that was taking place in the rural areas. In his report, he spoke of "magnificent" coffee plantations with many slaves.

5. The classification by categories used in the document was respected, but the data were selected and reorganized in accord with the interests of this work.

6. So far, no references proving that this order was carried out have been found.

7. The Benga el Sábalo plantation, in Mayarí—which has come down to us as the place-name Vengánzabalos—was not a runaway slave settlement but was attacked by a band of vagabond runaway slaves or runaways who lived in a settlement. Therefore, it is incorrect to speak of the Vengánzabalos runaway slave settlement.

8. E. Pichardo ([1875] 1986) marked the Candelaria coffee plantation on his 1:200,000 map, page 32-A, at coordinates 61 and 15, around five miles northeast of the Gran Piedra, but modern maps do not include references to it, so its location has been made in the conventional way.

9. The Providencia plantation is not marked on Pichardo's ([1875] 1986) map. Now the corresponding place-name is included at coordinates 624 and 160 on the Cuban Institute of Geodesy and Cartography map, page 5076-II (ICGC 1980).

10. The runaways living in the Todos Tenemos *palenque* also used this method, though the head of the settlement protected the women in a refuge that had been prepared ahead of time.

11. Pichardo marked the Filipinas plantation at coordinates 64 and 15 on his map on page 32-A. It was a coffee plantation on the side of the mountain and does not correspond to the present town of Filipinas, which is much farther to the east.

12. Pichardo ([1875] 1986) did not mark La Cueva on his map, which shows that, at midcentury, it had yet to be founded—or, at least, was not known. Now, however, several farm families live on the same place where the runaway slave settlement stood, according to the diary.

13. This attack—one of the few that caught all the runaways in their settlement—was carried out thanks to the assistance of a runaway who had been living in the settlement and who turned traitor and served as the slavehunters' guide.

14. *Vivíes* in the original. There were many Vivís in the eastern part of the island of Cuba. Research that ethnologist R. López Valdés did in the Tiguabos archives showed that there were many members of that group among the slaves in the area. The Vivís, who came from the southeastern part of Nigeria, near the Niger River delta, were famed as warriors. The fact that a runaway slave settlement was described as being theirs is quite significant, especially since it was the only one of its kind in Cuba, at least as far as current studies have discovered (López Valdéz 1986).

Chapter 3

1. It is noteworthy that slave plantations had been developing apace in the territorial division of Santa Catalina, mainly raising coffee and cotton. A census taken in 1823 reported the existence of about 43,700 acres of land being cultivated in that rural district. According to the calculations to which the data of that census were subjected, 85 percent of all the cultivated land was planted to cotton, 10 percent to coffee, and the rest to sugarcane and tobacco. Santa Catalina had a population of 2,367 inhabitants that year, 72 percent of whom were slaves (ANC, GG, leg. 491, no. 25,173).

2. The spelling of the *palenques* used in the document has been respected.

3. On the map that was drawn to show the route taken by this slavehunting militia, the locations of the runaway slave settlements and some of the plantations were inferred, because many of the places mentioned do not appear on modern maps, though they did appear on Pichardo's ([1875] 1986).

4. We may assume that this happened during the other slavehunting militia's operations, in Sagua.

5. Camagüeyan historian Gustavo Sed lent me the original of José Rafael Parrado's diary of operations (1830). J. Pérez Sánchez's diary of operations is contained in several different files in the National Archives. Both are now the subject of a special study.

6. The figure of 160 runaway slaves living in a single settlement seems a little exaggerated. In correspondence with the number of "houses," each with a living room and bedroom, there may have been between 100 and 120 runaways.

7. Emphasis by the author.

8. Esteban Ulloa had headed a band of slavehunters ever since 1823, so he had amassed a great deal of experience in this kind of activity.

9. According to the records of the Town Council of Santiago de Cuba, the execution of these three criminals cost sixty pesos, nineteen of which were paid for the construction of iron cages "with bolts for the heads."

10. This is corroborated by authorized sources. In addition, expeditions made to those mountain ranges in 1985 and 1987 showed that they had no caves.

11. The diary of operations kept by the slavehunter Francisco Estévez, who operated in the Vuelta Abajo region, in western Cuba, was an exceptional case, for C. Villaverde (1982) copied it and made it known in the nineteenth century.

12. The original spelling of names has been respected.

13. The operations of these slavehunting militias were recorded in notebooks whose pages were divided in five large columns. The first (on the left) contained the date; the second, the geographic points; the third, the distance covered each day; the fourth, a description of the area; and the last, the operations carried out.

14. The small plots of land were planted to vegetables. They were separated from one another, and each one had a hut.

15. The term "country" in the quotation was used in the document as a synonym for the Eastern Department.

16. When they had failed to catch any prisoners who could tell them the name of the settlement—and therefore did not know what it was called—the slavehunters resorted to techniques typical of the era for distinguishing among them and gave them plant names, such as La Yagruma (Trumpet Tree), La Palma (Palm Tree), and El Ocujal (Grove of Santa María Trees), or contemptuous names, such as Guarda Basura (Save Garbage), Come Berraco (Eats Boars), and Leva Buena (Good Clothes). The two mentioned in the text to which this note refers mean Muddy Stream and Milkman.

17. This settlement's name—Come Palma, or Eats Palm Trees—reflects the fact that many groups of runaways living in settlements used palm trees as a source of food. It was a custom that some slaves had brought from Africa to Cuba.

18. Micara was a plantation in what is now Mayarí Arriba, and the area around it was also called Micara. It should not be confused with the places close to Sagua that had similar names.

19. This area is still called La Zanja. It contains some widely scattered farmhouses now.

20. On place-names: through the oral tradition, the farmers of the Toa region have preserved the names of many runaway slave settlements, applying them to mountains, streams, and other geographic features. For example, there are streams called Bumba, Calunga, Todos Tenemos, Guardamujeres, and Ajengiblar.

Chapter 4

1. In general, Cuban historical studies have paid little attention to this aspect. The censuses show that this process of manumission of the offspring of interracial relations had considerable weight in the eastern areas of Cuba.

2. Partial results taken from the figures in the books of the El Cerro depot of runaway slaves (ANC, ML, no. 7,794, 7,795, 7,796, 7,797, 7,798, 7,799, 7,800, 7,802).

3. Only the captain general could authorize an attack on a runaway slave settlement.

4. On the plots planted to corn: *tarea*, the Spanish word for these plots, was used in the first half of the nineteenth century to mean an extension of land about 2,475 feet square.

It seems that there were possibilities for growing rice at the runaway slave settlements in the Toa River basin, since this grain was reported as very abundant at the Todos Tenemos *palenque*, as well. On expeditions made to this mountain range, I confirmed that it was possible to grow rice in those areas.

5. During the second attack on the El Frijol runaway slave settlement, which was made in 1816, the slavehunters found a skull hanging from a tree. When questioned about it, the runaways who were captured said that it was that of Ramón, who had been killed in the attack made the previous year and that "his marrow and hair were used to make false prophecies" (AHSC, GP, leg. 554, no. 22).

6. In their oral tradition, farmers living along the Toa River have preserved fascinating legends about the existence and destruction of the Calunga runaway slave settlement. I heard some of them when on an expedition to those mountains in 1985. The settlement was on a mountain with very steep foothills, in a place that was very difficult of access and where no other people lived. During fieldwork, I found the floors of the fourteen housing units in the settlement and some

crude cooking places made of three stones. Farmers had found the remains of machetes, clay pipes, and a rustic, crudely carved basin. Even now, coffee plants that the runaways planted can be found in the thick undergrowth, and wild ginger abounds. A year after this settlement had been studied on the basis of the oral tradition and fieldwork, the diary of operations of the slavehunting militia that attacked it was found, which made it possible to complete the picture of this runaway slave settlement. The spelling in the document (Calunga) has been respected here, even though it is really a Bantu term (Kalunga) that is associated with a deity of the first rank in many African groups.

7. Aspects such as this prove the tactical (and economic) nature of many temporary runaway slave settlements in relation to the permanent ones.

8. The slavehunting militia must have made a mistake about the location of this runaway slave settlement, confusing it with another that they found, for several diaries of operations refer to this settlement and state that it was between two branches of the Jaguaní River, a great distance from its confluence with the Toa.

9. This was a spelling mistake in the diary of operations. It should be the El Ocujal runaway slave settlement.

10. Because of the location of the Quemayal *palenque*, there is no confusion with the Quema Sal settlement, which is mentioned in another diary of operations and is located in another area.

11. It took the men in the slavehunting militia from El Cobre four days to get to the Sevilla plantation.

12. Pichardo ([1875] 1986) mistakenly said that this plantation was on the eastern bank of the Turquino River, but various slavehunters' diaries of operations stated that it was on the Bayamito River—that is, about eleven kilometers farther to the east.

13. There are many reports of guard dogs in runaway slave settlements, an aspect that deserves further attention.

14. Once more, the documents show that the runaways living in runaway slave settlements did not come from the western parts of the island.

15. The content and format of the information have been respected.

16. Fieldwork shows that the Guardamujeres runaway slave settlement was only two miles west of the Todos Tenemos settlement and could be reached from the latter by going along the Todos Tenemos Stream and then climbing to the base of Galán Peak. The Vereda de San Juan runaway slave settlement was on the highest point.

17. The official letters from the governor of Santiago de Cuba are dated March 31 and July 29, 1850 (ANC, GSC, leg. 621, no. 19,820).

18. According to the documents, this seems to have been the first time the El

Bruto runaway slave settlement was attacked. The others had been discovered and attacked previously.

19. Even though they clung to slavery, plantation owners often spoke out publicly against the slave trade—for example, when Captain General Leopoldo O'Donnell asked various institutions and individuals for their opinions of the draft of the Penal Law of 1845, two of the main conclusions were that the traffic in blacks should be ended (and be followed by a policy of natural reproduction among the slaves) and that the white population should be increased (Barcia 1987, 56).

20. The book by M. del C. Barcia that has already been cited (1987, 161–62) contains a table drawn up by the author in which she recorded the number of slaves brought to Cuba between 1815 and 1872. The same table contains the figures proposed by other authors, who were more specialized in this subject. Curtin, for example, estimated that the number of slaves imported from 1860 on was as follows: 24,985 in 1860; 23,964 in 1861; 11,524 in 1862; 7,507 in 1863; 6,805 in 1864; and 145 in 1865, the last year for which he gave figures. Cuban demographer Juan Pérez de la Riva gave the following figures for the number of slaves brought into Cuba: 15,000 in 1860; 10,000 in 1861; 8,000 in 1862; 7,000 in 1863, 1864, 1865, 1866, and 1867; 6,000 in 1868; 5,000 in 1869; 4,000 in 1870; 3,000 in 1871; and 2,000 in 1872. This last author (1979, 47) also stated that, as far as he knew, the last time that the authorities had caught slave ships bringing in slaves illegally was in 1873.

21. During the preceding decades, a number of attempts were made to produce sugar with free labor, but the replacement process could not be effected rapidly, so all those attempts failed. However, the number of free workers who were hired in the industry gradually increased. Thus, for example, 22 percent of the 1,136 workers in the sugar mills owned by the Aguirres in the western part of the island in 1877 were free blacks, and 58 percent of the Gran Azucarera Company's 838 workers were hired Chinese laborers, 37 percent were slaves, and 5 percent were free blacks (figures from tables in Friedlaender 1978, 538).

22. The books by M. del C. Barcia (1987), Moreno Fraginals (1986c), and especially Moreno Fraginals, H. Klein, and S. L. Engermann (1986) contain extensive studies on the changes in the prices of slaves sold in Cuba during that period.

23. The slave population on the island dropped from 344,615 in 1867 to 199,094 in 1877 (Ortiz 1975).

Chapter 5

1. Table 14 is based on figures taken from the diaries of operations.

2. All amounts are the figures and data taken from the diaries of operations and

other documents. In no cases were calculations made. The information was organized in descending order within each subregion. Whenever information on runaway slave settlements is not recorded here, it is because the information that was available was unclear. In the case of the El Frijol runaway slave settlement, the figures offered contradict what was stated in preceding historical studies; the information was checked very carefully, and the data used were taken from statements by the governor of Santiago de Cuba (ANC, RC/JF, leg. 25, no. 1,364, 8).

References

Aguilar Flores, R. n.d. *Lecciones de ingreso a la Escuela Profesional de Comercio de La Habana*. Havana: Cultural.

Aimes, H. 1907. *A History of Slavery in Cuba, 1511–1868*. New York: G. P. Putman's Sons.

Aptheker, H. 1969. *American Negro Slave Revolts*. New York: International Publishers.

Archivo General de Indias (AGI). Cuba.

———. Santo Domingo.

Archivo Histórico de Santiago de Cuba (AHSC). Administración regional. Cimarrones.

———. Gobierno Provincial (GP).

Archivo Histórico Militar de España. Fondo América Central. Cuba.

Archivo Nacional de Cuba (ANC). Asuntos Políticos (AP).

———. Correspondencia de los Capitanes Generales (CCG).

———. Gobierno General (GG).

———. Gobierno Superior Civil (GSC).

———. Miscelánea de expedientes (ME).

———. Miscelánea de libros (ML).

———. Real Consulado/Junta de Fomento (RC/JF).

Bacardí Moreau, E. 1925. *Crónicas de Santiago de Cuba*. Vols. 1–3. Santiago de Cuba: Tipografía Arroyo y Hnos.

Barcia, M. del C. 1987. *Burguesía esclavista y abolición*. Havana: Editorial de Ciencias Sociales.

Bowser, F. P. 1977. *El esclavo africano en el Perú colonial, 1524–1650*. Mexico City: Editorial Siglo Veintiuno.

Callejas, J. M. 1911. *Historia de Santiago de Cuba*. Havana: Imprenta de la Universidad.

Centro de Estadística, Cuba. 1862. *Noticias estadísticas de la Isla de Cuba*. Havana: Imprenta del Gobierno y Capitanía General y Real Hacienda por S.M.

Colón, C. 1961. *Diario de navegación*. Havana: Publicaciones de la Comisión Cubana de la UNESCO.

Comisión de Estadísticas, Cuba. 1829. *Cuadro estadístico de la Siempre Fiel Isla de Cuba correspondiente al año 1827*. Havana: Imprenta del Gobierno y Capitanía General.

———. 1842. *Resumen del censo de población de la Isla de Cuba a fin del año de 1841*. Havana: Imprenta del Gobierno por S.M.

———. 1847. *Cuadro estadístico de la Siempre Fiel Isla de Cuba*. Havana: Imprenta del Gobierno y Capitanía General.

Comisión de la Junta de Hacendados de Santiago de Cuba, Cuba. 1832. *Arreglo de las partidas para la persecución de negros cimarrones en este territorio*. Santiago de Cuba: Imprenta del Colegio Seminario.

Comité Cubano de Asentamientos Humanos. 1977. *Los asentamientos humanos en Cuba*. Havana: Hábitat.

Conrad, R. 1978. *Os últimos anos da escravatura no Brasil, 1850–1888*. Rio de Janeiro: Civilicao Brasileira.

Danger Roll, Z. 1977. *Los cimarrones de El Frijol*. Santiago de Cuba: Empresa Editorial Oriente.

Duharte Jiménez, R. 1986. *La rebeldía esclava en la región oriental de Cuba (1533–1868)*. Santiago de Cuba: Taller Unidad Gráfica.

Erenchun, F. 1856. *Anales de la Isla de Cuba: Diccionario administrativo, económico, estadístico y legislativo: Año 1855*. Havana: Imprenta del Tiempo.

Esteban Deive, C. 1985. *Los cimarrones del Maniel de Neiba*. Santo Domingo: Banco Central de la República Dominicana.

Franco, J. L. 1961. Afroamérica. *Publicación Junta Nacional Arqueología Etnología* (Havana): 115–31, 141–62.

———. 1973. *Los palenques de los negros cimarrones*. Havana: Departamento de Orientación Revolucionaria, Partido Comunista de Cuba.

———. 1974. *Ensayos históricos*. Havana: Editorial de Ciencias Sociales.

———. 1981. Rebeliones cimarronas y esclavos en los territorios españoles. In *Sociedades cimarronas: Comunidades esclavas rebeldes en América*, compiled by R. Price, 43–54. Mexico City: Editorial Siglo Veintiuno.

Friedlaender, H. 1978. *Historia económica de Cuba*. Vol. 2. Havana: Editorial de Ciencias Sociales.

García del Pino, C. 1985. *Morell de Santa Cruz: Visita eclesiástica*. Havana: Editorial de Ciencias Sociales.

Gebara, A. 1986. Escravos: Fugas e fugas. *Terra e poder* (Brazil): 16 (12): 89–100.

Gebara, A. 1986. *Escravos: fugas e fugas. Terra e poder*, Rev. Brasileira Hist., 6 (12):89–100.

Geggus, D. 1983. *Slave Resistance Studies and the Saint Domingue Slave Revolt: Some Preliminary Considerations*. Miami: Latin American and Caribbean Center, Florida International University.

Guerra Cedeño, F. 1984. *Esclavos negros, cimarrones y cumbes de Barlovento*. Caracas: Cuadernos Lagoven.

Humboldt, A. de. 1959. Ensayo político sobre la Isla de Cuba. *Revista Bimestre Cubana* (Havana) 5 (76): 190–425.

Iglesias, F. 1982. Población y clases sociales en la segunda mitad del siglo XVI. *Revista de la Biblioteca Nacional "José Martí"* (Havana) 73 (3): 101–32.

Instituto Cubano de Geodesia y Cartografía (ICGC). 1980. *Mapa de la República de Cuba 1/50,000*. Havana: Academia de Ciencias de Cuba.

Jerez de Villarreal, J. 1960. *Oriente (biografía de una provincia)*. Havana: Imprenta El Siglo XX.

Knight, F. W. 1970. *Slave Society in Cuba during the Nineteenth Century*. Madison: University of Wisconsin Press.

Kopytof, B. 1976a. The Development of Jamaica Maroon Ethnicity. *Caribbean Quarterly* (Kingston) 22 (2–3): 33–50.

——. 1976b. Jamaica Maroon Political Organization, the Effects of the Treaties. *Social Economic Studies* (Kingston) 25 (2): 87–105.

Labat, J. B. [1772] 1979. *Viaje a las islas de América*. Havana: Casa de las Américas.

La Rosa Corzo, G. 1986. Los palenques en Cuba: Elementos para su reconstrucción histórica. In Instituto de Ciencias Históricas, *La esclavitud en Cuba*, 86–123. Havana: Editorial Academia.

——. 1987. Algunos datos para la historia temprana de Holguín. *Revista de Historia*, Sección de Investigaciones Históricas del Comité Provincial del PCC en Holguín, 2 (2): 5–12.

——. 1988a. *Los cimarrones de Cuba*. Havana: Editorial de Ciencias Sociales.

——. 1988b. Sobre marcas de esclavos en Cuba. *Boletín del Museo del Hombre Dominicano* 15 (21): 59–67.

——. 1990. Componentes del sistema de asentamiento de los esclavos prófugos. Unpublished paper. Departamento de Arqueología, Academia de Ciencias de Cuba.

Le Riverend, J. 1965. *Historia económica de Cuba*. Havana: Editorial Nacional de Cuba.

López Valdés, R. 1986. Pertenencia étnica de los esclavos de Tiguabos (Guantánamo) entre los años 1789–1844. *Revista de la Biblioteca Nacional "José Martí"* (Havana) 77 (28): 23–64.

Macías, I. 1978. *Cuba en la primera mitad del siglo XVII*. Seville: Escuela de Estudios Hispano-Americanos.

Macías, J. M. 1866. *Geografía de Cuba*. Cárdenas: Imprenta del Comercio.

Martí, J. 1953. *Obras completas*. Vol. 1. Havana: Editorial Lex.

Moreno Fraginals, M. 1986a. Entrevistas. *Cuadernos de Nuestra América*, (Centro de Estudios sobre América, Havana) 8 (11): 294.

——. 1986b. *Hacia una historia de la cultura cubana*. Havana: Universidad de La Habana.

——. 1986c. *El ingenio: Complejo económico social del azúcar*. 2 vols. Havana: Editorial de Ciencias Sociales.

Moreno Fraginals, M., H. Klein, and S. L. Engerman. 1986. Nivel y estructura de los precios de los esclavos de las plantaciones cubanas a mediados del siglo XIX: Algunas perspectivas comparativas. *Santiago* (Santiago de Cuba), no. 63: 97–126.

Ortiz, F. 1975. *Los negros esclavos*. Havana: Editorial de Ciencias Sociales.

Parrado, J. R. 1830. Cuadernos de acientos [*sic*] diarios que tiene la cuadrilla desde el 1ro de octubre del año 1830. Typescript, courtesy of Gustavo Sed.

Patterson, O. 1969. *The Sociology of Slavery*. London: Associated University Press.

Pérez de la Riva, F. 1945. El bohío: Su origen y las influencias que modificaron su estructura primitiva. *Revista de Arquitectura* (Havana) 14: 247–57.

———. 1946. El negro y la tierra, el conuco y el palenque. *Revista Bimestre Cubana* (Havana) 58 (2–3): 97–139.

———. 1952. La habitación rural en Cuba. *Revista de Arqueología Etnología* (Havana) 7 (15–16): 295–392.

Pérez de la Riva, J. 1957. *El barracón y otros ensayos*. Havana: Editorial de Ciencias Sociales.

———. 1979. *El monto de la inmigración forzada en el siglo XIX*. Havana: Editorial de Ciencias Sociales.

Pérez Landa, R., and T. Jústiz del Valle. 1947. Los palenques en Cuba. *Nuevos rumbos* (Havana) 2 (5): 18–20, 32–33.

Pezuela, J. de la. 1863. *Diccionario geográfico, estadístico e histórico de la Isla de Cuba*. 4 vols. Madrid: Establecimiento de Mellado.

Pichardo, E. 1976. *Diccionario provincial casi-razonado de vozes* [*sic*] *y frases cubanas*. Havana: Editorial de Ciencias Sociales.

———. [1875] 1986. *Isla de Cuba, carta geotopográfica*. Havana: Editorial de Ciencias Sociales.

Pichardo Viñals, H. 1965. *Documentos para la historia de Cuba (época colonial)*. Havana: Editorial del Consejo Nacional de Universidades.

———. 1986. *La fundación de las primeras villas de la Isla de Cuba*. Havana: Editorial de Ciencias Sociales.

Portuondo Zúñiga, O. 1986. *Nicolás Joseph de Rivera*. Havana: Editorial de Ciencias Sociales.

Price, R. 1975a. *Guiana Maroons: A Historical and Bibliographic Introduction*. Baltimore: Johns Hopkins University Press.

———. 1975b. *Saramaks Social Structure: Analysis of a Maroon Society in Surinam*. Rio Piedras: University of Puerto Rico, Institute of Caribbean Studies.

Prince, R. 1981. *Sociedades cimarronas, comunidades rebeldes en las Américas*. Mexico City: Siglo Veintiuno.

Real Consulado/Junta de Fomento, Cuba. 1796. *Nuevo reglamento y arancel que debe gobernar en la captura de los esclavos cimarrones*. Havana: Imprenta de la Capitanía General.

———. 1846. *Reglamento de cimarrones reformado por la Real Junta de fomento*. Havana: Imprenta del Gobierno por S.M.

Rousset, R. 1918. *Historial de Cuba*. Vol. 3. Havana: Librería Cervantes.

Saco, J. A. 1881. *Colección póstuma de papeles científicos, históricos, políticos y de otros ramos sobre la Isla de Cuba*. Havana: Editorial Miguel de Villa.

———. 1960. *Papeles sobre Cuba*. Vol. 1. Havana: Dirección General de Cultura.

Sagra, R. de la. 1831. *Historia económica, política y estadística de la Isla de Cuba*. Havana: Imprenta de la Viuda de Arazoza y Soler.

Sánchez Guerra, J., N. Guilarte Abreu, and C. Dranquet Rodríguez. 1986. Los palenques de Guantánamo del siglo XIX. *El Managüí* (Guantánamo) 1 (2): 14–24.

Sociedad Geográfica y Centro Científico del Extremo Oriente de la Academia de Ciencias, USSR. 1984. *Geografía económica del océano mundial*. Moscow: Editorial Progreso.

Torres Lasqueti, J. 1888. *Colección de datos históricos geográficos y estadísticos de Puerto Príncipe y su jurisdicción*. Havana: Imprenta El Retiro.

Valle Hernández, A. Del. 1975. Nota sobre la introducción de negros bozales en la isla de Cuba y estado actual de la distribución de las gentes de color, libres y esclavos de ella. In *Documentos de que hasta ahora se compone el expediente que principian las cortes extraordinarias sobre el tráfico y la esclavitud de los negros*, 116–26. Madrid: Imprenta de Rupelles.

Vento, S. 1976. *Las rebeldías esclavas en Matanzas*. Havana: IHPCC.

Villaverde, C. 1982. *Diario del rancheador*. Havana: Editorial Letras Cubanas.

Wright, I. 1916. El establecimiento de la industria azucarera en Cuba. *La Reforma Social* (Havana), April–June, 26–42.

Index